Reshaping Fatherhood

Understanding Families

Series Editors: **Bert N. Adams, University of Wisconsin**
David M. Klein, University of Notre Dame

This book series examines a wide range of subjects relevant to studying families. Topics include, but are not limited to, theory and conceptual design, research methods on the family, racial/ethnic families, mate selection, marriage, family power dynamics, parenthood, divorce and remarriage, custody issues, and aging families.

The series is aimed primarily at scholars working in family studies, sociology, psychology, social work, ethnic studies, gender studies, cultural studies, and related fields as they focus on the family. Volumes will also be useful for graduate and undergraduate courses in sociology of the family, family relations, family and consumer sciences, social work and the family, family psychology, family history, cultural perspectives on the family, and others.

Books appearing in **Understanding Families** are either single- or multiple-authored volumes or concisely edited books of original chapters on focused topics within the broad interdisciplinary field of marriage and family.

The books are reports of significant research, innovations in methodology, treatises on family theory, syntheses of current knowledge in a family subfield, or advanced textbooks. Each volume meets the highest academic standards and makes a substantial contribution to our understanding of marriages and families.

The National Council on Family Relations cosponsors with Sage a book award for students and new professionals. Award-winning manuscripts are published as part of the **Understanding Families** series.

Multiracial Couples: Black and White Voices
Paul C. Rosenblatt, Terri A. Karis, and Richard D. Powell

Understanding Latino Families: Scholarship, Policy, and Practice
Edited by Ruth E. Zambrana

Current Widowhood: Myths & Realities
Helena Znaniecka Lopata

Family Theories: An Introduction
David M. Klein and James M. White

Understanding Differences Between Divorced and Intact Families
Ronald L. Simons and Associates

Adolescents, Work, and Family: An Intergenerational Developmental Analysis
Jeylan T. Mortimer and Michael D. Finch

Families and Time: Keeping Pace in a Hurried Culture
Kerry J. Daly

No More Kin: Exploring Race, Class, and Gender in Family Networks
Anne R. Roschelle

Contemporary Parenting: Challenges and Issues
Edited by Terry Arendell

Families Making Sense of Death
Janice Winchester Nadeau

Black Families in Corporate America
Susan D. Toliver

Reshaping Fatherhood: The Social Construction of Shared Parenting
Anna Dienhart

Anna Dienhart

Reshaping Fatherhood

The Social Construction of Shared Parenting

UNDERSTANDING FAMILIES

SAGE Publications
International Educational and Professional Publisher
Thousand Oaks   London   New Delhi

For information address:

SAGE Publications, Inc.
2455 Teller Road
Thousand Oaks, California 91320
E-mail: order@sagepub.com

SAGE Publications Ltd.
6 Bonhill Street
London EC2A 4PU
United Kingdom

SAGE Publications India Pvt. Ltd.
M-32 Market
Greater Kailash I
New Delhi 110 048 India

Printed in the United States of America

Library of Congress Cataloging-in-Publication Data

Dienhart, Anna.
    Reshaping fatherhood: The social construction of shared parenting / by Anna Dienhart.
        p.   cm. — (Understanding families; v. 11)
    Includes bibliographical references (p.   ) and index.
    ISBN 0-7619-0977-X (cloth: acid-free paper) —
    ISBN 0-7619-0978-8 (pbk.: acid-free paper)
    1. Fatherhood. 2. Parenting. 3. Sex role. I. Title.
II. Series.
HQ756.D52 1998
306.874′2—dc21   97-45392

This book is printed on acid-free paper.

    98 99 00 01 02 03 10 9 8 7 6 5 4 3 2 1

Acquiring Editor:	Margaret N. Zusky
Editorial Assistant:	Corinne Pierce
Production Editor:	Sanford Robinson
Production Assistant:	Denise Santoyo
Designer/Typesetter:	Janelle LeMaster
Indexer:	Molly Hall
Cover Designer:	Candice Harman

Contents

Preface   ix

Acknowledgments   xv

I. Background: Entering the Meaning-Making Loop   1

1. Introduction   3
    Fatherhood: Vignettes From a Researcher's Notebook   3
    Fatherhood: What Are We to Think?   4
    Finding a Language to Capture Diverse Fatherhood Images   6
    An Alternative View   9
    Dominant Discourses and Beyond   11
    Exploring Family Life for Other Possible Discourses:
        A Look Into Sharing Parenting   15

2. Academic Discourses: Interdisciplinary Perspectives
    on Fatherhood   19
    Historical and Cross-Cultural Discourses   21
    Men and the Provider Role   23
    Father's Involvement in Family Life and Child Care:
        Quantity-Quality Discourse   24
    Father's Influence on the Child   29
    Effect on Men of Becoming and Being a Father   31
    Revisiting Fatherhood Discourses: The Contribution of
        This Study   34

II. Meaning-Making   37

3. Diversity of Styles in Sharing Parenting   41
   Dan and Liz: Interchangeable Parenting Partners   41
   Rodney and Kate: Sharing Parenting While Reserving
      Certain Specialties   42
   Jason and Helen: Sharing Parenting With Accounting Equity   43
   Jack and Denise: Man as Designated Stay-at-Home Parent   44
   Todd and Collette: Woman as Designated Stay-at-Home Parent   45
   Descriptive Snapshots of Five Couples   46
   Styles of Sharing Parenting   47
   Reflections   53

4. A Diversity of Paths: What Influenced Men and Women
      to Move Toward Sharing Parenting   55
   Family-of-Origin Stories   56
   Co-Creating Sharing Parenting Possibilities: Some Prime Movers   65
   Distinctions and the Decision-Making Process   73

5. Guiding Light: Foundations for Sharing Parenting   76
   Commitment to Parenting   77
   Parenting Philosophy   82
   Goodwill   96
   Reflections   99

6. Tag-Team Parenting and the Mechanisms of Sharing
      Parenting   100
   What's in the Language?   101
   Tag-Team Parenting: Key Mechanisms to Making It Work   115
   Reflections   125

7. The Dance of Father Involvement: Men's and Women's
      Connected Experiences   127
   The Dance Metaphor   128
   Readiness to Dance: Some Differences Between Women and Men   129
   Solo and Partnered Dancing: Claiming Parts in the Parenting
      Repertoire   131

Women's Experiences in the Dance of Father Involvement   136
Men's Experiences in the Dance of Father Involvement   139
Reflections   146

8. Sharing Parenting and the Reciprocal Revisioning of
    Fatherhood and Motherhood   149
Revisioning Patterns of Leading-Following   150
Reflections   161

III. **Reflexive Commentary**   165

9. Sharing Parenting: Possibilities to Inform Alternative
    Discourse   169
What Makes Sharing Parenting Work?   169
Obstacles to Sharing Parenting   173
Gender Politics of Sharing Parenting   176

10. Revisiting Dominant Discourses and Final Reflections:
    Implications of Taking a Different View   183
Beyond the Dominant Discourse?   184
Final Reflections   200

Appendix A: Methodology   203

Appendix B: Research Informants: Biographical Snapshots   223

References   233

Index   241

About the Author   245

This book is dedicated to my young friends—*Avery, Chandler, Gideon,* and *Teresa* and *Kathleen.* May your generation of men and women reap the possibilities your parents envision for fatherhood and motherhood.

Preface

What do men experience as the joys and challenges of taking active and full participatory presence in family life? What can men tell us about the benefits to themselves and their families when they are involved and active in the emotional, as well as instrumental, aspects of family life? How are women affected by having a partner who is deeply involved in child rearing? Questions like these intrigue me. The general absence of these questions from current conversations on women's and men's issues seems important. For some time, I have been concerned about the potential polarization between the general women's movement agenda and that of various men's interests, whether they be traditional bastions of power or grassroots men's groups. It strikes me that both sides may have political reasons for an apparent disinterest in asking such questions. Yet, men who actively participate in family life may have some interesting perspectives on such questions—perspectives that could offer an expansive view of gender equality and inequality.

As a family science researcher and therapist working with individuals, couples, and families, I am fascinated by what I hear when I listen to stories located in the private lives of men and women. The private stories seem to be an intriguing conglomeration of what men and women have learned socially to expect of themselves and each other. Not surprisingly, it often sounds as if their socialization was more a process of osmosis than of intentional instruction. Yet, I also often hear men and women talk about trying to change those things they acquired through that osmosis, only to discover it is extremely difficult to hold on to the belief or behavior long enough to get a sense of what keeps it in place and makes change elusive.

When I encounter men and women who seem to be doing family life differently than they experienced growing up, I indulge in exploring what has allowed them to be different. Often their accounts challenge me to reflect on ideas encountered in academic work. I am struck by the persistent pull of cultural stories about how men and women in families are supposed to "be," how they are supposed to act and feel. At the same time, I am amazed at the myriad ways individuals do not conform to those cultural stories. Grand narratives, or our theories and research about families, seem simultaneously to reflect society and to influence individuals in society. For example, feminist-inspired social critique addressing the inequities between men and women has both reflected changes in society and contributed to changing the perceived and real possibilities for women in families, implying that men must change too.

Although women have moved en masse into the "public domain" of work outside the home, recent literature suggests that little has changed for women regarding their responsibilities for the family. The question "why not?" could draw my interest toward further socio-political-economic analysis of a power-based impetus for men's resistance (Goode, 1982). Yet, after listening to men's and women's stories about trying to make changes in their individual lives, I found I was drawn more toward exploring what allowed some men to resist resisting.

The opportunity to explore such questions formally and publicly came in the guise of a PhD thesis. Preparing for that endeavor, I needed to find some ways to combine my interest in the unique individual experience while valuing general tendencies found across a variety of people. I wanted to explore private narratives about the often inexplicable dance of men and women engaged in living together and raising the next generation, and my hunches about the intricate, reflexive loop people negotiate between their own life story and its fit with perceived cultural norms about men, women, and families.

A social constructionist perspective on foundational questions of what is considered truth (or reality) and the process of knowledge creation underpin this entire project. Having adopted a social constructionist perspective, I have been influenced by some core values and beliefs. As a social constructionist researcher, I believe humans are constantly making meanings of their experiences: "Meaning-making is always imbued with language, whether or not we use words" (Weingarten, 1991, p. 295). We generate meanings verbally, nonverbally, and symbolically. Ultimately, meanings are interpretations constructed in social interaction, and as such they are "interpretable only in the light of specific cultural practices" (Weingarten, 1991, p. 295).

I understand cultural practices to suggest several levels of the interpretive backdrop. There is the large cultural perspective associated with the dominant sociocultural group of the person's society or nation. There is the more local cultural perspective of the person's community or group identity. There is the even more local cultural perspective of the person and her or his unique experiential history, which serves as a multilayered interpretive filter in itself. Some argue that the personal culture (each individual) may very well contain all these layers. Thus, as one works to understand the personal perspective, one may uncover embedded specific cultural practices of a larger group.

Each person constructs her or his meanings against the intricately woven meaning space of her or his personal, interpersonal, and sociocultural experience. I believe the personal construction of meanings is intersubjective. We construct formulations; in interaction, we check out our formulations for fit with the cultural milieu in which we live. Thus, we negotiate our individual meanings in a social context (Gergen, 1985). The intersubjective construction of meanings does not necessarily suggest that each person in the interactive interpretive exchange arrives at the same meaning. Our subjective meanings are complexly located in the social context of our existence. Intersubjectivity also suggests that our personal meanings may be influenced by the degree of connection we have to a particular person or social context. The more connection we feel or desire, the greater the potential to be influenced by the other.

Weingarten (1991) argues that intersubjective meaning-making in any particular social interaction is sensitive to the stance each individual takes to the exchange. An open, curious stance void of efforts to impose meanings, restrict meanings, withhold meanings, or otherwise withdraw from a constructive meaning-making exchange is more likely to result in a co-construction of meaning. That is, a co-construction, or the process of arriving at shared meanings, more likely results from an open exchange of possible interpretations. It was this type of stance that I wanted to take to my research conversations. This stance has several implications for interpreting this research.

Essential to a social constructionist perspective is the belief that the observer cannot be objectively detached from that which is being observed: The mere activity of observing may influence the observation. Hence, it is imperative that I provide personal and professional contextual information underpinning my interpretive frame. My current status as a single, middle-aged woman with no children could give the impression that I have few connections to the research topic. My personal history, however, contributed to the original framing of my research interest. In short, I am not an objective observer of some distant phenomenon.

My interpretive lens has been influenced by having grown up in the 1950s and 1960s with a "stay-at-home mother" and a "provider father." The family life of my childhood both fits and does not fit with central themes identified in a critical feminist analysis of such a traditional family experience. Our family made several moves dictated by my father's advancing career because he strongly felt the economic imperative to provide well for his family. He spent his after-work hours relating with his children, sometimes through games, at other times through help with school work, letting us assist him with his chores, and many times just being there as we drifted off to sleep. I implicitly knew my mother had a great deal of influence and decision-making power in the family, and her constancy of presence at home was a great source of assurance and trust.

My mother and my father both lived out aspects of what we have come to call traditional family roles for women and men. Yet, they also each expressed individuality in parenting not adequately captured by the caricatures of the traditional mother or father. This awareness led me to want to explore the complexities behind today's caricatures of men and women in families.

Disappointment at the ending of my marriage, in which both my partner and myself worked outside the home, had equally high incomes, and managed to divide up responsibilities of family life and care for his daughter, initially led me to feminist literature for an understanding of family experiences. Exposure to that literature helped me appreciate aspects of socialized gender roles that can constrain both men and women. Yet, a feminist focus on patriarchal power, male privilege, and control did not fully capture the subtleties of my own marriage. I began to wonder if analysis of culturally embedded male privilege loses some of its power in the uniquely intimate interpersonal relationships of family. I now take a more curious stance about the subtle dynamics between men and women as they live and negotiate family partnerships.

Another important influence leading me to study men in families was a privileged experience of listening to men talk about themselves and their families in my career as a consulting economist to large international corporations and financial institutions. My colleagues, mostly males, often shared stories of their lives over lunch or while traveling on business. Remembering those men and their stories, I noticed a predominant strain of men feeling pulled out of their families by their work and struggling to create space in their lives to experience the deep meaningful connections with their children, as well as providing for them. From those men, I learned there was more to the traditional image of "father as provider" than met the eye.

Adopting a social constructionist perspective raised my awareness of and respect for the interpretive process of any research endeavor. I appreciated that my interpretive lens would need checking for where and how my focus was clear, where it remained fuzzy or notably distorted, and where I needed to find another lens to add perspective and understanding. I came to recognize the importance of having a consultant group serve as an external monitor on my interpretations. Thus, I asked several couples actively engaged in living the intricacies of family life and partnership to act as consultants to this research. These consultants asked me difficult questions; pointed out potential biases; provided inspiration through sharing the intricacies of their own experiences; and reviewed many of my ideas, then pushed me to go farther in my thinking.

Because a social constructionist perspective on research highlights the subjective and interpretive quality of any research endeavor, I chose to present this research in a style that I see as congruent with that approach. For the most part, this book is organized along traditional academic lines, with some notable exceptions. The primary departure from mainstream academic practices is found in style and language. I do not use strictly objective, third-person language. In keeping with a social constructionist stance, I generally adopt a first-person, narrative style.

Furthermore, the interpretative nature of this research is highlighted throughout. In doing so, I adopt two practices: First, I introduce the language of *meaning-making*. The chapters traditionally called results or findings are included in a six-chapter section labeled "Meaning-Making." This heading stresses the socially constructed nature of this research and the centrality of the researcher's subjective presence in the interpretive process that shaped the research narrative (this book). I include a description of my methodological approach (Appendix A) to substantiate the research practices that guided my interpretative process. Second, the writing style stresses the distinction between narrative "accounts of experiences" and "experience" in the sense of a "reality." Narrative accounts of experience include the narrator's meaning-making.

As I came to the conclusion of this book, I realized I could go back to the beginning and search deeper into the phenomena discussed—such is the excitement of research. I have paused here, just long enough to go public in the form of this book. I offer these ideas for you to ponder. As you construct your own interpretations of my research interpretations, see where you take these ideas from where I have left off, at least for now.

Acknowledgments

A book is prepared with the support and contributions of many people. I wish to give special recognition and thanks to the men and women in the 18 couples who so generously shared their time, stories of their family life, and ideas with me, and whose faith and resourcefulness in making sharing parenting work are reflected in the results of this study. I thoroughly enjoyed meeting each one of you and still carry around images of your families and memories of our conversations. You, individually and collectively, made this research possible, and share in whatever contribution it makes to our field.

Special recognition also goes to the men and women in the four consultant families. You were the initial inspiration for my research, and later gave generously of your time, ideas, and reflections on my ideas. Beyond your direct contributions, your images and family stories often served as my touchstones. Watching from the sidelines as you co-create parenthood's sharing potentials always helped me regain energy, confidence, and courage to keep going with this project.

I was fortunate to meet Dr. Kerry Daly several years ago when I returned to university in search of a new career. For me, he modeled a different way to express consummate professionalism, with humor and humanity. Kerry shared his skills in qualitative research, an interest in men's stories of fatherhood, and supported my journey into the realm of social constructionism. I appreciated his choices to privilege his parenting over our appointed meeting occasionally when family life veered off its predictable course, because it suggested to me that he personally knew something about living shared parenthood. His questions and challenges invited me to look at ideas I had not considered, and thus moved this research along. Kerry gave of his time graciously; he welcomed me as a colleague and encouraged me to value my own ideas. For all this, I am ever grateful.

Several other colleagues at the University of Guelph contributed valued critical perspectives: Drs. Jean Turner, Claude Guldner, and Michael Sobol each brought unique interpretive perspectives and raised challenging questions while supporting my developing ideas. Dr. Theodore F. Cohen of Ohio Wesleyan University challenged and affirmed my ideas about alternatives to traditional models of family life. Tara Curtis provided skillful and thoughtful transcription, capturing the rich texture of people's narratives and adding insights to my reflections. My colleague Dr. Dalia Restrepo Ramirez helped sustain me with encouragement, intellectual challenge, diversions, laughter, faith, and most important, friendship.

My family of friends in Guelph—Susan, Fred, Nancy, Patsy, Stepanie, Peter, Sharon, Paul, Jean, Janet, Kim, and Dave—stood patiently by me through many months and shared the sustenance of close families—encouragement, acceptance, conversations, food, flowers, fun, dancing, and a loving faith in me; these connections pulled me out of the isolation of writing and gave me energy to continue. My parents—John and Barbara—and siblings—Janice (and family), Lucy, and John (and sons)—though they are all geographically distant, helped me find the courage to set out on this journey and the fortitude to finish with a new beginning. I trust your loving.

Finally, an award cosponsored by the National Council on Family Relations (NCFR) and Sage Publications, Inc., brought life to a once-distant hope, giving me the chance to make public what had been an exciting journey into research. This annual award—the Sage/NCFR New Professional Book Prize—acknowledges the contribution of new authors and supports them as they learn to edit, refine, clarify, and transform ideas. For me, those ideas were often so close I could not know what others might interpret. Dr. Bert Adams (University of Wisconsin) and Dr. David Klein (Notre Dame), editors for the Understanding Families Series, helped me see ways to convey what I really thought so that others might gain new appreciation for diverse possibilities in the private lives of families. This has been rich journey into ideas I thought I already knew well, and will remain a touchstone through my academic career.

PART I

Background: Entering the Meaning-Making Loop

Entering the meaning-making loop in any social science research endeavor is typically preceded by many hours of noticing, considering, and questioning phenomena encountered in everyday living. Before entering the field to study involved fathers, I had been noticing that my everyday life was filled with stimuli about men in families. I kept coming back to questions about what fathers today experience in their connections to their children. Once my attention was turned to these interests, there seemed to be myriad bits of impressionistic data coming into focus. Approaching this research project, I organized some of these impressions by searching the extant research literature and comparing my everyday observations. This two-chapter part summarizes some observations, thoughts, and questions that led me to search deeper into the lives of men and women who are sharing family life in interesting, and perhaps unique, ways. Information included in these chapters is by necessity partial and selective, and as such, is both representative of my entering process and does not exactly replicate that process. I have chosen to give you, the reader, selected bits that survey the landscape but do not provide all the details. There is a large body of research on

fathers, fatherhood, and men in families; this literature is now a focus
of active interest and increasing debate. The selected, partial list included
here is meant to locate my work in a broader context, without pretending to be all-inclusive. I have chosen to feature work that gives you a
view of what existed before I entered the field and spoke with men and
women living the everyday experience of sharing parenting.

1

Introduction

Fatherhood: Vignettes From a Researcher's Notebook

A first-time father enters the nursery of a prominent teaching hospital and informs the duty-nurse that he will be taking the baby to the room to be with his wife. The nurse says okay, then adds, "Since I have only your baby to look after just now, I'll just change the diaper." At this point, she takes the baby over to a changing table, leaving the new father waiting to connect with his son beside the now-empty bassinet. (Hospital scene: an everyday observation)

Several mothers chat at the school bus stop as they wait with their children. A man and his three children approach the bus stop; they are all engaged in animated conversation. The mothers begin to talk about him and try to hush their giggles at what his children are wearing, noting how their clothes don't match, commenting on how they dress differently when their mother brings them to the bus. The chatting stops as he nears the corner to wait with his children. (Bus stop experience: an everyday observation)

A child is ill and cannot stay at day care. The day care provider calls the father to come and get the child. The father is in a meeting; his secretary suggests that the day care call his wife. When the father returns to his office, the secretary informs him of the call. He rushes to the phone to check on his child. (Business world experience: an everyday observation)

A judge makes his decision on a child custody case, pronouncing that the father will need to find a job, keep it, and settle in a "suitable" home before joint custody arrangements will be considered. The judge gives the man 3 months to accomplish these major lifestyle changes. (Film depiction: *Mrs. Doubtfire*)

Driving along a freeway, I notice a black-and-white billboard featuring a man (naked to the waist) holding an infant; the look of delight and love in his face catches my attention. Then I notice that it is an advertisement for Calvin Klein jeans. (Advertising media: an everyday experience)

"Because fatherhood is universally problematic in human societies, cultures must mobilize to devise and enforce the father role for men, coaxing and guiding them into fatherhood through a set of legal and extra-legal pressures that require them to maintain close alliance with the children's mother and to invest in their children" (Blakenhorn, 1995, p. 3: an academic view).

"Moving beyond the deficit models of fathering, we believe, means acknowledging that most fathers have the desire, ability, and sense of obligation to care effectively for the next generation" (Hawkins & Dollahite, 1997b, p. xiii: an academic view).

Fatherhood: What Are We to Think?

Observers of family life in the past several years have been confronted with a barrage of fatherhood images. The meanings one could create from these images are quite mixed. A sampling of these images has the potential to create a rich mixture of hope and despair. What hope and what despair can we find in these simple observations of men as fathers?

The hope in the hospital scene may be that fathers are now a familiar presence in an activity once declared off limits to expectant fathers. Men are now actively participating in the birth and immediate after-birth care of their infants. The despair may be that the nurse seemed to privilege her job, her exclusive responsibility, to care for the infant in the nursery rather than to create an inclusive moment for the new father to see how an "expert" handles the task. She may have missed a "teachable moment" with this new father; a moment that may have encouraged him to take on new responsibilities. If she had seized that teachable moment, he may have left the hospital with a sense of having developed some new skills necessary to accomplish what will now be routine tasks in his family life. An embedded question may be, what do we really expect men to be as fathers? Only distant observers, perhaps!

The hope I find in the bus stop scene is found in the man's participation in the daily routine of getting his children to school; he is involved in the flow of their lives; he is engaging with his children conversationally, not only directing them on how to behave; he is willing to enter the world of women waiting with their children. I despair at the hidden judgment that he is not as good as the mother in caring for the children, disguised perhaps in the conversation about dressing them for school. I despair that the women even take special notice of the man participating in routine activities of family life. Would men even be noticed if more were participating in the public routines of children's lives? Does it matter how many men participate if we secretly harbor beliefs that family and children are really a woman's domain?

In the business world scene, hope may be found in the fact that the day care attendant called the father at his place of work. This could suggest that day care personnel see fathers as responsible for their children's health and care, as well as suggesting that it is appropriate to interrupt a man's workday. I find it despairing that the man's secretary did not offer to interrupt him at the meeting. I wonder if the secretary would have interrupted a mother if she was in a meeting and the day care called about her sick child. I wonder if the secretary was unaware of the extent of the man's involvement in his child's life. I wonder what the man's coworkers, especially his boss, would think of him if he instructed his secretary to interrupt him whenever the day care called. I despair that policies and the social environment at the workplace are changing very slowly, if at all, for working parents, especially for men who want to be involved in their children's lives.

Hope may be found in this courtroom vignette from the film *Mrs. Doubtfire* in the fact that the father is seeking joint custody. Despair may lie in the message that the father will be considered eligible for joint custody only if he almost immediately takes on the trappings of a successful working man. Imagine if a stay-at-home mother were given just 3 months to prove she could financially provide for her children.

Advertising seems to have discovered the potential joys of fatherhood to sell everything from jeans to automobiles to life insurance. Although trying to sell their products, advertisers are also projecting the value of men as fathers—this may be hopeful in suggesting that the macho male image is not the only way to reach American men today. The advertisements typically depict the joyful sides of fatherhood, or draw on the image of men as responsible providers for their children's futures. Why don't we see advertisements depicting the not-so-fun sides of being a multifaceted father in the complex, shifting terrain of child-rearing responsibilities? Are we to conclude despairingly that if we project the darker sides of parenting, we will not attract men to the image?

In his book *Fatherless America*, Blakenhorn (1995) urges Americans to take fatherhood on as a social cause in need of attention. In tracking what he sees as men's sociohistorical move away from the responsibilities of family, the author offers hope that men should be seen as vitally important in children's lives. Critics may despair, however, at the implied message emphasizing financial responsibility and the strong-armed measures Blakenhorn suggests are necessary to keep men connected to and involved in their families.

In contrast, the alternative view offered by Hawkins and Dollahite (1997b) is hopeful in its contention that most men have the desire and ability to care for the next generation. Generative fathering, in their view, can and will emerge as a dominant image of fatherhood if we stop looking for and focusing on the flaws. This may be, but it is despairing to think that the political profile of fatherhood as an important social issue might be submerged once again as policymakers and employers eagerly grasp at any suggestion that nothing needs to change.

Finding a Language to Capture Diverse Fatherhood Images

Depending on one's perspective on the collage of fatherhood images currently available in North American culture, one could conclude that fatherhood is in vogue and men are readily embracing the life of the "enlightened father." Alternatively, one might conclude that men are reluctant participants in changing social conditions that increasingly demand that they conform to their social responsibility. Supporting this latter view is a large academic literature looking at women's changes and experiences of taking on nontraditional family and work roles, whereas men's shifts in family and work are documented minimally at best (Benokraitis, 1985; Lamb, 1987; Pleck, 1987).

The more hopeful view comes most obviously from selected media depictions of prominent men who model ways for men to be involved fathers (e.g., Bill Cosby in *The Cosby Show;* Robin Williams in *Mrs. Doubtfire*). Emerging academic literature adds some documenting evidence for this view, at least in limited measure (see Cohen, 1987, 1991, 1993; Hawkins & Dollahite, 1997b; Marsiglio, 1991, 1993; Snarey, 1994). Typically, this view casts involved fathers as nontraditional and searches for new ways to describe families and the men in them. Some of the alternatives suggested by various academic authors include the following.

• *New father.* Authors suggesting this language talk about men sharing in the housework and child care in homes where both parents are in the labor force and are moving forward in their career choices. The message here is that both men and women can experience satisfaction in their work life and a rich and rewarding family life. This lifestyle may require careful arranging of schedules and efforts to find good day care for the children. This language implies that the man is highly nurturing with his children, and is increasingly involved in their care and the housework (see Bloom-Feshbach, 1981; Bronstein, 1988; Lewis & O'Brien, 1987; Pleck, 1987). This language also implies, however, that men in the past have not engaged in this way in families, a view La Rossa (1997) critically challenges.

• *Hands-on fathering.* Daniels and Weingarten (1988) suggest that this is the kind of father involvement seen in families where both the woman and the man participate in child care, though this may not be a 50-50 arrangement.

• *Enlightened father.* Some authors recognize that there is a variety of forms of participation that likely have different determinants and different associated patterns and consequences. In this view, men are seen as actively participating in child rearing. Sharing parenting is viewed as beneficial to men and women, as well as the child(ren), even though men and women face many challenges in negotiating their shared and coordinated parenting efforts. These authors focus on institutional obstacles and speculate that we would see more enlightened fathers if they were removed (see Barnett & Baruch, 1988).

• *Modern father.* In contrast to images of the traditional father, some authors suggest that a modern father is more involved in the daily routines of child care and is not experienced as the family expert or hero. This view includes ideas that children will benefit from models of men as fathers who do not always have to be in control; do not always have the final solution to every problem; can be in error and learn from others; know comfort in expressions of love, anger, joy, fear, and sadness; and recognize that the expression of a range of feelings does not detract from masculinity (see Giveans & Robinson, 1985).

• *Third-stage father.* Barnett and Baruch (1988) suggest that academic interest in men as fathers has evolved historically from seeing fathers as barely represented in psychological research about parenting, toward notions of glorifying men's active involvement in families. The tendency to glorify men's involvement assumes an assured positive benefit to women and children. It also assumes that men's participation in child care and household care generally eases the stress and tension experienced in dual-wage families. In contrast, third-stage fatherhood connotes a recognition that increased male participation in the daily activities of families has both positive and stressful consequences on some aspects of family life: that it will solve some problems and create other challenges.

Despite this proliferation of new descriptions, there is still much debate about men's readiness and willingness to leave behind traditional ways of being a father. Often these debates center on the prevalence of certain types of fathers to support a "state-of-the-family" conclusion. Researchers often ask what model of fatherhood is more prevalent in families today, and what this implies about the future. Given these types of questions and the evidence then documented, it seems the more despairing view carries significant weight.

What about asking different questions—questions that explore the diversity of father presence and participation in family life? What limits our curiosity about men who are not represented in the majority view? Although perhaps not in the majority, men who are active in parenting and participating in all aspects of family life may enrich our understanding of what encourages, as well as potentially encumbers, men as they change their presence in families and lead us to entertain different conclusions. Would exploring this possibility carry weight only if it could fully and convincingly dethrone the view of the reluctant or recalcitrant father?

An Alternative View

Do we really have to choose one of these images over the other? In a postmodern view of the world, no! The predilection to choose dominant images of what fatherhood is seems based largely in preferential practices that stress generalization from central tendencies found in society. The tendency toward such practices seems to be most clearly rooted in the modernist view of the world, a view that searches for "foundational forms and [rests on a] belief in linear progress through more knowledge" (Kvale, 1992, p.3). Alternatively, a postmodern view challenges conceptualizations of the world as having objective truth underpinning one reality, and replaces it with a distinctly pluralist approach. A social constructionist lens, associated with postmodernism in the fields of sociology, psychology, and family therapy, recognizes the heterogeneity of local and global societies, and focuses on flexibility and change rather than control and stability. In a social constructionist view, we are seen as active in constructing our social realities, with subtle processes of social consensus underpinning the creation of ideas about "what is" or "the way things are in the world." Some of these ideas may, over time, become reified in popular or dominant views. Once reified, these dominant views may obscure their socially constructed bases.

As a researcher engaged in a study of fatherhood, I began to recognize the power of language to shape our ideas about the world. The language of both traditional fatherhood and, in contrast, the variations on nontraditional fatherhood represents common depictions of men in families. Both these descriptions of fatherhood are products of simplified and generalized ways of thinking about families in American society. As reified ways of viewing fatherhood, these descriptions are part of our social discourse.

Discourse is a way we talk about something. A discourse is more than a simple description of a set of behaviors. A discourse may be considered a set of ideas; a "main-line story" that conveys common values, constructs and reflects a specific worldview, and consists of ideas and practices that constrain what we feel, think, and do (Weingarten, 1991). A dominant discourse is a set of explanations, or a generalized story, that gains prominent status or privileged distinction. The process of gaining privileged distinction is largely embedded in social consensus. Social consensus likely reflects implicit power structures in society.

If we construct our realities in social interchanges and create social discourse across a spectrum of activities and interactions, then the theories and knowledge about fatherhood become an important type of discourse: a type of discourse inherently located within the reflexive loop of looking at images of fatherhood found in our culture, interpreting them against what we think we know to be possible, then reinterpreting them for possibilities not yet widely entertained. The possibilities may be thought to be endless. Yet as researchers, not fiction writers, science fiction authors, filmmakers, nor advertisers, we are constrained by what we can observe and what we can elicit from the people engaged in creating versions of fatherhood in their daily lives. Exploring their everyday experiences and meanings can open our view to subjugated, or heretofore obscured, discourses about fatherhood possibilities.

By no means do I consider the discourses of traditional and nontraditional fatherhood false, but they may severely limit our ability to capture the complexity and diversity of fatherhood in research. As commonly used, dominant traditional and nontraditional discourses describe only two alternatives for men and how they perform fatherhood. The two alternatives are often set up as if they are mutually exclusive, and generally obscure the inherent complexities of men's family involvement by focusing merely on role profiles. As such, these discourses privilege distinctions made to simplify and generalize about family functioning. Does this language allow us a lens for viewing the multitudinous and intricate transactions and negotiations that spontaneously and regularly occur in everyday family life? Can we know that what we may see in one family will mean the same thing if observed in another family? These are questions central to the inquiry of fatherhood from a social constructionist view.

A social constructionist view embraces a reexamination of popular or dominant discourses. A social constructionist view encourages us to look beyond surface similarities across people's lives. A social constructionist view opens the exploration to diverse and pluralistic experiences of people in their daily lives. It opens the way for us to explore a chosen phenomenon for complexity, intricacy, and contradictory facets. Released from some of the constraints of reductionistic thinking and the imperative to generalize to a universal explanation (discourse), we can talk about multiverses, or the many possible stories, of fatherhood from a social constructionist perspective.

Dominant Discourses and Beyond

In the past several decades, family science researchers have participated in the creation and promotion of some dominant discourses of fatherhood, particularly the traditional and nontraditional father discourses. These discourses seem to rest largely on analysis of the separation between the public and private domains (men's work outside the family and family life, respectively), and on a fascination with differences between men and women. This body of knowledge purports simultaneously to reflect the general culture of fatherhood in postwar America and to present evidence for critical cultural analysis of what "should be" in the future. These discourses reflect embedded cultural values—implicitly mirroring the images seen as possible for men in families from the large sociocultural domain—and lead us to believe that it reflects they way men actually live in families. Discourses about the traditional, and in contrast nontraditional, father typically convey generalized characteristics or norms, suggesting that what holds true for most men on average should hold true for all men. These discourses typically do not explore in detail the experiences of men who may not be adequately represented by the dominant experience. As such, these discourses are limiting. As we entertain an increased acceptance of the plurality in our society, expanding our view of fatherhood's diversity seems imperative.

The following study took as a central departure point an interest in some men who may not consider their experience of fatherhood to be either traditional or nontraditional. As a researcher, I took this departure based on some conviction that some men see themselves as being engaged in family life that is complex, multidimensional, and responsive to fluctuating demands. My departure from dominant traditional and nontraditional father discourses also led me to wonder whether these men would compare their parenting to that of their female partners, and view themselves as inadequate in the comparison.

I have talked with men and women in 18 families whose experiences are not adequately depicted by the discourses currently found in the extant academic literature. At the same time, I came back to the question of what influences these discourses about men in families have on men. Although I approached this research from an initial conviction of finding men who are doing things differently, I also remained open to observing, or hearing about, aspects of their lives that are clearly within main-line cultural stories. Although I was interested in what lay beyond current academic discourses, I repeatedly asked what would be considered beyond both by these men and women and by the larger community and culture. At the conclusion of the book, I revisit these questions.

INFLUENTIAL DISCOURSES: COMMON THEMES

Discourses about fatherhood found in the media, everyday social exchanges, and academic literature share a few common themes: These discourses are generally critical of men's attitudes toward the family side of life, their style of parenting, and the amount they participate in the myriad aspects of daily family life. In this, they could be considered part of what Doherty (1991) calls a "deficit model" lens for characterizing men and masculinity, focusing as they do on what men are not doing or are doing poorly. Hawkins and Dollahite (1997a) refine this view by adding analysis of a "role inadequacy perspective" (p. 3) as the center-piece of the deficit model lens. They believe that most studies of fatherhood cast men as playing mere roles in family life. They suggest that we are held captive by the tendency to simplify and stultify the deep texture of men's experience of and contribution to family life.

A connected theme found in all three contexts implicitly suggests a "woman as the standard for comparison" discourse. Men, as fathers, are usually compared to women, as mothers; it is against women that they come up short in their participation and contributions. Our ideals and cultural models of motherhood seem to be the template for men as they fashion ways of participating in family life, as if motherhood is itself a universal experience. Furthermore, although some idealized mother-hood template may be useful in building and understanding aspects of what parenthood entails, it likely limits the scope of inquiry into unique experiences of fatherhood. Using a motherhood template may implicitly lead researchers into the easy comparative trap. Comparative analysis is ultimately valuable, but the trap lies in the tendency to privilege one way over another rather than value both ways for their similar and unique contributions.

Cultural Discourses: Some Views From Popular Media

Popular culture currently has a fascination with fatherhood. Several weekly news magazines and most women's magazines have recently featured "fatherhood." There is also a growing list of popular films exploring various types of father roles. These media features often present idealized images of the new involved father. He is pictured holding an infant, soothing a hurt child, preparing meals. He is written about with emphasis on how special he is and the rewards he reaps from being a "good dad." He is also depicted as struggling with changes in his marital relationship. Often the changes reported focus on the loss of the sole devotion and attention of his partner. At the same time, anecdotal stories highlight how some men may experience feeling closer to their wives, drawn together in a new bond through their child.

In contrast, media also run feature stories on the "deadbeat dad." These are men who do not maintain connections with their children, and do not provide economic support to their families. They are usually depicted as scoundrels who are only too willing to get away with the minimal demands placed on them legally and socially. One may be led to believe that cultural values let these men off the hook, so why would they behave otherwise. Little to no attention is paid to the complicated beliefs and events that lead to such estrangement.

Everyday Social Discourses:
Some Observations

I became interested in men's stories about making changes in their lives, especially stories about being husbands and fathers. I noticed many men talking about desires to participate actively in all aspects of family life. I also notice many women talking about wanting their partners to be more involved in all aspects of parenting and family life.

I often hear men relate feelings of uncertainty and ineffectuality. At times, I sense they seem unsure how to go about doing and managing child care, meal preparation, daily household maintenance, and other routines of everyday family life—all while remaining committed to their work outside the home and respecting their partner's ways of doing these things. My female friends, colleagues, and clients often talk about networks of women who can identify with and share their struggle of juggling it all. My male friends, colleagues, and clients talk of having virtually no models, nor any perceived support network. I also notice that, basically, each family feels like it is in this alone. Families are isolated and are trying to marshal their resources as best they can to figure out what will work for them no matter what others are doing. I hear people talking about the pragmatics of handling the busyness of daily living. It often sounds to me that it feels like this busyness is a great deal to handle.

I have also heard men and women talk about the higher "rewards"—both tangible and intangible—for women who have moved into traditional male worlds (i.e., work outside the home) than for men moving into traditional female worlds (i.e., work inside the home). I detect a general devaluation of family work in our culture. Feminist discourses have long pointed to the insidious presence of this cultural message. The cultural message is reinforced by prevailing economic practices—family work is valued in the monied economy only when someone outside the family is paid to do it (Garbarino, 1994). In the everyday lives of men and women, these cultural practices become real considerations and constraints in their freedom to make decisions about how to juggle family and work outside the home.

The changes women are making inside the family continue to be invisible, yet the changes men are making are lauded, seen as special. Initially I too was captured by this "these men are special" message. I saw men's willingness to engage in family life and parenting fully with their partners as special. As I continued to talk with men and women, I became increasingly aware of an associated cultural bind that may trap both men and women. It seems that men both want to be seen as doing some things differently and not to be seen as special. Some men recognize how being seen as special tends to make their partner's changes invisible. Other men mention not wanting to be held up as models lest the public gaze become too critical. Still others mention how characterizing their involvement as special may limit others' appreciation of just how possible it is for all men to take on and share full responsibility for child care and family life.

Women, too, want to be visible in their family involvement, and in having made changes in both their private and public lives. But women, too talk of feeling the pressure of the public gaze. Women are readily noticed for their handling of both worlds and are encouraged to "get their men to share" the responsibility. Some women fear critical judgment when they feel reluctant to relinquish their privileged status in the private sphere of the family; they are admonished to just "let it go—give yourself a break!"

Exploring Family Life for Other Possible Discourses: A Look Into Sharing Parenting

Discourses about men in families often focus attention on average practices found in a majority of families. It seems to me that discourses about family life still include strong messages that family work continues to be primarily women's work. Measuring the average time spent and typical activities in which women and men are engaged provides a clear documentation of the seemingly marginal change in men's presence in families. Research has also provided a particularly clear idea of the increased demands on women's lives as they juggle both family work and work outside the home. Though more recent research has begun to focus on the deep texture of men's experience in families, most of the research to date does not yield a thoroughly grounded understanding of the why or how of men's participation in sharing parenting.

In this book, I bring men's and women's own stories to our understanding of men's full and active participation in parenting. These men have engaged in actively creating family involvement in their everyday lives. They have done so in the face of potentially constraining cultural and personal discourses about what men are and how they should be in families.

An interest in how men and women experience themselves, each other, and their children in everyday family life led me to work within a qualitative research framework. Qualitative methodology facilitates tapping into complex constructions of the participants' worlds, and opens the research inquiry to an explication of how men and women make sense of their life experiences (Denzin, 1994; Marshall & Rossman, 1989; McCracken, 1988; Moustakas, 1990; Strauss, 1987; Strauss & Corbin, 1990). These ideas and research practices match the foundational tenets of a social constructionist paradigm.

This study took as its starting point a specific focus on the "everyday world as problematic" (Smith, 1987). Having been trained in systems thinking, I believe that when one member of a family changes, the change affects other members of the family. I also believed that men and women do not create their visions of fatherhood and motherhood in isolation from each other, nor in a cultural vacuum. Thus, I wanted to view fatherhood from both men's and women's perspectives. This led me to interview both the man and the woman in participant families. I also wanted to take a fresh look at men's and women's experiences of family life and sharing parenting, especially taking a proactive focus on their resourcefulness and success.

My focus was on families in which the man and the woman have negotiated a relationship of sharing parenting, with both being generally satisfied with their participation in the full spectrum of caring for and rearing their children. My primary focus was on fatherhood. The specific orienting research questions were as follows:

- What are men's experiences of fatherhood when they are active and fully participating in parenting and daily family life?
- How do men and women come to create a sharing parenting family? What are the influences in their individual lives and marriage that led them to organize their sharing parenting family?

- What are the experiences of men and women as they work out sharing parenting arrangements? How do they work out the processes of keeping their parenthood experiences shared?

Both partners were engaged in open-ended conversations about the man's general involvement in family life and his involvement in parenting. The man was asked to speak directly to his experience and to his perception of his partner's experience of his parenting and involvement in family life. The woman was asked to speak to her experience of his involvement in family life. She was also asked to speak to her experience of sharing parenting and how it affects her sense of being a woman, wife, and parent.

This research study explored the resourcefulness of men and women in 18 couples, selected specifically for their self-reported commitment to share parenting responsibilities and activities fully. The men and women were interviewed, both individually and in couples, to explore the ways they construct fatherhood—their beliefs, expectations, behaviors, and reflective experiences. A sample drawn from convenience referrals met three criteria: 1) both partners agreed that the man was an active and fully participating father in everyday family life; 2) the focus was on the years of high-demand parenting, so the couple had at least one child between the ages of 2 and 6; and 3) the research participants were a first family with biological children.

The average age of the couples in this study was 38 and 36 years for men and women, respectively. The men and women were generally from the dominant Caucasian culture, and were generally well educated. There was a range of educational and occupational experiences among both the men and the women. The 18 couples represented several different configurations of family structure: three families had dual incomes of roughly balanced proportions; three families job shared; the woman worked part-time in four families; the man worked part-time in two families; and there were three stay-at-home fathers and three stay-at-home mothers. The annual income for the 18 couples was reported to range from $10,000 (one family) to just over $140,000 (one family), with an average income of approximately $50,000. Two families had only one child, 11 families had two children, and 5 families had three children.

The research design (Appendix A features a full explication of the research methodology) followed the open and emergent tenets of grounded theory (Glaser & Strauss, 1967; Strauss, 1987; Strauss & Corbin, 1990) and the long qualitative interview (Marshall & Rossman, 1989; McCracken, 1988). Thematic and constant comparative analysis of the 36 narrative accounts revealed diverse possibilities for men and women to recreate fatherhood in the interactive environment of sharing parenting.

2

Academic Discourses

Interdisciplinary Perspectives on Fatherhood

Family scientists have long considered men's contribution to and participation in family life to be important. Over the years, the study of men in families, as fathers in particular, has evolved to a current interest in the complex and diverse ways men contribute to, are potentially challenged by, and benefit from fatherhood experiences. Current research spans a broad spectrum of interests from diverse ethno-cultural experiences (e.g., Chicano, black, Asian fathers), different age cohorts of fathers (e.g., adolescent fathers, middle-aged first-time fathers), and different family forms (e.g., single fathers, noncustodial fathers, fathers with joint custody, primary parent fathers, fathers with a special needs child). Some academics have also begun to critique the tendency of researchers "to reduce the activities of parenting to who-does-what-how-often" (Thompson & Walker, 1989, p. 861) and have begun to set out revised and expanded conceptualizations of fatherhood (Hawkins & Dollahite, 1997b; Palkovitz, 1997).

Being rooted, for the most part, in a modernist paradigm, much of the extant research and theories likely rests on what, over time, have become hidden cultural assumptions and practices. One such practice is the tendency to seek understanding of a phenomenon by juxtaposing it with a seeming opposite. Such practices certainly may help clarify. Yet, embedded in this type of analysis are simplifying assumptions that reduce to narrow differences and assign them to apparently distinct groups. When two groups are seen as being mutually exclusive or contradictory, we have set up a simplistic dichotomy. A tendency to view phenomena through a dichotomous lens seems apparent in some of the research concerned with men in families. I noticed that tendency particularly in research concerned with comparing men as fathers to women as mothers, comparing families with fathers to families where no father was present, and comparing the effect of fathers versus others (usually mothers) on the sex role socialization of children.

In family theory and research, one may particularly note hidden and dichotomous assumptions about the complementarity of gender roles and the neat separation between the public and privates spheres. Messner's (1987) critique of this literature focuses on how it "simply mimics the dominant theoretical and methodological conventions of the various academic disciplines" (p. 338) without incorporating considerations of the ideological and structural contexts of the sociocultural arena. Messner calls for a reexamination of what has been alternatively depicted as 1) no differences in men's and women's experiences in families, or 2) an excessive focus on men's and women's experiences as separate and distinct differences. The no differences portrayal typically presumes that either parent (but usually the mother) can fully represent both parent's experiences. On the other hand, dichotomous portrayals of differences between men and women have a tendency to ignore potential similarities between women and men. These tendencies may lead to the creation of the dominant discourses resting on a deficit model perspective and a sex role paradigm.

Exploring the sex role paradigm against the backdrop of a deficit model perspective, Hawkins and Dollahite (1997a) suggest that much of the research focus on fathers and fatherhood has been based in a *role inadequacy perspective,* or RIP (note an interesting play with words and cultural symbols). Central to this view on the role inadequacy perspective is a critique of how much of the fatherhood research generally suggests that men have not adjusted to sociohistorical change; that men have, indeed, resisted change in contemporary family roles; and that, as a result men enjoy significant privilege in family life and at the worst are ignorant, incompetent, or slothful in caregiving arenas. Hawkins and Dollahite believe that much of the research is nondevelopmental in that it does not pay adequate attention to the processes of a man's growth and maturation once he becomes a father; it is inadequate and misconstrues men's motives, feelings, attitudes, and hopes about being fathers; it tends to be unmotivating because it suggests significant barriers to men's personal transformation; and, finally, it is narrow in its focus by holding up some limited external standard of paternal care. That standard is often based on idealized models of motherhood (Day & Mackey, 1989).

As a researcher interested in social constructionism, I am aware of the power of privileging certain stories about "how things are in the world." In the tradition of Michel Foucault, I have come to think about and talk about explanations of how things work as *discourses.* Discourses are more than mere objective perspectives; discourses contain embedded beliefs, values, and practices that serve to shape our sense of the possible explanations. When a discourse gains credibility in society, it may be thought to represent a dominant (or favored) explanation. Keeping in mind all the foregoing ideas, a critique of academic discourses on fatherhood follows.

Historical and
Cross-Cultural Discourses

One of the most striking themes repeatedly found in the historical literature is the idea that fatherhood, generally and specifically, has changed quite dramatically over the course of Western history. The changing roles and activities performed by men in families are explained as being closely associated with the changing economic structure of preindustrial, industrial, and postindustrial societies as families responded to the move away from subsistence economies. Economic industrialization increased the gender separation in family roles, and eroded the interdependent contribution of both men and women in the day-to-day providing for and caring for their children (Bloom-Feshbach, 1981).

Historical analysis suggests that the gender separation of care activities and involvement in family life first came with the introduction of agrarian societies, and then, with much more pronounced effect, at the introduction of paid labor outside the family group accompanying the industrial revolution (Bloom-Feshbach, 1981; Coltrane, 1988; Harkness & Super, 1992; La Rossa, Gordon, Wilson, Bairan, & Jaret, 1991). As men began to venture farther from the family to earn a living, the dominant story of what men "do" became one of provider, whereas what women "do" remained nurturing and caring for children, as well as servicing the family's basic daily needs. Men worked outside the family environment, whereas women remained home; this created a socioeconomic ideology that served to distance men from their children (Zaretsky, 1976).

Since the industrial revolution has given way to highly diverse postindustrial economies, social historians suggest there has been an evolution back toward a sociocultural ideology that values men's active role in families. Social historians remark on several shifting nuances in the discourse of the distant father. Historians note that sociocultural ideology seems to have moved from a prominent discourse of fathers as the moral overseers in the 18th and early 19th centuries (Lamb, 1987; Pleck, 1987) to the dedomestication of fathers as they were pulled out of the family to perform paid work in the factories of the industrial revolution, to fathers as breadwinners until the mid-20th century (Lamb, 1987; Pleck, 1987), to the mid-20th century, when fathers were seen as crucial models in the sex role socialization of children (Lamb, 1987; Pleck, 1987), to the present, when researchers are searching for ways to understand the changes in families that came on the heels of women's massive entry into the paid labor force (Bloom-Feshbach, 1981; Bronstein, 1988; Lamb, 1987). Now that both men and women have been dedomesticated to a great extent by their work outside the family, the focus on father participation and involvement may again have new meanings for families.

An emerging theme in recent literature is that of researchers trying to capture new images that connote the multifaceted, complex, and diverse images of men in families (Lamb, 1987; Lamb, Pleck, & Levine, 1986; Parke, 1988; Pleck, 1987; Schwartz, 1994). La Rossa and his colleagues (1991) remind researchers to revisit their historical perspective before becoming too enamored with new images of men in families, however. La Rossa (1997) stresses how men's earlier experiences of family life was unlikely to have been as monolithic as historical accounts suggest, and that currently there is a discrepancy between what men say they choose as their roles in family life and what they actually do as fathers.

Men and the Provider Role

Structural-functional theory (Parsons & Bales, 1955) became a dominant and idealized template for the analysis of family life in the 1950s and 1960s. As a dominant theory, structural-functionalism supports thinking about normal family functioning, treating any departures from that model as nonnormative or dysfunctional. Though prone to Eichler's (1983) four biases (monolithic, conservative, sexist, and microstructural), structural-functional theory was the genesis for active research regarding the father's role in the family.

In the structural-functional framework, the father is depicted as the "instrumental-leader" of the family, whereas the mother, as the "expressive" parent, is seen as providing care and nurturing for the man and their children (Parsons & Bales, 1955). The emergence of the good provider role (Bernard, 1981) accompanied the trend toward men's dedomestication in family life. Despite women's massive entry into the paid labor force, social discourse about the good provider role for men still seems deeply entrenched. Hood's (1993) edited volume, *Men, Work, and Family,* devotes the entire opening section to research on fatherhood and providing. Hood extends Bernard's (1981) observations on the good provider role, and concludes that this relationship is rather complex. Both qualitative (Cohen, 1991, 1993; Ishii-Kuntz, 1993; Williams, 1993) and quantitative (Stier & Tienda, 1993) studies suggest that men view themselves as involved psychologically; providing for the family's economic welfare may be part of that psychological involvement.

Father's Involvement in Family Life and Child Care: Quantity-Quality Discourse

Questions of how much and what kinds of activities men perform in the everyday life of the family became more interesting to researchers as record numbers of women entered the paid labor force in the 1970s and 1980s. When researchers ask "What do fathers do?" the findings tend to suggest variations on "not enough" (Benokraitis, 1985).

QUANTITY DISCOURSES

General survey studies suggest that men's proportional involvement in family time and activities has increased only marginally by taking on responsibility and activity in family work despite women's increased labor force participation (Atkinson, 1987; Barnett & Baruch, 1987, 1988; Benokraitis, 1985; Carling-Fisher & Tiedje, 1990; Gershuny & Robinson, 1988; Lamb, 1987; Leslie, Anderson, & Branson, 1991; Model, 1981; Pleck, 1984, 1987, 1993). On the other hand, several studies that intentionally looked at families where men were responsible for at least 40% to 45% of child care and general family life have found benefits for all family members (Lamb, Pleck, & Levine, 1987; Radin & Russell, 1983; Russell, 1983, 1986). Men in egalitarian families tend to be more involved than other men, though not as involved as their wives.

This research generally has not examined differences in men's responses to women's changing employment status according to age cohort or by employment status. As such, averages across all generations may distort the phenomenon and contribute to the discourse that men resist changing or relinquishing their privileged access to inequitable sharing in the family. The response in younger cohorts may be different than that found in older cohorts. Looking specifically at subsets of the population and age cohorts may modify understanding of men's purported recalcitrance to be equal partners in family life. For instance, research specifically comparing dual-income families with single-income families reports differences in men's relative participation. Men in two-wage families spend more hours in a week handling family care relative to men in single-earner families (Lamb, 1987; Lamb et al., 1987; Pederson, 1981).

QUALITY DISCOURSES

Studies exploring changing patterns of family life have also looked into the types of child care routines and household activities performed by men and women. Generally, these studies also suggest that men's and women's child care and household routines continue to reflect more traditional gender separation and specialization patterns (Blair & Lichter, 1991; Coverman & Sheley, 1986; Levant, Slattery, & Loiselle, 1987; Perry-Jenkins & Crouter, 1990; Pleck, 1982, 1985). Despite increased involvement by the men, the women remain predominantly the "psychic parent," or the parent who holds the children's well-being foremost in mind and takes responsibility for ensuring that needs are covered regardless of who performed the task (Barnett & Baruch, 1988). Because the time survey studies generally do not simultaneously report satisfaction ratings, it may be too easy for us to speculate that these seeming inequities are always unsatisfactory for women.

More interesting are studies identifying a number of factors explaining how maternal paid employment affects gendered patterns of child care. These studies begin to get at some of the meanings men and women may place on various activities and time commitments when they engage in family decisions about who does what and how. Some interesting factors include the importance of the number of hours the woman works (Leslie et al., 1991); the proportional earnings differential between husband and wife (Model, 1981); the balance of perceived importance between direct and indirect involvement in child care and family life tasks (Atkinson, 1987); men's provider role attitudes (Perry-Jenkins & Crouter, 1990); the woman's sex role attitudes (Barnett & Baruch, 1987); both the woman's and the man's experience of fathering in their respective families of origin (Barnett & Baruch, 1988); the father's perceived competence in child care and household tasks (McBride, 1989); marital harmony (Crouter, Perry-Jenkins, Huston, & McHale, 1987); the husband's marital satisfaction (Levy-Shiff & Israelashvilii,

1988); balancing the advantages and disadvantages of dual-wage life-styles (Skinner, 1980); the father's personality dimensions of autonomy, sensitivity, perception, and openness to experience (Levy-Shiff & Israelashvilii, 1988); and the family's contextual and developmental status (Volling & Belsky, 1991). These studies suggest that much more may influence men's participation in child care and family life responsibilities than simple time use surveys can explain. Expanding the view to include research exploring the meanings men and women hold for their own and their partner's participation in and contribution to the complex tangle of family responsibilities and activities may result in some interesting revisions to popular academic discourses.

ALTERNATIVE PERSPECTIVES ON
THE QUANTITY-QUALITY DISCOURSES

Looking at men who are primary parents offers another perspective for exploring alternatives to the dominant discourse about men's taken-for-granted privilege to spend less time than women in family work. Radin (1988), in a study of primary caregiving fathers (i.e., "house husbands," or men who took more than 50% of the responsibility for child care and general family work), found both the woman's and man's attitudes and characteristics to be important in determining their alternative family life arrangements, but those of the women proved to be more salient. Factors contributing to the women's adjustment were 1) having had a positive relationship with a nurturing father, and 2) having had a mother who worked outside the home. For the man, having had a mother who participated in the paid labor force also seemed to be an important factor in his adjustment.

Generally, research on men's relative contribution to child care and family life could suggest that sociocultural discourses about family being women's work remained largely intact through the mid-1980s. They may also echo popular discourses regarding men deriving their greatest satisfaction from their work lives, and thus not desiring greater involvement in family life. Several studies have found otherwise. Pleck (1985) reports that men derive greater satisfaction from their involvement in family life than from their work. Bloom-Feshbach (1981) also notes that although it can increase the stress experienced in balancing family and work, increased family involvement is generally satisfying for men.

Research exploring the attitudes and factors that encourage and discourage men from active involvement in child care and general family work suggests a complex web of interacting influences. Lamb (1987) and Benokraitis (1985) conclude that four primary areas may discourage men: 1) Men may feel uncomfortable in active fathering roles; 2) friends, peers, and relatives may be suspicious or feel threatened by the man's family life involvement if they are not as involved; 3) structures for balancing work and family life are not flexible or conducive to accommodating family life demands; and 4) government policies are not particularly supportive of men's active involvement in family life.

Pleck (1985) also reports a startling finding suggesting that only a minority of women desire increased involvement from their husbands in child care. Increased involvement of men in child care does not have unambiguously positive effects for these women. Although women generally noted their relief in sharing the total family life and work overload with their husband, they also noted the loss of their exclusively close relationship with their children. This finding lends some credibility to speculative observations that women may subtlety, and perhaps unknowingly, be acting as gatekeepers, constraining men's increased involvement in child care and family life. Women's resistance may slow the pace of change in the general pattern of men's active involvement in daily family life (Lamb, 1987).

In contrast, research in both the United States (Lutwin & Siperstein, 1985; Radin, 1988) and Australia (Russell, 1987) suggest that men who are the primary family caregivers are both competent and satisfied with their family life. Generally, the factors reported to be associated with these men's satisfaction suggest relatively high socioeconomic status and education (Lutwin & Siperstein, 1985; Radin, 1988; Russell, 1987); a high degree of freedom of choice in taking on the family role (Lutwin & Siperstein, 1985; Pruett, 1989; Radin, 1988); flexible work hours (Radin 1988; Russell, 1987); both the husband and wife tend to reject traditional sex roles (Russell, 1987); the husband both enjoys his children and may have more experience with children than his wife (Russell, 1987); and wives are involved in the primary caregiving role for only a relatively short period of time—not more that 18 months (Radin, 1988). Both Russell (1987) and Lutwin and Siperstein (1985) report that men experience some negative aspects of their active and involved parenting and family roles. Interestingly, the negative aspects echo the issues widely reported in the literature on women's experiences—such as loss of freedom, problems of adjusting to being at home, lack of "work status," general lack of social support, the desire for greater community support, and the need for more flexibility in balancing work and family life.

These findings offer an interesting perspective on what may facilitate a man's move into a primary parent position in the family. Generally, they suggest that at least some men and women are actively pursuing a family lifestyle that lies outside the main themes in our social discourse about men's interest in family involvement. The focus in these studies is generally limited to the attributional explanations of what led men to such involvement, however. The studies to date have not generally explored how men and women approach their parenting involvement when the man is more involved in the daily care of the children than the woman. Is there an embedded assumption hidden in the discourse that parenting is really only "mothering," whether women or men are doing it (Kraemer, 1991), that men will not handle the primary caregiver responsibilities and activities as a stay-at-home mother will? Expanding the parenthood discourse beyond a maternal-centric perspective seems necessary; what might we learn about fathering and fatherhood if we look deeply into and beyond this potentially limiting discourse?

In summary, research focusing on the quantity and quality of men's participation in child care and family work has had a tendency to rely on survey research. This reliance may have a distorting effect on academic discourses regarding men's participation in family life. The dominant emphasis placed on "doing"—that is, what men are doing in the family relative to women—obscures other aspects of fatherhood. Many aspects of parenting are expressed not so much in the mere activity being done as in how the activity is done, or how the man thinks and feels about his parenting activities. The embedded attitudes and emotional tones expressed (verbally and nonverbally) while accomplishing any particular task are not revealed in simple time and activity studies. A focus on the nuances in the quality of doing certain parenting responsibilities, as well as attending to the meanings they give to such activities, may further enrich our understanding of the complex experiences of being a father.

Father's Influence on the Child

In reviewing the history of child development theories, Lamb (1981) and others (Lewis, Feiring, & Israelashvilii, 1981; Pederson, 1981) note the early focus on mothers and the absence of or peripheral interest in fathers' influence during infancy, the toddler stage and preschool years. Psychoanalytic (Freudian) and attachment (Bowlby) theories contributed to a dominant discourse relegating the father to the mostly ignored background of family life (Lamb, 1981; Lewis et al., 1981; Parke, 1981; Pederson, 1981). Later, Parsonian theory showed more interest in the father, though it was primarily as a detached socializing agent readying the child for the outside world (Lamb, 1981). Social learning theory (Bandura, Kohlberg, and Deutsch) then took an interest in fathers for their "novel" modeling influence in the socialization of children due to their limited amount of contact (Lamb, 1981). Research in the 1970s began to focus more clearly on the father's effect on child development, initially observing fathers' patterns of interaction with their children (especially newborns) and later moving further toward appreciating the complex and interwoven interactions and relationships in the family (Lamb, 1981; Lewis et al., 1981; Pederson, 1981). Increasingly, researchers appreciated the family systems perspective and its ideas about the difference between interactions and relationships (Lewis et al., 1981), the potential for both mothers and fathers to have direct and indirect effects on their child (Lamb, 1981; Lewis et al., 1981; Pederson, 1981), and the direct and indirect effects the child has on both the mother and the father and their relationship (Clarke-Stewart, 1978; Lamb, 1981; Lewis et al., 1981; Pederson, 1981).

Traditionally, this literature has compared and contrasted men's parent-child interactions with that of women, and concluded that men are generally less involved and are deficient in their ways of interacting. Palkovitz (1997) critiques the limited perspective researchers have taken, and offers six misconceptions that distort our ideas and the resulting research: 1) more involvement is always better; 2) involvement requires proximity; 3) involvement can always be observed or counted; 4) involvement levels are static, and therefore concurrently and prospectively predictive; 5) patterns of involvement should look the same regardless of culture, subculture, or social class; and 6) women are more involved with their children than men are.

An area in which fathers have typically been seen as more involved than women is in the domain of play. Earlier discourse regarding men and play seemed to imply that men's relatively greater involvement in this domain was basically entertainment and had little developmental effect. Parke (1990), reviewing his own groundbreaking research on father-child interaction, notes the need for further study into how play interactions contribute to the development of children. Parke's call for attention to this area may be seen as a critical move toward valuing an area where men consistently demonstrate significant involvement with their children. Parke suggests further examination of how play contributes to children's development that may increase both appreciation for and understanding of gender differences in how women and men interact with their children.

Along with Parke, several researchers have moved in the direction of valuing the ways men, as different from women, engage in parent-child interactions. Starrels (1994) suggests that informal marital and family power, which tends to favor women's decision-making authority, may serve to keep the locus of father-child interactions and relationship in traditional gender domains, such as fathers focusing their attention on instrumental and play interactions. Snarey's (1993) multigenerational research examines typical father-child interactional modes by recasting them in an Eriksonian generativity model. He concludes that typical father-child interactions—such as playing games, going on outings, providing enrichment programs and lessons, teaching athletic skills, and verbal play—make significant contributions to children's 1) social-emotional development, 2) intellectual-academic development, and 3) physical-athletic development. Snarey's extensive list of father-child activity possibilities begins to get at nuances of how instrumental and emotional and nuturing aspects of parenting are blended in complex interactional packages.

Biller (1993) also considers the potential developmental contributions men can make in their children's lives by interacting across a broad spectrum of daily activities. Biller goes somewhat beyond Snarey (1993). He introduces systemic conceptualizations of parent-child interactions, noting how the father-child interaction and relationship is influenced by and mediated through the mother-father-child system. He suggests that parent-child attachment is not an all-or-nothing quality, and that the mother's and the father's experiences of their partner's interaction can influence the quality of the child's developmental interactions with that parent.

Snarey's (1993) work served as a springboard for Dollahite, Hawkins, Brotherson, and Jensen's (1994) and Hawkins, Christiansen, Sargent, and Hill's (1993) focus on how fathers' parenting stories reveal their generativity. These researchers are intentional in their turn away from a deficit perspective (Hawkins & Dollahite, 1997b). Their research moves away from seeing men's nurturing through a lens focused on whether men do the same things women do in caring for children. The focus in their work is on what, in men's ways of being in the family and interacting with their child, can be experienced as providing nurturing in a very broad sense of care and upbringing. Their conceptualization of effective parental nurturing includes broad and inclusive definitions of behavioral and affective indicators of connection, care, communication, consecration, creativity, commitment, and change. These aspects of effective parental nurturing expand the conceptualization of parenting beyond observable behaviors, potentially broadening the field for researchers to explore more of the deep texture of men's parental participation and involvement. Men's narrative accounts of raising a special needs child suggest that men include aspects of all these elements in their self-definitions of being a nurturing parent.

Combined, these findings seem to extend the view of father involvement beyond the previous discourse of dichotomies. These research questions and findings point in a direction of considering a father's presence and effect on a child's development as complex and multidimensional, as well as embedded in an intricate system of family life.

Effect on Men of Becoming and Being a Father

Early research exploring the transition to fatherhood and its effect on men's lives was embedded in discourse assuming the transition would be difficult for men. In contrast, social and academic discourse about the transition to motherhood generally stresses joyful anticipation. For men, the transition-to-parenthood research focused primarily on the challenges, often referring to "crisis" or a "stressful turning point," while ignoring the (perhaps) more illusive joy and opportunity for personal growth (P. Cowan, 1988). Several major findings (C. P. Cowan, 1988) suggest that men can experience the blues or symptoms of depression; men report a decline in their marital satisfaction; men note that their marital communication is reduced in both quantity and quality; men take on smaller shares of housework and child care than either they or their wives had predicted; and men who report being "not ready" for the birth of their first child were found to have lower self-esteem and greater dissatisfaction with their marriage and suffer more symptoms of depression.

In contrast, research from the late 1970s and the 1980s reports some of the positive aspects of becoming a father. Cowan and Bronstein (1988) conclude that some aspects of current research invite us to appreciate the ideas that fatherhood, as a major adult role in men's lives, can be a generator of men's continued development. Several authors call attention to the importance of studying fatherhood across the life span, as opposed to only at the transition points, because it is a continuously evolving process with many opportunities for growth (Cowan & Bronstein, 1988; P. Cowan, 1988; Daniels & Weingarten, 1988; Dollahite, Hawkins, & Brotherson, 1997; Hawkins & Belsky, 1989; Hawkins & Dollahite, 1997a; Hock, McKenry, Hock, Triolo, & Stewart, 1980). Other authors seem to be taking a reflective look at how they conceptualize ideas about the effect on men of becoming and being fathers. Newman and Newman (1988) explore attachment ideas, suggesting that attachment is bidirectional, with each parent forming an attachment to the child. They posit that parent-child attachment grows out of responding to the child and is shaped in an ongoing process through ever-changing parent-child interactions. They suggest that both women and men experience significant adult development cognitively and emotionally through this process. In research on the transition to parenthood, Palkovitz and Copes (1988) echo these ideas, suggesting that men begin to experience changes in self-perception more intensely once the baby is born. They suggest that the ongoingness of being a parent constantly challenges men (and women) to draw on resources, supports, and accumulated experiences to deal with the unexpected. Hawkins and

Belsky (1989) suggest that the dynamic experience of fatherhood can yield rewards for the actively involved father, as well as disappointments.

Krampe and Fairweather (1993) extend Belsky and Volling's (1987) work on the systemic connections among marital relationship, parenting, and infant behavior and development. Focusing on the multidirectional (mother-father-child) and multidimensional interactions of family dynamics that are the milieu of fatherhood, Krampe and Fairweather suggest that men's involvement in the family formation process and child care goes beyond observable behavior and direct parent-child involvement.

Feminist discourse often suggests that men are overidentified with their work and that their relatively limited participation in their children's lives stems from lower interest relative to their work. Some findings in the transition-to-fatherhood literature challenges these conclusions. Fatherhood may bring a shift in a man's sense of self, with the salience of work and partner identities giving way somewhat to an increase in parent identity (P. Cowan, 1988). Daniels and Weingarten (1988) remark that although the primacy of men's work identity changes little, their focus on work often takes on a new perspective with fatherhood—that of increased motivation to be a good provider because the welfare of their child(ren) depends on their ability to support the family. Men also notice changes in their sense of self-boundary to include awareness and sensitivity to others (Daniels & Weingarten, 1988), and report that they experience a surprising level and intensity of emotional involvement with their child(ren) that seems to generate their emotions continuously (Lewis, 1986); that their sense of increased responsibility makes them perceive the world differently; and that they invest a great deal of themselves in their child(ren).

Broadening the discourse beyond the transition-to-parenthood perspective, the life span approach to studying fatherhood has the potential to increase appreciation for and understanding of the bidirectional process of parenting and men's adult development. Lamb et al. (1987) identify a number of themes: Men who highly value parenthood and family and are more involved parents experience greater satisfaction in their family than men who feel parenthood is less intrinsically important. Involved fathers across several cultures experience increased satisfaction in life from feeling close to their children, their opportunity to observe and participate in their children's development, and their sense of feeling intrinsically important to their children. Involved fathers gain a sense of accomplishment and increased fulfillment when they are involved, effective, competent caretakers.

Revisiting Fatherhood Discourses: The Contribution of This Study

The authors reviewed above have made significant contributions extending the understanding of the complexity of men's involvement in child care and family life beyond the simple notions of who does what how often. The evolution of research on fatherhood has undergone several important shifts in focus. These shifts are reflected in what seems to be a move away from earlier research that tended toward dichotomous thinking about fathers—that is, father absence/presence, good/bad fathering, positive/negative effect on child development, and either/or ways of seeing men's participation in family life (Biller, 1993; Furstenberg, 1988). Researchers also seem to be making a departure from an earlier propensity to take either a deficit model perspective on masculinity and men's presence in families (Doherty, 1991) or a comparative model perspective, juxtaposing men's and women's experiences and interactions with children (Belsky & Volling, 1987; Day & Mackey, 1989; Kraemer, 1991). Several researchers are beginning to look at men's experience through a lens championing fatherhood's potentials and men's success as fathers (Biller, 1993; Dollahite et al., 1994; Hawkins & Dollahite, 1994; Hawkins & Roberts, 1992; Palkovitz, 1994; Snarey, 1993).

In framing this study, I responded to several aspects of critique embedded in these earlier studies. Most notably, I was influenced to think about alternatives to the deficit model (Doherty, 1991) and comparative model (Belsky & Volling, 1987) frameworks often used to study men's involvement in parenting. To this end, I was challenged to consider further ideas about the multi-interactional parental system (Belsky & Volling, 1987); ideas about how women may influence, directly and subtlety, men's adopted fathering style (Marsiglio, 1993; Starrels, 1994); and Hawkins and Belsky's (1989) reflective comments noting the potential multidimensional developmental effects for men who are involved fathers. I also noticed that the authors of the most recent research critiques suggest that the study of men's involvement in parenting and general family life needs to listen directly to the voices of men and explore the deep texture of men's own experiences of parenthood.

Work expanding the conceptual framework of father involvement caught my attention. Hawkins and Dollahite (1994; Dollahite et al., 1997) detail aspects of fathering they call "generative" (borrowing from Erickson's theory) that specifically incorporate a positive frame on an "ethic of care." For these authors, *generative fathering* means child-centered fathering that meets the needs of the child by ongoing work to create and maintain the relationships between the father and child. These authors' multidimensional framework recognizes the conditions and constraints of the context, the corresponding necessary categories for generative fathering work, stewardship work, relationship work, and the responsibilities and capabilities of generative father work (see Dollahite et al., 1997, for a complete description of the framework). Palkovitz's (1994, 1997) reconceptualization of father involvement also expands the discourse to include consideration of the behavioral, cognitive, and affective domains, while considering moderating factors (such as individual differences, specific contexts, temporal fluctuations) and several continuums of factors addressing the texture of various types of involvement. Palkovitz concludes that there are myriad ways for men to be involved in a child's life.

Like Dollahite et al. (1997) and Palkovitz (1994, 1997), I set out to explore what alternatives to the deficit model and comparative model discourses there may be in men's and women's narratives. My study extends the extant research by 1) specifically using a social constructionist perspective to explore the multiple realities of parenthood for men and women; 2) purposely seeking to give privilege to the voices of men who are highly involved in parenting; and 3) approaching the study of men's experience of fatherhood from a systemic perspective that brings together the voices of both men and women. I worked with narratives of both men and women, whereas earlier studies focused on men's experiences. I was particularly interested in the experiences of people who were deliberately sharing parenting. In this, my work adds perspective on how fatherhood and motherhood are intricately interwoven, and how changes in men's approaches to father involvement affect women in their approaches to mothering, and vice versa. Although I was well acquainted with the research literature on father involvement, I endeavored to allow the narratives heard from these men and women to shape the theoretical framework I share here. The themes and patterns that were repeatedly voiced became the basis for the theoretical framework I later developed. This was a grounded theory study (Glaser & Strauss, 1967; Strauss, 1987; Strauss & Corbin, 1990), which means that I did not develop hypotheses and then test them against the data generated. I worked with narratives men and women shared about their collaborative parenting experiences to construct a framework located directly in their own stories, rather than taking a reflective conceptual position from the outset.

This research is positioned to challenge and expand academic discourse regarding fatherhood. It contributes to furthering understanding of the deep and complex texture of fatherhood by exploring the experiences of men and women in the context of sharing parenting. This study was framed to look at potential systemic conceptualizations and explore alternatives to dichotomous (either/or), segregated, and complementary views of men's and women's involvement in the intricate moving landscape of family life. The conclusions I reach offer alternatives to the traditional and nontraditional conceptualizations of men's presence in families. The spectrum of potential organizing arrangements created by families suggests there are many ways to structure equitable involvement of women and men in family work. Beyond the organizing arrangements, the study discusses what emerged as some crucial mechanisms that allow parents to keep their "tag team" in place. As well, I suggest that scholars of family relations consider expanding our language, specifically adopting language that begins to break down embedded assumptions that family work is women's work. The conceptualization of an active and interactive process between men and women offers an alternative to common practices of studying fatherhood and father involvement in isolation from motherhood and mother involvement.

PART II

Meaning-Making

As a researcher, I was interested in the meanings men and women ascribe to their everyday experiences of sharing the intimate, intricate, subtle experience of raising children together. Recognizing that their meanings would have been socially constructed between them against the backdrop of predominantly Western cultural practices, I endeavored to access multiple perspectives. Particularly, I wanted to hear men's meaning constructions of their fatherhood experiences; women's constructed meanings about fatherhood; and men's and women's constructed meanings about how each perceives the effect of their ideas, behaviors, and feelings on their partner as they share parenting. I wanted to understand their meanings, rather than impose some preconceived notions, so I adopted the practice of open, unstructured interviewing. I also frequently checked out my evolving interpretations with the participants during the course of each interview. I wanted to keep the research meaning-making endeavor close to their constructions.

My position as researcher was one of privilege and power. The process of conducting the research conversations, although open ended and responsive to what people shared with me, was, in the final analysis, directed by my general research questions. Those questions primarily focused on my interests in the social construction of fatherhood. The questions I asked, the clarifications I sought, the connections I queried imposed brackets around what people might be prone to tell of their everyday lives. People often commented that they seldom thought about the kinds of questions I was asking, and did not think I should make too much of their answers. Their narratives about, and their reflections on, their experiences were so much a part of their everyday world that it seemed I was in the position of making "problematics" out of their taken-for-granted experiences.

The information people shared with me is, not surprisingly, partial, reflective, and reconstructed. Thus, I think of these narrative accounts as "story bits." They are the men's and women's reconstructions after the events, reconstructions that I further extracted from the context of lived experiences. That is, I worked with the narrative accounts removed from the conversational context of the telling of the story. Then I imposed another layer of reconstruction associated with the analytical research endeavor. Thus, the research story presented here, although located in the narratives of the 36 men and women who participated in this research, is essentially my reconstruction of their partial reflections and reconstructed meanings.

As the researcher, I report, interpret, analyze, and comment on the narrative accounts. My interpretations and comments are influenced by 1) the narratives I heard from all 36 people, 2) my interpretations of other research literature, and 3) my interpretations of the local, community, and socio-cultural perspectives. The research interpretations are also influenced by my own life story, particularly my interest in this piece of research, especially my preference to take a proactive view on men's and women's resourcefulness in an attempt to give voice to what I saw as a potentially subjugated story. The resulting research story is a product of interpreting through coding, comparing, organizing, analyzing, and imposing abstract conceptualizations.

In this meaning-making endeavor, I have experienced a layered and reflexive process. In each conversation, my listening was guided by my interest in how each man and each woman came to construct his or her life as a full partner in parenting. I listened for how they explained and made sense of their unique experience. At the same time, I listened with an ear tuned to the similarities and differences between the man and the woman in the couple, as well as comparing their story bits with the story bits I heard from other men and women, both in this study and from previous research literature. I found the reflexive path both rich and illusive. My analytical process worked simultaneously on the individual and couple and across sample levels (see Appendix A for further description of the reflexive analytical cycle).

In choosing where to begin telling these constructed meanings, I had to pick a point in the many reflexive loops that shaped this research story. I was eminently aware that the sequencing of the writing could not duplicate my research process because it was constrained by the linearity of writing. I had the privilege of going back and forth between the tapes, transcripts, and my telling. You, the reader, do not have that privilege or potential advantage. In this regard, the sequencing of my telling shapes your meaning-making.

I chose to sequence the telling somewhat reflexively, moving from telling selected bits of individual and couple history, to abstracted shared concepts, back to more full exploration of selected couple stories. I present six conceptual frameworks developed as part of this research endeavor. As the reader, you will also have the choice to access bio-graphical information on all the families in the study, because Appendix B includes brief sketches of each family. In choosing to present my telling in this way, I hope to give you, the reader, a sense of both the unique experiences and the shared possibilities for men and women creating collaborative parenting. When reading the next six chapters, please keep in mind that what is presented is a result of multiple layers of meaning-making, starting with the individuals' meanings, then the couple's intersubjective meanings, and finally, privileging my interpretations of their meanings.

An important contextual perspective to keep in mind as you read the next six chapters has to do with the genesis of this work. I was working from a grounded theory perspective. As such, I have endeavored to stay close to the research participants' language. Hence, the general analyti-cal framework and the specific themes reflect something of the richly textured meanings I heard about. I often found it difficult to find language that could capture the intricately interwoven textures of meanings. It was tempting to impose familiar language of roles and role complementarity, but this language does not capture the richly textured nuance I heard in these men's and women's narrative accounts. I introduce new terminology as an attempt to distinguish meanings from previous conceptualizations. Thus, in endeavoring to stay close to meanings, I use language that is often laden with complex connections. When doing so, I try to lead you through the nuances so that you, the reader, are invited into their dense meaning space. I trust you will arrive at an appreciation of why I rejected more familiar language.

3

Diversity of Styles
in Sharing Parenting

Dan and Liz: Interchangeable Parenting Partners

Dan and Liz, over 15 years of marriage, have co-created a sharing pattern that intersects their family life and their career work. Both Dan and Liz are in their mid-30s and work in the same human services field. Until recently, they job-shared, both working half-time in the same job. They came to their job-sharing arrangement before they began having children, deciding early on that if they planned and budgeted carefully, they could live on one salary. This decision yielded the potential to give them both equal time for family life, an idea and practice to which they are firmly committed. Over the years, they have arranged their work commitments so that one or the other could always be home with their children, ages 8, 5, and 3 years. Recently, because of threatened cuts in their salary, Dan left "their job" to take a half-time position in a neighboring community. This shift brought a reorganization to some of their family patterns. Most notably, Dan is now home with the children about 60% of the time, and they now have their youngest child in day care 2 half-days a week. Liz now works their job alone, which means she is working full-time, but with some flexibility in arranging her hours. She uses this flexibility to allow her to be with children on the afternoons and early evenings when Dan is working and to schedule one morning as "couple time." They consider their "child-free mornings [as] an oasis in the fortnight . . . [which has] become something sacrosanct."

Dan and Liz also share the routine household work. Now that Dan is home more than Liz, he has taken up most of the cooking, daily tidying, and supervising of after-school routines. They share the weekly cleaning and laundry. They occasionally enjoy having an "adult dinner" after the children are in bed and do the dishes together, when they can, because this is another time they can share work and share talking about the happenings in their respective worlds. Liz has now taken the bath-time routines, because this gives her time with the children, time to listen to their worlds, time to play while accomplishing routine self-care. They alternate story time and bedtime, mostly determined by who may have to be out in the evening for work.

Rodney and Kate: Sharing Parenting While Reserving Certain Specialties

Both Rodney and Kate are in their early 30s, with two children ages 7 and 5 years. Over their 11-year marriage, theirs has evolved into an arrangement that allows them both to work full-time. When their children were younger, Kate moved between full-time work and periods of staying at home with the children. Both Rodney and Kate work in a social services agency. Rodney's work schedule is less flexible than Kate's during the 10 months when their children are in school, but he has the summer months off with the children. Kate's work schedule is flexible throughout the year. Her work flexibility often means she can contribute to the children's parent participation school activities and have after-school time with them. It also means she often works evenings, plus she has extra contractual work one evening a week. Rodney and Kate prefer to minimize their use of day care, and use their different work flexibilities to manage this over the year. When Rodney and Kate both have evening commitments, usually once a week, they handle child care arrangements on an ad hoc basis: "who[ever] had it written in their book first, the second person [who] didn't have it in their book first has to find the care [for the kids]."

Rodney and Kate split the household maintenance and family chores primarily based on preference. Rodney does the household cleaning, the family laundry, and other home maintenance routines. Kate does the weekly shopping and cooks when she is home; Rodney cooks on nights Kate is working. Neither Rodney nor Kate likes doing the family finances, so Rodney does that because Kate believes he manages it better. An area that tends to bring out their differences most clearly is the children's health and medical care. Kate handles most doctor visits and administering of medicine. Her primary involvement in this area started when the children were infants, especially their second child, who had several bouts of illness when he was very young. Kate felt at the time, "I needed to sort of keep on top of that, and I needed to be with him . . . it wasn't that Rodney wasn't involved, it was that I couldn't not be involved."

Jason and Helen: Sharing Parenting With Accounting Equity

Jason and Helen are both in their early 40s, with two children ages 12 and 4 years. Married for 20 years, they have been through a couple of configurations of family life. Jason is an owner-executive of a successful business. Helen is finishing her doctoral education, and works a few hours a week in her professional field. After the birth of their first child, Helen found herself taking most of the responsibility for the daily child care, whereas Jason was dedicating his time to building up his new business. Before they decided to have a second child, Helen requested that they seek counseling because she wanted some things to change. Jason and Helen significantly renegotiated their parenting arrangement to allow Helen to go back to school and to reinvolve Jason in the daily routines of family life. Many things changed before and after the birth of their second child. Four years later, they continue to work toward realizing their commitment and agreement to equal parenting. Jason says, "It's still a balancing act, each of us kinda keeping score, keeping parity in the situation. I feel with Mike [our second child], we at least entered into having Mike with the concept that there would be equal parenting."

Jason and Helen currently negotiate their schedules on a weekly or biweekly basis to juggle both their professional work and their family commitments. Helen has a more fluid schedule than Jason, but Jason has found he can build in flexibility if he plans well. Both Jason and Helen alternate cooking and have agreed on tasks they do on a routine basis (e.g., making school lunches; driving children to school; taking children to lessons; evening child care, including dinner, bath, and bedtime routines). As part of the changes they made several years back, and in recognition of some realities of managing one's own business, Jason and Helen also employ a housekeeper to relieve them of most of the household maintenance tasks and provide some child care during the weekdays. Often, Jason and Helen negotiate their weekend schedules with each having some off time, especially to allow Helen to spend extra time on her studies and professional development.

Jack and Denise: Man as Designated Stay-at-Home Parent

Jack is in his mid-40s and Denise is in her late 20s. In their 8 years together, Jack and Denise have traveled the world, living in a tent for 2 years, and later settled in a university community so Denise could pursue her dream of a medical career. Denise said she came to accept and understand how fully Jack was committed to their "joint project of her career" after the birth of their first child, Jessica, who is now 2 years old.

Over the past 2 years, Jack and Denise have worked out a pattern of sharing parenting that allows her maximum flexibility to accomplish her studies. Jack took paternal leave from his job in retail sales 2 years ago and decided not to return. He now stays home with their daughter and runs a small retail business out of their home. Jack and Denise started their business during the first summer after their daughter's birth, when Denise had some months off from school. At that time, they both realized their infant did not require full-time care from both of them. Jack also recognized his decision to be a stay-at-home father meant they needed some other source of income. Denise is at school long hours most days during the week, and often has studying to do in the evenings and on weekends. Denise contributes to family income with work during the summer months.

Jack, as the designated stay-at-home parent, covers the routine daily child care tasks and the household and family maintenance requirements. He does most of the cooking and daily tidying, as well as the weekly cleaning and laundry. Both Jack and Denise mention squeezing in couple time over the evening dishes. Denise, upon returning to school full-time over a year ago, announced she would clean the bathrooms and prepare some meals on weekends so as to feel she carries a share of the load. She also tries to schedule her studying time after Jessica's bedtime, so she can have a few hours each evening to be with their daughter. Denise also usually has Jessica alone on Friday evenings and on some Saturday mornings, when Jack is out working in their business.

Todd and Collette: Woman as Designated Stay-at-Home Parent

In their early 30s, Todd and Collette have been married for 7 years. They started their family soon after marriage, and now have three children, ages 6, 4, and 2 years. Collette worked full-time until their first child was born, when she took maternity leave. She was uncertain whether she would return to work when her leave was over, and took most of that time to decide not to go back, though her employer was anxious to have her return. In making the decision, Todd was supportive of whatever Collette wanted to do, believing if she "really thought she needed to go back to work, then [he] would have been happy, but, [he] also let her know that [he] would rather have her at home with the kids."

Todd works in the construction trade in his father's business. He also has a contract cleaning business with a friend that brings in extra money occasionally. Collette, self-described as "domestic goddess," has stayed home with their children for the past 6 years, and does not anticipate returning to the workforce in the near future. Collette covers most of the caring for the children and coordinating of their activities during the day. She notes how busy she is with the children's school and other child-oriented activities. Todd is involved in both the morning and evening routines. He gets the kids up and feeds them breakfast while Collette gets dressed in the morning. He is involved in the evenings at dinner, family time after dinner, getting the children bathed, and putting them in bed. They both participate in story time before bed, each reading a story to one or two of the children. Collette handles most of the household maintenance tasks and the routine cooking of meals, but Todd often assists with meals and does the vacuuming weekly. His involvement in the evenings has increased in the past couple of years because economic conditions softened the market for his contract cleaning business, and Collette let him know how important his presence is in her and their children's lives. Collette also notes that Todd makes sure she has some hours to herself on weekends, when he takes over with the children. His personal time usually comes after the children are in bed.

Descriptive Snapshots of Five Couples

All the men and women self-defined their family pattern of parenthood as one where the man was "fully involved" and "active" in daily family life and parenting their children. In asking people to describe a typical day and a typical week in the life of their family, inquiring about who does what, I heard about a variety of ways men and women live their involvement in family life. I noticed five general styles these 18 couples have come up with to organize their family life.

For these families, as with most, notions of a monolithic structure did not fit their diverse experiences. There were differences between the man and woman in each couple, as well as differences across the men and the women in this study. There was not one way to organize men's full and active involvement in family life, but many variations considered acceptable to men and women across these families. I began to think in terms of dominant themes and descriptors that might capture some primary aspects of this variety. I looked to categorize and compare dominant themes and emerging descriptors. Looking for similarities and differences, I clustered the 18 families in groupings of similar styles and patterns as an heuristic schema.

A DISCLAIMER

In selecting these five families to feature in introductory profiles, I hope to give you, the reader, a sense of the complexity and diversity of lived experiences, both within individual families and across several families. Each of the 18 families who shared bits of their stories offered a rich and interesting collage of experiences and meanings. Each family's story warrants full telling, yet I have chosen to tell only five stories here. I have considered the heuristic potential of each family experience and selected those that allow differences to be highlighted clearly. These five profiles focus on some tendencies toward prototypic aspects. I have thought of them as exemplars, or good models to illustrate some of the dynamics I heard about in other families; families that, although different in specific details, tend to organize their sharing parenting arrangements somewhat similarly.

These five snapshots are merely descriptive and are intended to provide some sense of the real people behind the conceptualizations. They may also provide a hint at the diversity of ways parents have constructed their family life. Like photographs, these descriptive snapshots are posed, perhaps stilted, and frozen in time. Like photos, these constructed snapshots are both representative of the real people and not. They are representative in that they sketch, in simplistic and basic outlines, the family's present organizational structure from a simple overview perspective. They capture only one view—a descriptive overview. From a closer, in-the-moment perspective, they are not really representative of lived experience. Living in families is typically more complex; intricately woven between individuals (parents and children); and fluid over myriad opportunities of interaction daily, weekly, and yearly than an overview picture can provide. It would be necessary to create a multiperspective, rich collage of moving pictures to begin to capture the deep texture of these complex family experiences. As a start, however, I will build from these selected snapshots.

These snapshots are not representative in another important way: They focus on the instrumental and behavioral aspects of managing the flow of family life and formal work outside the home, rather than on the deep texture of affective experience and interactive meaning-making between the members in the family. Nonetheless, I offer these descriptive snapshots as an opening introduction to the potentials of living and co-creating sharing parenting.

Styles of Sharing Parenting

As I listened to the 18 families talk about they way they organize their sharing patterns, I heard them use language that hinted at their beliefs about both the woman and the man being equally responsible for their children. Their talk suggested that they often planned and organized how they, as two parents, would cover all the bases of managing the daily flow of life, as well as how, in the larger scheme of their child's life over many years, they wanted to shape parenthood for themselves to reflect, in intentional living patterns, their sharing of responsibilities and activities. These men and women do not view these responsibilities or activities as belonging in the sphere of one or the other of them. They do not experience their participation in family life as mere roles. Rather, they view the myriad aspects of family life as their joint responsibility. Further, they recognize that these are complex responsibilities about which they often have to make pragmatic decisions. In the spirit of their rich narratives, I have chosen to introduce new language—or labels I heard embedded in their narratives—to describe their styles of sharing parenting. This language reflects both their sense of joint responsibility and ongoing pragmatic organizational decisions.

I call the five clusters of dominant styles *man as designated stay-at-home parent, interchangeable parenting partners, parents with certain reserved specialties, parenting partners in an accounting equity pattern,* and *woman as designated stay-at-home parent.* These thematic labels are meant to represent a tendency toward a diversity in style and variations in how men and women organize their involvement. Although these five styles are presented here as distinct, in lived everyday experience, the complexity of family values and myriad life situations means they are likely less distinct than defined and presented here.

INTERCHANGEABLE PARTNERS

The descriptive snapshot of Dan and Liz suggests it is possible for couples to organize their family life so that both the woman and the man are participating in an interchangeable manner across a wide spectrum of activities and responsibilities. In Dan and Liz's case, over the 8 years they have had children, both have had the responsibility and experience of being the at-home parent about the same amount of time. They have had periods when Liz was at home with the children a greater amount of the time, especially in the early months following the birth of each of their three children. More recently, Dan has become the parent who is at home a greater proportion of the time.

Dan and Liz, along with the other two families in this style cluster, organize their family life and their work outside the home so both of them may be involved in their careers and in raising their children. Their sharing style typically has each being the designated at-home parent according to a fairly fixed schedule each week, determined largely by their respective work requirements. During times when both parents are at home with the children, they typically both participate in what needs to be done. At times when both parents are available to be involved, they may work out a schedule that allows each to have a period of "down time," time to oneself to relax or to pursue personal interests.

In families where the father and mother tend to be highly interchangeable, generally both the man and the woman are equally involved in the daily and weekly routines and nonroutine tasks and events with the children. Both also participate in managing and performing the household maintenance tasks. They have co-created their family parenting philosophy, and are equally committed to and competent in carrying out all aspects of implementing it in their daily lives. Typically, the couples in this configuration have made career choices to maximize their involvement in family life. This often means negotiating work arrangements that are flexible in their hours (full-time/part-time possibilities) and financial potentials. Both the man and the woman typically contribute more or less equally to the family income.

RESERVING CERTAIN SPECIALTIES IN SHARING PARENTING

Rodney and Kate's snapshot suggests the potential for both the woman and the man to be involved, but to have their involvement differentially distributed over daily family life. The reserved specialties dimension comes to light when they talk about certain areas of family life they do not open fully to equal and interchangeable sharing. That is, there are some aspects of parenting that one partner or the other "reserves" for herself or himself. In Rodney and Kate's family, the children's health and medical care is an area where Kate reserves a right to more, though not completely exclusive, involvement.

In the general flow of daily life, Rodney and Kate each take an active part in being an at-home parent, but their availability for being the designated at-home parent is largely determined by their work schedules. Kate maximizes her flexibility to spend some hours every week in the school with each of their children, plus to be available to be with them at home after school, by working a four-fifths week at the social service agency. She brings her work hours back up to full-time by regularly doing contractual work in the evenings. Her flexible availability is constant over 12 months, whereas Rodney's flexibility is concentrated in the evenings and over 2 summer months when school is out. He is then available to be with the children all day and most evenings. Rodney and Kate spend about the same amount of time with their children over the course of a year, but they do so in quite different time frames. Rodney and Kate have also organized their division of labor for family maintenance and household tasks to allow each to do what he or she prefers. They do not expect each other to share each and every job, but to do those tasks that are their individual specialties. They each acknowledge that the other is capable of doing any task or performing any child care responsibility, but they typically agree to specialize in a few reserved areas when and where possible.

There are three other families in this configuration cluster. In each, both the man and the woman are highly involved in the daily and weekly routines and nonroutine events and tasks with their children. In their pattern of involvement, there are certain domains or tasks that one or the other claims complete or greater jurisdiction over, or declares outside his or her jurisdiction. Their pattern, in effect, creates certain reserved specialties for one or both partners. These specialties may occur in parenting and family and household maintenance areas. In these families, both the man and the woman contribute to family income, but in some cases, one or the other partner potentially contributes more than 55% of total family income. When there is a significant disparity in income-generating potential, providing for the family may be considered one area of reserved specialty.

ACCOUNTING EQUITY PARENTING PARTNERS

Jason and Helen's transition to sharing all aspects of family life has not been particularly smooth. They have been through many discussions, agreements, renegotiations, and refinements. As Jason works to live up to his commitment to be an equal parent, he is at pains to reconcile within himself whether he is indeed truly living up to his partner's idea of being an equal parent. His questioning of himself suggests that he is unsure, and his partner is the key to monitoring how equal he has become. He said,

> I think I share in some of the responsibilities, but I'm not, I certainly don't have the total awareness of the things that Helen is aware of when it comes to our children's behavior or responsibilities. So I don't know if I'm— maybe I was trying to force my characterization, my role of parenting into equal parenting. I don't know if I'm an equal parent.

For Jason and Helen, and the two other couples in this configuration cluster, the man and woman have worked out rather formal agreements and arrangements as to who will handle various aspects of the routine and nonroutine child care, family care, and household maintenance responsibilities. The flow of balancing family work and child care between them seems to be monitored regularly by one or both partners, with negotiations occurring frequently to ensure that "equity" or "fairness" is maintained. The impetus for bringing them to the current arrangement has typically come from the woman, with the man making an honest effort to become more fully engaged in family work and child care. The man may not have questioned earlier arrangements, but often felt his commitment to family life—though perhaps not his instrumental involvement—has always been equal to that of his partner's. He is now in the position of bringing his instrumental involvement in line with his self-perception and commitment to sharing parenting.

MAN AS DESIGNATED STAY-AT-HOME PARENT

As the descriptive snapshot of Jack and Denise suggests, in families where the man is the designated stay-at-home parent, the couple's organizational structure may resemble what much of the academic literature refers to as "traditional family structure with the roles reversed." In talking with Jack and Denise, however, I came to appreciate that they do not see themselves in a reversal of roles. They do not see parenthood as primarily the woman's domain or role, nor did they experience Jack to be in some reversal of roles as he took on the designation of being the parent who would carry the bulk of the daily interaction and care of their child. In fact, they were clearly opposed to the idea that their complex lives could be reduced to a set of roles to be divided between them. Their pattern is one of coconstructing a division of labor that has allowed Denise to be involved in an intensive training program while they started having children. Jack manages the daily flow of life at home, while Denise has the time to concentrate on her career studies, be away from home long hours every day, and be assured that their daughter is experiencing primary nurturance and socialization from one of her parents.

In man-as-designated-stay-at-home-parent families generally, the man takes much of the responsibility for organizing and carrying out the daily and weekly routines and nonroutine tasks with the children. He also manages most of the daily and weekly household maintenance tasks. Generally, the woman is formally engaged in daily activity outside the home. She participates actively in child care during her at-home hours, and is very involved in co-creating the family environment and parenthood philosophy. For Jack and Denise, as with other families in this configuration cluster, Denise wants to be more involved in the parenting, family maintenance, and household tasks than is often typified of men in similar positions (i.e., as the partner who works outside the home or is involved in career training). At the same time, Denise notices that Jack does not usually request her to be as involved in these tasks as she believes she should be; he leaves it to her initiative to decide how involved she wants to be on a daily basis. Often in the man-as-designated-stay-at-home-parent families, the woman's income is primary, whereas the man's income is likely to be supplemental.

WOMAN AS DESIGNATED STAY-AT-HOME PARENT

Generally, Todd and Collette's family looks very traditional when focusing on the surface organizational structure of who provides family income and who takes care of the children. That is, Todd is the designated provider, and Collette has chosen to stay home with the children. I heard this couple talk about a crucial difference in how they think about their reasons for organizing their family life in this manner, however. The twist in what we think of as a traditional family structure appears when you look under the surface of the provider and caretaker organization to discover nontraditional attitudes and parenting behaviors.

Todd has intentionally adopted an attitude and the behaviors of being an active parent. To make this happen for himself, his partner, and his children, he purposefully creates many opportunities, in both routine family life and nonroutine opportunities (e.g., coaching his son's baseball team), to participate, interact, and be available for his children. He makes sure he is home in the evenings and on weekends to "be with his kids" so he "will know them and they will know [him]." Collette also expects Todd to be involved. She wants him to share in family life. To encourage this, she does not try to do all the family chores while the children are around because she believes this diverts energy and attention from them. She welcomes Todd's presence at the end of the day, when he can take over with the children to give her some time to herself.

For the five families in this configuration cluster, the man is generally very involved with the children outside his formal work hours (mornings, evenings, and weekends). He and his partner value sharing the responsibility for the children. That is, they both expect him to be highly involved in the noninstrumental aspects of creating an environment to raise their children—planning, guiding, and nurturing their growth—as well as the instrumental activities when he is home. The man has typically taken specific positions with his paid work to minimize his absence from the family. He often provides the primary care for the children for periods in the evenings and on weekends so his partner can be engaged in other interests or activities. The woman, although a stay-at-home parent, has not assumed that this is her primary responsibility or her exclusive role; she has typically chosen to be the designated at-home parent, and often expresses a sense of privilege in having this choice. The men typically consider themselves to be an equal parent with their partner with "unequal exposure to parenting opportunities" (Sam).

Reflections

In the disclaimer statement, I mentioned the idea that the lived experience of these 18 families was likely less distinct than the examples and the imposed definitions I suggest. Now I want to go back somewhat, to revisit my declared distinctions between the style clusters and suggest a more complex representation of these ideas.

In constructing the sharing parenting style clusters and my working definitions, I often found it difficult to fit each of the 18 families into one, discrete category. This was not a particular surprise, nor was it a function of my relative research experience or intellectual ability. It was more a function of complexity. People's lives are not as simple nor as linear as researchers (myself included) want to make them seem. The men and women who shared parts of their lived experience through reconstructive telling for this research are no exception. Indeed, in the ways they have tried to manage life's complexity—by co-creating a sharing parenting experience—they may have increased the complexity of family life. These women and men have chosen to decide and negotiate how they will organize their experiences of parenthood, rather than fall into typical sociocultural patterns that simplify negotiations and guide people in knowing what they are expected to do as men and women. Each of the 18 families has created a unique way to coordinate and manage the myriad activities and responsibilities encountered daily in family life. As such, none of the families represents an exact "fit" in any the five configuration clusters sketched above, especially if the clusters are thought of as discrete and mutually exclusive categories. Indeed, even proposing these configurations as a way of organizing an academic understanding of how families live out sharing parenting risks creating another stereotypical characterization of families and the individuals in them—characterizations that inevitably misrepresent the complexity of lived experiences.

Revisiting my constructions of these sharing parenting style clusters, I offer them as a method to conceptualize possible ways couples are organizing their coordinated contributions to keeping their families going, day in and day out. I do not think of these style clusters as mutually exclusive or discrete categories along a linear continuum. I think of them more in terms of a circular, multilayered spectrum. For any particular family, one configuration style may be the most apparent currently. Over time, however, the family may go through transitions when its most prominent style could shift. At any given moment, the most prominent style could be blended with subtle aspects of any one or more of the other styles.

4

A Diversity of Paths

What Influenced Men and Women to Move Toward Sharing Parenting

I was very interested in the background, or the paths that may have led these men and women in the direction of co-creating their working vision of sharing parenting. Asking these men and women about what led them to this place in their family lives, I heard them describe a number of processes. Behind the structure of their current family life arrangements lies a dynamic interplay between individual histories of the man and that of his partner, and the history of their life together as a couple and a family. In listening to all 18 families' partial stories, my attention was initially drawn to what in the man's life may have primed him to move toward actively participating in all aspects of family life and child rearing. Later, I also asked the woman what in her life primed her to organize her partnership this way. When I spoke to them as a couple, I asked what in their life together spurred this to become their shared reality.

My lines of inquiry and the story bits I heard led me to focus on two levels of analysis: 1) tracing some family-of-origin precursors that might be thought of as an impetus; and 2) what was, and perhaps continues to be, the prime mover behind their constructing together sharing parenting possibilities and arrangements. Both analytical levels contribute to an understanding of how and why these people came to organize their family lives along sharing parenting lines. Both levels of analysis are intricately woven and connected to the other. For heuristic purposes only, I present each level of analysis here as separate influences.

Family-of-Origin Stories

My curiosity about the general experiences in each parent's family of origin initially focused on what kinds of models their own parents had been for them; how their experiences growing up influenced their ideas about how they wanted to be in their adult family of choice. Later, I became interested in what other ideas or people influenced both the man's and the woman's path toward co-creating sharing parenting. Below, I focus most fully on the family-of-origin influences, and later speculate about how these may have influenced the formation of ideological positions about male-female partnerships.

Women's family-of-origin experiences seemed to influence these couples' stories both directly and indirectly. I think of the direct influences as being the ideas and models of parenthood a woman shaped coming out of her family of origin. At the same time, I heard men describe their partner's family of origin as a surrogate model or, more significantly perhaps, seeing their partner's way of parenting as a primary model. I think of this dynamic as a indirect influence of the woman's family-of-origin experiences.

Asking people to talk about what kinds of things influenced them to create this living vision of sharing parenting, I often heard men's family-of-origin experiences highlighted as a primary impetus, whether those experiences were satisfactory, not particularly satisfactory, or quite negative. The meaning clusters below are based on my reading of how much those experiences were highlighted as *antimodels*; *good, but not good enough to emulate, models*; or some combination of influences that have been overshadowed by a declared ideological position—*beyond family-of-origin models.*

ANTIMODEL FATHERS

Several men in the study offered stories about unsatisfactory and negative experiences in their families of origin. Recalled experiences with their fathers ranged from severely physically abusive, to emotionally abusive, to emotionally and sometimes physically absent, to quite distant and unconnected. Generally, these men recalled making decisions not to repeat this experience with their own children, vowing early on to father differently. Most often, the women mentioned satisfactory relations and experiences with their mothers, and in many cases with their fathers also. Only one woman mentioned growing up in an abusive environment. Nonetheless, they made similar decisions to do things differently. Women frequently mentioned not wanting to be as isolated and housebound as their mothers were.

The number of times men mentioned their family-of-origin experiences being instrumental in their decision to "do things differently" caught my attention. The frequent mention of this idea indicated the seriousness of those early shaping experiences, especially their potential to push these men to find other ways to be in families. The number of times men mentioned their commitment to themselves, their partners, and their children not to be like their own fathers also caught my attention. It convinced me of the sanctity of their commitment to be a different kind of father. The prevalence and passion of the antimodel father stories men told suggest how unsatisfactory family-of-origin experiences can be a major impetus in men's lives. It is an impetus influencing men to find the energy and resources within themselves to be highly involved in family life and in their own children's lives.

Three of the five selected exemplar families told antimodel father stories about the man's family-of-origin experiences in particular. Of these three, I selected Rodney and Kate's story to feature here. Their story provides some detail about physical, emotional, and psychological abuse or neglect and how those experiences drove Rodney to break the pattern in raising the next generation.

Rodney and Kate

Rodney: I think a combination of a couple of things [influenced me to
be involved with my kids]. I think one is the way I was reared
as a child. In that my dad wasn't a lot involved with me. He was
always sort of out doing his own thing, even on weekends he
would do his own thing and not necessarily family-type of
things. That was one of the reasons that kind of motivated me
to think that if I were to have children, I would definitely be
more involved or whatever. Spending a lot of time with my
mother as well, I think there [I had] more respect for my mother
than I had for my father around how she sort of kept the house
running, and kept things in check, and I mean it was a lot of
work. Typically I'd help her out a fair bit. Another thing was,
after meeting Kate, her father was quite involved in the home.
He was retired at the time, and he did a lot of the work around
the home, which was kind of neat for me to see as well. . . . He
did a fair bit of the chores and basically ran the home, and I
thought that was great too. So, I mean again that just kind of
reinforced my thoughts of, yes, it's okay to do it, it's not
something you know that you're going to be kind of teased or
taunted for by other people. The way my dad was, well you're
supposed to do manly thing, and looking after the house isn't
one of them. . . . Whatever we did, it didn't matter what we
did, it was just never the right way, it was never good enough.
You know, we'd never get any sort of empathy or love from him,
it was more always yelling and his low tolerance and frustra-
tions . . . I mean, my relationship with my father is, there
basically isn't one. In my family growing up, there was a lot of
family violence, and there still is, and again that was something
that really affected me. I was always sort of protective of my
mother, in a sense, but I couldn't protect her, so you know,
growing up, I'm always sort of telling myself that this isn't going
to happen with me, it's not going to be, these types of things
aren't going to happen with my family. So telling myself, I'm
going to be more involved. I want my children to be able to
come to me and be able to show them empathy and caring and
love. I mean, that word was never used in our family, I mean,

it wasn't even heard of . . . again, telling myself, this isn't going to happen type of thing, it's going to be different. Basically, what motivated me was the things that happened to me as a child, I didn't want to happen to my children.

Kate: Rodney lived at my parent's house for a little bit, and in my parent's house because my dad was retired and my mom was still working full-time, my dad did cooking and cleaning and stuff like that. So I think that was sort of the beginning, because then Rodney saw a difference between his family and my family, and I just sort of assumed that's the way it was. I was 10 when my dad retired—when I remember home, that's what I remember. My dad was sort of puttering around and my mom gone.

Rodney's family experience growing up was a major factor in his decision to forge a different path for himself, his partner, and his children. His father was not only physically abusive, he was severe in his criticism and his humiliation. Rodney recalls his experience of not knowing his father loved him; nor does he remember any positive times when he was able to connect with his father. He laments that he has never had a relationship with his father. He found more positive parental models in his own mother, and later in Kate's father and mother. Here he learned about feeling connected in a relationship and the potentials of creating a different life for his family. Rodney's vow to himself to do it differently was emphasized several times in our conversations. Kate's family experience gave her a grounding to appreciate that men could be very involved in home life and women could be involved in their work outside the home. She found it difficult to imagine it being any different, which reinforced Rodney's initially tentative steps away from traditional male posturing.

Eight other men in the study related family-of-origin experiences that echoed themes found in Rodney's story. The men related family-of-origin stories they experienced as emotionally isolating and as psychologically impairing their sense of what it meant to be a man in the world, even if physical abuse was not present. These men spoke of longing to be connected to their undemonstrative, seemingly uninterested, peripheral yet overbearing fathers. In my conversations with these nine men, I heard them voice how those experiences lead them to vow to themselves that they would build relationships with their children, be available in body and spirit, and work to build their children's self-confidence. Their vows were all voiced in direct reaction to how they were fathered —voiced out of the harm they felt they experienced in their families of origin.

GOOD, BUT NOT GOOD ENOUGH TO EMULATE, PARENTING MODELS

For several men and women, conversation about their family-of-origin experiences suggests they had satisfactory to quite positive experiences with their fathers and mothers. Generally, their fathers were seen in the traditional mold. These older generation men worked outside the home, providing a basic sense of well-being and financial security for the family, while their partners (the women) were in charge of the home and children. The father's interaction with the children was mostly remembered by these men as special events or family outings.

Although the men in these families usually did not use the strength of language about vowing to do it differently as did the men who had antimodel fathers, they also suggested that they know their children are having a different experience because of their more active involvement in sharing parenting. As I listened to the stories of these men, I thought of them as having good experiences with their fathers, but not good enough for the fathers to be models for their fathering. These men did not convey a strong commitment to being different in the antimodel sense of reacting against their childhood experiences; they talked of finding more potential in fatherhood than they thought their fathers had experienced. Of the families in which men told good, but not good enough to emulate, father model stories, Jason and Hillary's story is featured here. Jason and Hillary related how they each wanted more "connection" and "freedom of self-realization" for themselves and for their partner and children than they felt their parents' models could give them. They seem to recognize how the expectations in their parent's generation constrained their potential as parenting partners.

Jason and Hillary

Jason: If you're brought up in a traditional family and your father was a traditional father [which mine was], and all your male peer group are in a traditional setting, there's tremendous amount of pressure to stay traditional. . . . I had a comfortable childhood, though my parents divorced when I was a teen. I had all the financial security in the world. That was never an issue, but I think now the financial security was there in lieu of the real emotional attachment, and I think my kids will have the emotional attachment. They know that they have parents who are there for them. . . . From time to time my mother would kind of get on me about certain traditional things—"Aren't you doing this, you're doing that?"—I just let it go. From my father, I get the typical dose of—"You're doing such a great job as a father"—I think that would come no matter what I was doing. . . . It was not easy to break out of that traditional mold, but boy I'm glad I'm not there! I've gained life experience. Life experience and connection. If it's only better connection with the kids, that's more than enough to have gained. It really is, yea!

Hillary: I didn't really want to have [children] for a long time, I think because I was the oldest of four and felt sort of that it was way too many kids for my parents to handle. I ended up being very responsible for raising my siblings. But when I was 29, I just decided that I would do that, and Jason had never pushed for kids and didn't object, so I'd say it was certainly my decision and he was kind or going along with it. . . . I was pretty much raised to be a mother and all that, and I'm just one of those people that I think I didn't settle in on anything—a major in college or a job afterwards, or anything. Then about a year after [the birth of our first child], I got depressed, because I realized that my life was going exactly the way my mother's had gone and it scared me.

My conversations with Jason and Hillary (and others in this cluster) were remarkable in that their families of origin were seldom mentioned. When asked directly, Jason mentioned his traditional upbringing and his feeling of having had a comfortable childhood. He mentioned his father's support of whatever he does, and conveyed a sense of appreciating that support. In retrospect, he also laments that the financial security he knew as a child was likely in lieu of what he now knows as a father's emotional connection with his children. Hillary's experience as a "parentified child" was instrumental in her initial reluctance to start a family, and later in seeking to change her experience as a mother and partner significantly. Hillary's family-of-origin experience, although not abusive, served as a major impetus in pushing for difference in her family of choice; she did not want to repeat the seemingly oppressive experience she saw in her mother's life.

Other men and women in the study conveyed a similar good, but not good enough to emulate, kind of experience with their fathers and mothers. As men talked about their childhood experiences with their fathers, I often felt a sense of calm, knowing that their fathers represented a sense of family security and had presence in creating the family's comfortable atmosphere. When asked about specific interactions with their fathers, most people's responses echoed Jason's: The father was there, often on the periphery, but his occasional involvement was noted (e.g., "He'd come home and sit and read his paper and on weekends he'd often take the family on outings in the country"—Rick; "On Friday nights he'd come home from work with Coca-Cola, he would make popcorn, and we would watch TV together as a family"—Patrick).

One man, Erik, had a more significantly positive experience with his father. He remembers his mother becoming chronically ill when he was a teenager; he and his father then worked together to run the family and home life. He remembers, fondly, that time of forging a closer bond with his dad, who had been more of a disciplinarian until then. His vision of parenthood comes more from the time of working with his father than the earlier experience of him as a disciplinarian. Erik says that, though his experience with his father was quite positive in his later years at home, his current sharing parenting partnership stems primarily from developing an egalitarian ideology as a young adult.

Of the 18 women I spoke with, all but one spoke of her experiences with "good enough" fathers and mothers. These women, although acknowledging basically good childhood experiences, also declared that they wanted to have a different experience of parenthood than they observed their fathers and mothers having. They typically spoke of wanting their partners to be involved in sharing all aspects of parenthood with them. These women suggested, directly and indirectly, that their mothers carried the primary responsibility for child rearing and family care. When women spoke of their mothers, I heard stories of predominantly stay-at-home mothers. Although the daughters (the women I spoke with) remembered their childhood experiences fondly—offering several versions of "knowing their mothers were there to care for them"—they also spoke of an awareness that their mothers paid some costs in being the primary caregiver, and that their fathers lost out because of their peripheral involvement in family life. These women did not want to repeat that experience in their own lives. The women who had mothers who worked outside the home depicted their mothers (with one exception, in Kate's story) as carrying a double load. These women spoke of not wanting this to be their experience in their family of choice. I came to think of the women as having both male and female models in their parents (whether antimodels, good, but not good enough to emulate, models, or good models). For the most part, these women generally described their mothers as good, but not good enough to emulate, models. Their mothers modeled ways to interact with children and care for the family that these women appreciate, but they want to find alternative ways—ways to have their partners more involved so they do not have to do it all.

BEYOND FAMILY-OF-ORIGIN MODELS— ADOPTING EGALITARIAN IDEOLOGY

For several families, the most prominent strand in their path to sharing parenting seemed to be having purposefully adopted an egalitarian ideology. Consideration of their family-of-origin experiences seemed somewhat secondary in their stories. What sets this group of families apart from other clusters is the emphasis on an adopted ideology. Many of the women in this group hinted at being influenced, directly or indirectly, by the woman's liberation movement. Many of the men spoke of their life philosophy and its egalitarian ideals. In offering this meaning cluster as separate from the other two categorizations, I am not suggesting that family-of-origin experiences have not been influential in these people's lives. Rather, their stories "low-light" their family-of-origin experiences and highlight their ideology. These parents stressed that family arrangements are ideologically driven on some level other than in reaction to family-of-origin experiences. They clearly declared their egalitarian ideology as an impetus in coming to their current positions.

In the illustrative example found in Dan and Liz's story, I focus on both family-of-origin history and egalitarian ideology as the key threads in creating their version of sharing parenting.

Dan and Liz

Dan: I don't know that my parents particularly liked having children. They've shown astonishingly little interest in their grandchildren, and no interest in anybody else's children. My father was an only child, and I don't think he liked children at all. . . . My parents were not monsters, I grew up in a normal dysfunctional family. . . . I think probably the person that is my chief role model for how to be now is not so much my mother, but I tend to think what would a woman be doing now? . . . Liz and I, we're kind of pinko-leftist-Christian-vegetarian type freaks. . . . I suppose my generation has been able to fall a step back and do some critical thinking about the way we live our human lives . . . the feminist movement strongly saying to our generation, think about it . . . and feminism leads you into a vision of creation which is egalitarian. . . . I see it in spiritual perspective, and that's important. I mean it really shifts everything . . . it affects a lot for me. The way I see the world has altered in the last 10 years . . . [it's] allowed me to be very involved in raising my children.

Liz: I think I have more models to draw on because I was the second oldest of five, and I think mine [family of origin] was a more normal family in some ways than Dan's. . . . My father was very much the traditional father who was out of the home and very, very far removed from the child care. He didn't enjoy small children, and he made that quite plain. He would just remove himself. I suppose my mental image of my mother and the model that she [represents] was of somebody omnicompetent who would work and come home and do, well, do both of those things single-handedly without ever complaining as far as I remember. I often, in a sort of primitive way, call on her spirit, as it were, to enable me to cope when I'm feeling stretched or when the demands of home and work are conflicting. . . . So, I

think in reaction against that, I badly wanted a partnership
where my husband would be an active father. . . . Let's see, what
else drives me? A certain theoretical outlook which believes in
this very strongly. I think my brand of feminism is more a sort
of humanism. I believe that this [partnership and sharing par-
enting] makes both Dan and myself whole human beings in a
way that wouldn't be possible otherwise, or wouldn't be so easy
if we weren't able to do this.

Both Dan and Liz mention experiences with distant, traditional
fathers. Liz had a more positive image in her mother, but she also saw
that she did not want to replicate her mother's "double shift." She
talks of strongly desiring it to be different for her: wanting a partner
who would be active in family life. Dan mentions his mother, but looks
to other women to give him a more positive model of parenthood.
Both Dan and Liz talked less about their families of origin than they
did about their egalitarian ideology and how it fits with their life
philosophy and spirituality. Liberal ideology, in particular humanistic,
or ecological, feminism (in Dan's terminology), guides both Dan and
Liz in their partnership as husband and wife and as mother and father.
They both find egalitarian ideology to be a foundational touchstone,
especially when they are working through the challenges of living out
their partnership day in and day out.

Although the particulars differ, the stories of the other families I
include in this cluster resonate with strong ideological chords. About
half the families in this group told stories echoing the antimodel father
themes found in Rodney's story. From the other half of the people in
this group, I heard good, but not good enough to emulate, themes similar
to those found in Jason and Hillary's story.

Co-Creating Sharing Parenting
Possibilities: Some Prime Movers

In listening to people share pieces of their process in creating sharing
parenting possibilities for themselves, I began to think of themes that
could represent some of the paths I heard them describe. I settled on

three themes: 1) a co-construction responsive to circumstances; 2) a co-construction initially encouraged by the woman; and 3) a co-construction rooted in shared ideological ground.

Initially, I thought of these three predominant pathways as circumstance-determined, woman-driven impetus, and co-construction. As I went back over the transcripts, however, I became more open to the meaning-strands suggesting that both the woman and the man intentionally made choices to shape their family life together. Indeed, I found that all the couples were engaged in a co-construction process. A *co-construction* is an interactive meaning-making process between people. It is a process in which people create shared meanings that may lead to coordinated actions (Weingarten, 1991).

I found that these 18 couples were involved in a co-construction process as they negotiated decisions about family life together. In making intentional decisions, each person seemed to be balancing individual preferences with the larger family picture and individual and collective commitment to the family's well-being. I think of these processes as co-constructive in that I did not hear talk suggesting that either the man or the woman had imposed meaning, rejected meaning, misunderstood the other's meaning, or refrained from meaning-making with his or her partner (Weingarten, 1991).

For example, in response to a circumstance such as the birth of Jack and Denise's daughter in the middle of Denise's semester, each decided on a certain course of action. Denise decided she wanted to finish the term; Jack decided his commitment to Denise's career training and having one parent at home with their infant was more important than his current job. When it came time for him to go back to work, they had another decision to make. Together they decided the months with Jack as the designated stay-at-home parent had gone well; that Denise would lose too much if she took a leave of absence at that point in her training; and that neither really wanted the infant to go to day care. Both had the opportunity to make different decisions. The circumstance presented certain opportunities. Jack and Denise worked together to co-construct a response that worked for everyone in the family, although it had different effects on them individually. These subtle meaning-strands and the absence of impositional stances by either partner led me to refocus my meaning-making to highlight the co-constructive elements of the path toward sharing parenting.

Below, I offer illustrative examples of the three predominant pathways from the five selected exemplar couples. Later, I revisit the three pathway clusters, and suggest that they are not necessarily discrete nor mutually exclusive. Indeed, depending on one's level of analysis, these three pathway clusters might be collapsed into the general idea of co-constructing sharing parenting in the face of life's flow. The heuristic distinctions I make here highlight and clarify individual differences. These individual differences are found in nuances in the ways men and women described their decision-making processes.

CO-CONSTRUCTION IN RESPONSE TO A CIRCUMSTANCE

Circumstances constantly present people with opportunities to chart the next steps in the course of their unfolding life. For the five couples in this cluster of probable paths, certain life circumstances—and their responses to the situation—were seen as a primary impetus to co-creating sharing parenting experiences in their family. In responding to the circumstances life presented, both the man and the woman seemed to be aware that he or she had choices to make, and that his or her individual choice affected the partner's choice at the same time the partner's choice affected his or her choice. In the face of impelling circumstances, both the men and the women seemed to convey their keen awareness of their potential effects on each other and the course they were setting for their family. Below, I share the words Jack and Denise spoke that conveyed this theme.

Denise: I guess it was June or July when I found out I was pregnant. I thought, "What, I can't be pregnant, I'm going back to school!" Calculating the dates, [I knew] that it was like February, right in the middle of the term, and even then I said, "Well I'll just go to school and see how it goes, and I'll try and we'll have the baby." Jack was working at the time in sales, and we decided he would take paternity leave at that time, when and if the baby arrived. I would continue going to school. Basically, we decided that once I was done at school for the summer, he was going to go back to work. Then I finished the term basically exhausted. Actually, there was no way I could have done it without Jack.

Jack: Denise had thought that the only way she could afford to have
          children would be in the early years of med school, not in the
          later years. So we tried for a couple of years. We had hoped the
          timing would be better, but it turned out that instead of having
          the baby in summer, we now had a child in February. So with
          her in med school, it wasn't a viable alternative for her to stay
          home. I wasn't doing anything careerwise that mattered that
          much to me at the time, so I decided that I would stay home.

Denise: When summer came we got to spend time together and he
          basically decided he wasn't going to go back to work. Then we
          got to thinking about September and what we were going to do
          then. We started thinking about what he was earning and how
          much day care was going to cost, and we thought hold on, like
          go out and get a job and it's something he didn't really know
          that he wanted to do . . . and spending most of our money on
          day care while somebody else was looking after your child. We
          thought, this is silly. So we decided he would stay home. None
          of this would have worked if it hadn't been for Jack.

One of the circumstances mentioned by Denise—the financial costs
of day care weighed against each partner's earning potential and job
satisfaction—seemed to be a central consideration for each of the
families in this cluster. Each couple also mentioned its strong preference to have one of the parents be the primary caregiver for their
children. Three of the couples responded to the circumstances by
weighing the financial and emotional cost of child care and then
designating the man the at-home parent; one couple decided the
woman would be the designated at-home parent.

CO-CONSTRUCTION ENCOURAGED
BY THE WOMAN

Women have typically been seen as the primary caregivers in families.
It is also commonly thought that the impetus for change in families
comes from women, especially women who have taken on provider
status in the family by entering the workforce. When I talk to people—
both in the academic community and in my everyday community—
about my research, I typically am asked if it is the woman who demands

that her partner get more involved. Some people have suggested a "reverse caveman" image of the woman dragging her reluctant partner into a more involved role and active participation in the day-to-day activities and responsibilities of family life.

Given the prevalence of these ideas, I expected to hear many families talk of the women being the prime mover in bringing their families to sharing parenting experiences. Although several families spoke of the woman's influence as a central impetus, they typically told stories of cooperation in which she encouraged her partner to become more involved and he found ways to be more engaged. Again, I found nuances of a coconstruction process. The woman initially pointed out how she, their children, and her partner would all benefit by doing some things differently. Later, the man acted in respect of her position and found ways to get more involved. Typically, the men in these families also wanted to be involved fathers. The men seemed to respond to their partner's encouragement by pragmatically shifting their instrumental activities to match their self-perception of being involved fathers. Both the man and the woman seemed to acknowledge that each had an opportunity to move toward more sharing of parenting and general family responsibilities or not. In choosing to move into greater sharing, the men seemed to acknowledge the legitimacy of their partners' requests, and made decisions to enhance the family's quality of life. In all cases, the men spoke of how important it was for them to become more involved.

These co-construction stories ranged from the woman's strong encouragement with clear consequences for not cooperating (resonating with notes of demanding more sharing), to encouragement to enhance already notable male involvement, to the woman's initial encouragement and later the man taking the initiative to request changes that created more opportunity for his involvement. I offer two illustrative examples: Jason and Hillary's experience seems to exemplify the "woman-demanded" process. Rodney and Kate's process seems to exemplify more clearly the woman's initial request, followed by Rodney's initiating later changes.

Hillary: [I] demanded! I mean it [my decision to demand changes] had to do with a basic, "Wait a minute—why should I as a woman be the underdog in everything and do all the invisible stuff of raising the children—there's not much credit in that." It's not that there aren't rewards, but it's just not acknowledged, and a lot of the time it's just hard work and frustrating. . . . I think it kind of came out of a feminist kind of thing and a realization that I wasn't going to go through life being a nobody. I had made changes, went back to school, and now have a career direction.

Jason: When I wanted to have a second child, we went into therapy and worked out agreements that would involve me more in the ins and outs of family, of actively parenting the children. . . . We at least entered into having Mike (second child) with the concept there would be equal parenting. . . . Now I'm very thankful Hillary did have the insight or the tenacity or whatever it was, tenacity not to put up with the traditional parenting situation, to say "This is how it has to be." I think I resented it at first. I fought it, I felt she was saying I wasn't a good father and I thought I was a good father. But that's not what she was saying, and that's why I said initially it's kind of been a transition to get where we are.

The transition for Jason and Hillary took some time. Jason suggests that his resentment came not from not wanting to be more involved, but from feeling he was being criticized for not being a good father. Once he could see that he could be an even better father by being more involved, he made the transition. It seems his traditional ideas of what it means to be a good father shifted once he could hear Hillary acknowledge that he was a good father, and he could be an even better father if he participated more in the daily management of family life and child care. He then acknowledged that he needed to find more ways and time to be with his children.

Kate: I didn't really want to be at work, but financially we needed for me to work, and I also thought I needed to work. So, I juggled things for a while and that was really, really, really difficult. I would start a job and then everything would get really compli-cated, and then I'd quit, and then I'd start another job, and it would get really, really complicated, and I'd quit. When I started to work [where Rodney was working], I can remember saying, "These are your colleagues, your friends, and I will get support and everybody's going to know why I quit this job (laughing)." So, I think that was one of the things. And then the other big change that I can see is when Rodney started to get involved [as a volunteer] at C.W. (a resocialization program for men who have abused their partners), he would come home and say "Remember when such and such, well that was not okay for me to do." I see a big change just in what he feels is very important. I think he always sort of had an attitude, "Well this kind of works and this really feels good [to be involved with the children]," but when he was a [volunteer] at C.W., there was a lot of him saying "I need to do this because this is what needs to be done." That was very different, and that made a big difference, I think. The last set of changes have been all Rodney's initiative. I probably wouldn't even have thought of them.

Kate's story suggests her ambivalence about working while their children were young and how that seemed to play into her early cycle of working for a while, then staying home with the children for some time. She suggests that she pointed this out to her partner most clearly when they began to work for the same employer, and used it as a way to request more support and involvement. Kate also acknowledges how the influence in Rodney's life of another perspective on men in families later became an important source of ideas about how he thought he should be involved. He now takes a lot of initiative in making changes in how they co-create sharing parenting. Rodney now takes more initiative than Kate anticipated was possible.

The co-construction stories shared by the other families in this cluster also highlight how it may take some time to come to a place that is satisfactory for both partners. The women often spoke of being in the position of inviting their partners to revisit their arrangements. It seems that these men both want to be more involved and continue to rely on their partners to signal how involved they should become.

IDEOLOGICAL CO-CONSTRUCTION

Several couples in the study seemed to come to their pattern of sharing parenting through ongoing decisions in which their co-constructive process seemed ever present. They both seemed committed to intentionally constructing a sharing pattern from the outset. In telling their stories, they stressed their ideology of sharing. They were in this together, they both wanted and benefited from cooperating with each other to make their vision of sharing work for them. I heard men and women in this cluster openly declare forms of living egalitarian ideology, whereas for many of the couples in the other two clusters, egalitarian patterns were only suggested by their living examples. Typically, the people in this cluster told stories that had strands of creating their sharing vision before they began to have children; once they did have children, they intentionally made decisions to realize their vision.

Dan: The process of training together [at university], and always having studied the same stuff and done the same stuff in our work, the equality of us as two human beings was really very obvious, and there wasn't any obvious division. The theory had been that we would job share and parent share. I think in our move to Canada, I stood to lose a lot and Liz stood to gain a lot and it became quite clear to me that I had quite a powerful hand to enable or disable Liz's chances in her career. I didn't want to disable it, and so that was quite a change for me. That was the changing point where I realized that I could lay aside this power and control for myself or use it creatively. When our first child came along, it was again a decision, that I knew I could probably have Liz work a quarter-time if I'd pushed—it wouldn't have been difficult—but again it was quite clear to me that that wasn't what Liz had been called to do, and by then I was beginning to understand that.

Liz: In some ways, I think it seems apparent that Dan gave up some things to be at home. I think he gained some things being at home and I don't think there's the same sense that I had to give anything up. I am not the sort of person who's endlessly satisfied with being at home with a small infant. I find it very isolating, draining. . . . It was always a relief to get back to work [part-time]. So I'm not sure. I don't feel I've done anything heroic to enable this to come to be. It suited me very well . . . and I think [it's] been wonderful for him. I don't think we would often sit down and negotiate, but there were certain moments. There were certain turning points.

Liz gives extensive examples that demonstrate that there are times when they sit down and talk and listen to each other and come to new understandings and new ways of doing things. Her examples illustrate that sometimes she brings things up, sometimes Dan brings things up.

Dan's retelling of how they came to co-construct sharing parenting stresses his appreciation of their equality in both the family world and their formal work world. He talks of being acutely aware of opportunities for him to violate their vision of equality; potentially acting to misuse power and privilege sanctioned for men in a provider roles while closing options for his partner to balance her career-family choices. Liz talks about knowing there were apparent costs for her partner, whereas the benefits are more apparent for her. She emphasizes that they both gained by being collaborative in their decision making.

The families in this cluster told stories that echo repeatedly the sense of regard and respect for each other's perspectives. Like Liz, the men and women spoke of how they can listen to each other, appreciate what constraints and opportunities may exist in a situation, and work cooperatively to construct options that allow them to come to new understandings and new ways of doing things in and for their families.

Distinctions and the Decision-Making Process

As researchers studying the "everyday world" (Smith, 1987), we are at risk of overlooking the significance of commonsense meanings. Embedded in the everyday world and common sense are intricate beliefs and meanings foundational to each couple's ability to realize its vision of family life. These foundational commitments sustain the couples through the changing rhythms of daily dancing through mundane activities and negotiations.

Although it may seem like just plain common sense, family decision making is usually an intricate and delicate process for the people involved. Decision making about structuring family time, family resources, and family work may be the basis for how the family experiences daily life. Although foundational, these types of decisions may be constrained by considerations beyond the individual's and the couple's control. For example, employed individuals usually find that degrees of freedom about when and where they work are limited; options for child care may also be suboptimal or constrained by availability, quality, and cost considerations. Changes in external circumstances or unanticipated family events may challenge or even crack the foundation a couple had previously built.

One could argue that circumstances are a primary driving force behind the family's ability to set, and keep intact, its base. Such an argument focuses on the potential that, at any point in time, a family may be facing circumstances beyond its control that potentially invite a realignment in the foundational structure. One could also argue that a couple's decisions about how it will structure parenthood, if truly foundational, are not too likely to be affected by changing circumstances. I thought about both these arguments as I constructed distinctions between particular decision-making processes. Certainly, these 18 couples talked about how their decisions were a blend of intentional, foundational decisions and decisions made in response to life situations as they arose.

The distinctions made here simplify the stories people shared. Each family experience was told with nuances of ideological coconstruction, coconstructions responsive to circumstances, and co-constructions encouraged by women's desires for their partner's increased involvement. In my choice and depiction of exemplars, however, I focused only on the most prominent threads as I understood them in each of the families' tales. In revisiting these distinctions, I call attention to missing nuances. Each family, no matter what decision-making cluster I placed it in, could also be seen to have experienced aspects of the processes represented in the other decision-making clusters.

The clusters are neither mutually exclusive nor discrete. When faced with an impelling circumstance, each couple in the co-construction-in-response-to-a-circumstance cluster would likely find itself, collectively and individually, considering and reconsidering the foundational and ideological bases. For example, going back to Jack and Denise's decision-making path, Jack seemed to reaffirm his commitment to Denise's career training when he decided to be the designated at-home parent. His commitment to Denise's education for her professional career was initially based on his ideological commitment to both partners having the opportunity to seek personal fulfillment in their relationship and in their careers. My decision to place Jack and Denise in this cluster, as opposed to the ideological co-construction cluster, was based on the way they presented the circumstance as a prime mover, or perhaps a prime opportunity, to realize their commitment in their everyday lives. My decisions about placing people in the other decision-making clusters were made similarly. I listened for how people sequenced and emphasized the influences in their stories. The placement of each family is suggestive of how it highlighted some prominent strands in what was otherwise a complex weave of individual, collective, and external influences.

5

Guiding Light

Foundations for Sharing Parenting

All my conversations with the 18 families resonated with themes of how these men and women came to organize their current family life. Talk of "life philosophy" and "family values" was embedded in their descriptions of arrangement patterns and their individual and collective histories. Both men and women talked about what they believed was important for them to bring to their parenting experiences. Commonly, I heard things like, "They [children] don't raise themselves, we raise them" (George); "Spend time together as a unit, I think that's important. Be aware of what's going on in your kid's lives . . . just being available for your kids and not being selfish" (Rodney); "I think when you raise children, you've got probably somewhere in the region of 4 years where you pour the foundation of the building of that human being, after that, the stuff that goes on after that, it's increasingly from peers, from school, from culture, from society, but the basement is yours" (Dan); "[We] both want to take part in raising her, and being part of it all the way . . . we both wanted this so much, its never been a chore to do what Anita [child] needs to have done" (Phil).

These ideas caught my attention. Initially, I almost passed them by because they sounded so familiar, so much a part of everyday common sense. It was almost like hearing the "mom and apple pie" statements everyone makes when you ask them about family. Later, as I tried to piece together what allowed these families to create sharing parenting experiences that worked for them, I began to appreciate important nuances in these statements. These simple statements enticed me to explore a deeper texture of what may go into creating a living philosophy for everyday life. The beliefs and commitments these men and women make to each other and to their children are essential lights guiding them through everyday sharing parenting experiences.

Commitment to Parenting

All 18 couples know a basic economic or financial necessity for one or both parents to work outside the home. Work in the outside world provides the income needed to sustain daily living—the basics of shelter, food, and clothing. Although all these families certainly live well above the poverty line, they also speak of their real concerns with making a living. Comments like "There's the necessity for some more money too" (Rick) and "You're always short [of] money" (Karen) are typical of the way people talked about the financial backdrop of their decision making about family life. Thus, juggling the competing demands of family work and work outside the home for time, energy, and personal resources was a very real part of their everyday lives. These issues became even more pressing when the couples began to have children, and they were faced with family decisions about who and how they would care for their children on a daily basis.

MAKING CHOICES

All 18 women had worked or been formally involved (e.g., schooling) outside the home before their children were born, as had all 18 men. The women generally talked about the decisions of who would look after their children, how and where, if and when they returned to work. Their talk echoes a general assumption of having a right to choose.

Women felt they had, at some very basic level, a choice between family and work. If their family could afford to have a designated at-home parent, it would be acceptable for them, as women, to stay home with the children. The men, although voicing a serious commitment to parenthood and to parenting actively, seemed less aware initially of having a choice to stay home with the children. Rather, they seemed to assume, at least initially, that they would continue to work outside the home, at least in some capacity. Phil, a man in his mid-40s who has one child and works as an executive in a service industry company, said,

> [I think] it would have been nicer to come into this world as a woman because then you do have [a choice], I think, having kids and being a parent is more important than being out working, whatever you might achieve, and men—I don't think many women would agree with this—but [men] kind of get short changed in that sense, that we have to just keep on working.

For the men, their commitment to be involved confronted them with decisions about how to make this happen while juggling family life with outside work.

MAXIMIZING PARENT CARE—
MINIMIZING DAY CARE

Women and men came to their decisions about how to provide daily care for their children from different preconceptions about their parts in providing that care. Yet they ultimately converged on some primary assumptions about their commitment to be the primary care givers for their children and about co-creating their version of sharing parenting. One prominent theme I noticed was that both women and men agreed that the child's parents should be the people most influential in the child's life. This kind of commitment seemed to drive their decisions, whether they ended up co-creating patterns of interchangeability, male or female as the designated stay-at-home parent, accounting equity, or reserved specialties as ways to operationalize their beliefs. For example, Rob's (interchangeable) and Cheryl's (woman as designated stay-at-home parent) words capture these ideas vividly. Rob, a man in his early 40s with two children and co-owner, with his wife, of a specialty retail business, said,

When we had a second child, it put a lot of demands on us all and we came to the conclusion jointly, although I think Donna (partner) was much more perceptive than I, that something had to give. I was quite willing and ready to leave the financial industry. I then went to work at the store, and consequently we were able to come to a plan where we would share the store and the kids because we both felt strongly that we wanted to raise our children and not have 12 nannies looking after them [while I stayed] in the financial industry and she in the store. . . . We both naturally felt from our upbringing and beliefs that that was the thing to do. In fact, we saw each other and lived together before we got married and we really got married in order to have children. So we had children because we wanted to look after them.

Cheryl, a woman in her early 30s with three children, who is starting a retail business out of her home, describes the decision she and Erik made:

We both decided that we wanted me to be home, have the children raised with what we wanted their background to be and what we wanted to give them as their values, [rather] than give them over to a baby-sitter and let them grow up with the baby-sitter's values. That was after we decided it didn't matter whether we had money or not. It was just a matter of making sure the kids were well looked after by the best caregivers we thought we could find. Him and [me]!

INTENTIONAL LIFESTYLES

Cheryl mentions money, suggesting that part of their decision was consideration of the financial and lifestyle implications of having parents be home with the children as much as possible. All the couples mentioned considering the financial dimension in making their family decisions about who would work outside the home. Both men and women talked about how to balance the economic imperative to support their family with how they would provide daily care for their children. Regardless of the configuration they eventually arrived at, these people talked about intentionally making lifestyle decisions to allow them to interact as a parenting team and to be the primary care takers of their children.

In making these family lifestyle decisions, these men and women were aware that other families might pay more attention to materialistic considerations. At times, these men and women spoke with hints of disdain in their voices for the materialism that they saw as so pervasive in our culture. In contrast, they stressed their desire to minimize that cultural influence in their family. Karen, a woman who works part-time in retail trade and is home with her children, mentioned a family move made so they could afford to have each parent be more involved with the children:

> We'd been living in Anyville, and we moved to Sometown, where it was cheaper, because we made this decision that we had to reduce our expenses [so that I could cut back to part-time work]. . . . I work some evenings and on weekends when Rick can be home with the children.

Families made intentional decisions to be the primary caregivers for their children. They made clear commitments to parenting and to share parenting, and made adjustments in their lifestyles to enable this to become their daily reality. The theme of intentionality in decision making and daily living surfaces again and again in their family philosophies.

FIRST-LINE CONTACT AND VICARIOUS CONNECTION

Decisions about how to provide daily care to children means that parents switch on and off being the designated at-home parent. This typically means that the mother or the father is physically absent from the home for several hours each day. Listening to the descriptions, I began to think about how important it is for these men and women to have a parent be on the spot with young children. While one parent was working in the outside world, the other parent is with the child: "It's mostly just being that first line, you know the first contact the [child] has" (Phil). Absences—to provide income primarily—mean that a parent often misses both mundane and special opportunities to experience the unfolding of his or her children's lives. Both men and women mentioned their sense of loss in missing parts of their children's lives. Yet, they also talked about the benefit of at least one parent being there to witness and interact with the child, and later being able to report it to the absent parent as a way of including her or him. Women's and men's talk of wanting to be included, even if they were absent because of work commitments, suggested to me their desire to build connections vicariously, given that circumstances precluded direct connection for some parts of their children's lives.

Sam, in his early 40s with three children, who works full-time as a management trainee, mentioned repeatedly how torn he felt about being away for long hours during the day. At the same time, he struggled to take some comfort in knowing that his partner's moment-to-moment presence with the children would allow him to experience secondhand what he missed. His words also suggest that he felt that this vicarious connection was not enough. He strives to maximize his contact and interaction with his children when he arrives home.

> It's sad, it's very sad for me. I like my job, but part of it's sad. There's not one—I think I can't describe one emotion. The thing that makes me happy also takes me away from the kids. . . . I do believe these years are really important for the kids. I was happy that I didn't have to make the decision—Meg was happy to stay at home. I'm happy with that—I'm very happy with that decision. I mean as far as them being my kids, I trust her with my kids. I think she's a wonderful mother, and I personally believe the years from 1 to 5 especially are really important for kids. So if that's the trade-off I have to make, if I can try to give them as much love and she can give them all her love during these times, that means a lot to me. That's the thing that kind of keeps me going. . . . I miss them, I really miss them. . . . I feel confident that our communication—my communication with Meg is that I can at least pick up on what's going on [when] I am out of touch. I at least get to get a glimpse every night [into] the things [that] are going on. I am now getting reports directly from Katlin (daughter) about her day.

Helen's narrative echoes Sam's; she notes how important it was to her that their commitment to parenting included one parent being there to catch the other up on their child's day. She, like other parents in this study, would not want always to hear these pieces of her children's lives from an outsider. Helen, a woman in her mid-40s who has two very young children and works full-time as a middle-level manager in the financial industry, said,

> I'm missing things in their lives, and I just think I'm glad Bill is seeing that because it's not a stranger that's doing this [child care]. So he can tell me, you know, what goes on, and usually in our evenings he'll say "Oh, so and so did this and then so and so did this." That's the part that I'm missing.

So, I'm glad that it's not somebody—a baby-sitter—telling me about this. It's Bill!

Parenting Philosophy

The underlying notion of intentionality in their decision making seems critical to the way these men and women shaped their sharing of parenthood. I noticed how often words like *team, tag team, spelling each other*, and *shifts* appeared in their talk. I also noticed a sense that both men and women conveyed their commitment to do whatever has to be done to make it work, especially making it work in the best interest of the child. It seemed to me they were talking about another element in their guiding light, a notion of working in partnership toward a shared goal. Generally speaking, their goals centered on that most taken-for-granted notion of raising their children well. Dan spoke of the attention it takes to accomplish this most touted of parenting goals. Dan, a man in his late 30 with three children, who works part-time in the human services field and is home with his children part-time, said,

> To lay the ground, you need to be awake and rested. You need to have a good breakfast yourself, and not be stressed out, and not be preparing lunch while thinking about work or thinking about something else, because if your attention is either jaded or distracted, you're not doing the work of parenting. [Parenting] requires full attention and full presence of mind and being, I think, to do it well. I think men tend to have been brought up to think of child care as a bit like looking after a row of cars, and as long as you're there, they're being looked after. I mean [the notion] of as long as you are around, that's all that's necessary. It isn't! It works with cars and computers and pieces of paper, but it doesn't work with children. Just having your face there isn't enough!

PARENTING GOALS: FROM THE MUNDANE DAILY TASKS TO NURTURING SELF-ESTEEM

As parents talked about their efforts to raise their children, they hinted at myriad goals in the moment-to-moment events of everyday life. Parents spoke of a range of goals in the most micro sense of certain routine tasks and events of basic daily living, such as getting the child fed, clothed, and in bed. Dan has three young children; in describing their typical daily routines, he said,

> At 5:00 to 5:30, somewhere in that point, Liz returns home and we have a welcome home Liz time, the kids are excited about her reappearance, and we have a cup of tea at about that time, the same time the children are being fed something more substantial. That tends to be the big meal of the day. 6:30's bath time, so we get scrubbed, cleaned up, and then story time runs from about 7:00 onwards.

Their goals often go beyond achieving the functional aspect of these tasks to appreciating the match between the mood, method, and underlying message to the child. In a sense, they seemed to be conveying a complex awareness about how they are experienced by their children. This awareness spans from the general tone of their parenting objectives to the minute details of daily human interaction. These men and women conveyed an acute awareness of how all their interactions with their child contribute to the child's sense of belonging and self-worth. Steve, a man in his mid-30s with two children, who works out of his home as a computer industry consultant, said,

> I know they need to feel like they matter. They need to feel like they're an important part of this family. You can't tell them, "Hey, you know, you gotta do some chores, and you're part of this family," [trying to get] them to do the work when they also don't feel they're part of the family as far as being valued.

In this way, men seemed to see their microinteractions as closely linked with the grand-scale goals of their parenting philosophy.

PARTNERSHIP: WE'RE IN THIS TOGETHER

Both men and women mentioned the importance of being together in their parenting, but I had the sense that they were talking about more than simply agreeing with and supporting each other. These people talked about their commitment to a team effort or partnership. They view partnership as a central ray shining through their guiding light. Partnership is the key to living up to their philosophical goals in the face of everyday challenges and distractions. The strength of language men used conveyed the seriousness and sacredness they feel is embedded in the pledge partners made to each other and to their children. One man, Erik, who has three young children and works in the human services field, said,

> Cheryl and I have covenanted together, and I use that word intentionally, covenanted for me to be around home, to be involved . . . I think we're very much in partnership in terms of work around the house and whatnot. Our whole marriage and family is pretty much egalitarian. We're trying to base it on a partnership model. . . . My relationship is based on our understanding that we're both equal persons, that, you know, she's not subservient or any of that kind of crap, to be straight out about it.

Erik's narrative, along with many others, suggests that egalitarian ideals shine brightly in his guiding light. He also suggested that these ideals pertain to the whole family, not just his partner. His words and the words of others led me to think about other aspects of their parenting philosophy. When asked, men articulated several key rays that light their way in parenting their children, and their partners echoed these guiding beliefs.

RESPECT FOR THEIR CHILDREN

At the core of all the narratives about guiding beliefs is a commitment to gain respect by showing respect to their children. Specifically, these parents talked about treating their children as individual human beings who are taking shape as they grow. Their talk conveys deep-seated respect for their children as individuals, not at appendages of them as parents. Their talk often highlighted this kind of respect in contrast to what they experienced growing up. Bill, a man in his mid-40s with two very young children, who was designated the primary stay-at-home parent, but who also worked part-time in the retail trade, described his belief that the secret to getting along with his children and ultimately influencing them was to show respect for their capabilities. He said,

> I get along with children because I don't relate to them as children. I don't talk down to them. That's what I found out very early with children. You don't [talk down to them], you treat them like people, not, perhaps adults, but you treat them as human beings and then react accordingly. . . . When I see children in Leslie's (child) nursery school, I treat them just like they

are older people. I say "Hi, how [are] you doing and what's new?" whatever. I don't say "Are you playing with your toys? Are you being a good boy?" I feel that's talking down to them, and kids can act much more maturely than you think if you give them the opportunities to do that. I feel that if you give them the opportunities to do that, um, I feel that as you treat the kids better that way, it's better for the kids and better for you with interacting with them. I don't think it's fair to talk down to them. If you talk to a 6-year-old—not that you would get the same reaction that you would with an adult—but you can't treat a 6-year-old like a baby—a 6-year-old has verbal skills; he has some ability to think, and some of the answers they come up with are incredible!

Bill's statement conveys a sense that part of raising children well is an ability to go to their level without pandering to them. He, like other men in the study, conveyed an awareness of children's developmental stages, suggesting that being sensitive to the child's world is a crucial part of parenting. Steve offered a starker declaration about the importance of respect:

What we've tried to do is be as fair and democratic as possible with the kids. Treat them with respect and dignity and like they're intelligent people capable of learning and making their own decisions, but trying to keep it always on the proper side, I mean, at the end of it all, we are the parents.

MAXIMIZE CO-CREATIVE OPPORTUNITIES
WITH CHILDREN: IMPOSE WHEN NECESSARY

Closely aligned with respecting children are ideas about parenting, including opportunities to co-create relationship and life experiences with the children. This means parents being open to being influenced by the child's perspective and experience. This requires parents (particularly men) to set aside control and power in some interactions with their children. At the same time, parents spoke of their keen awareness of stepping away from the co-creative stance to exercise adult responsibility and decision making when necessary.

Steve's words above hint at this balancing between relinquishing power and control in the service of respecting the child's being, and coming in when adult perspectives are necessary for the child's well-being. This balancing is not a simple act. Dan's description of learning play from his son captures some of the complexity and challenge of relinquishing his control and power. Dan, a man in his late 30s with three children, who works part-time in the human services field and is at home with his children part-time, said,

> You know my son's baseball is great fun now that I'm slowly learning how to play. . . . We were playing catch with a tennis ball using his baseball hat and I said, "No, no, no, what we should be doing is practicing with a softball with the glove, and you should be catching with your left hand, not your right hand." So we had a discussion about this, and I could see that he wanted to have fun and I wanted to teach him how to do softball. I wanted to do the adult "teach you how to do softball thing," he just wanted to throw the ball and have fun. So we kind of compromised. He started off his way, and I slowly leaned him into my way. Later we sat down and we were talking about it and I said, "You know, Tom, I have this problem that I need to try and do things right because I'm very oriented towards these goals, and I know it's very adult," and he took a wad of chewing gum out of his mouth and said, "Put this in your mouth and put my baseball cap on backwards and you'll be a kid!" I said I don't like to be a kid. I had to tell him that I'm not a kid. I'm an adult. I like being an adult. And we laughed about it . . . he thinks it's a huge joke that he knows how to be a kid and I don't.

Dan's narrative of his experience, like that of several men in this study, conveys a sense that he is challenged to step out of his parental authority in a play situation. He knows that he needs to do this to be able to connect with his son in different contexts. He believes his son knows the difference between adults and children, especially with regard to adult responsibility for children's protection. He also seems to think his son knows the difference between playing together and circumstances that require adult decision making. Yet, Dan believes it is his responsibility to keep the rules clear as to which context they are in. In taking responsibility for making this clear for his son, Dan is both exercising adult responsibility and signaling contexts where he will try to enter into the co-creative domain of play, but he recognizes his limits in truly entering the child's domain. Nevertheless, in clarifying the contexts, Dan may signal to his son the co-creative potential and its limits:

I tend to think it would be false of me to go into his world because I'm not a kid. I'm an adult, and I think the important thing for me to be able to say [is], "I'm an adult and you're a kid. When it's time for you to go to bed, you brush your teeth, go to bed, and that's that. When the rules of the adult world are appropriate, I'm the adult and you're the kid, and when we're playing catch together, this is a game and the kids' rules apply and I'm an adult and you're a kid." . . . The one thing that children, well I think that everybody sees it, the children name it, is when people are pretending to be something they're not.

Men's talk was also suggestive that they were keenly aware of their limits regarding their ability to get into the child's world. Dan's conversation indicates this, and highlights his awareness that it is a parent's responsibility to take a clearly hierarchical position at times to impose structure and rules. Steve talked at length about how he knows he takes nonnegotiable positions at times, as well as how he tries to balance freedom and compassion for his children with his parental responsibility by giving them information and helping them understand why he is taking an impositional stance. Steve, a man in his mid-30s with two children, who works out of his home as a consultant to the computer industry, said,

At the end of it all, we are the ones that are in charge. At the end of it all, sometimes it just comes down to that's what we think and believe and that's what's going to happen. Sometimes it comes to, we'll be this way and we'll do whatever it takes to have it be this way, but as long as everything's staying on this side of the line. I think its important for them to understand why it's this way and what makes that work because it lets them start making decisions for themselves. So that's kind of what we've done. We give them a lot of freedom and compassion [but at the end of it all we are the parents].

Steve's stance, along with what other men described, is suggestive of an authoritative parenting style—or parenting with flexible, sensitive authority acknowledging the child's position and perspective—as opposed to an authoritarian parenting position stereotypic of traditional fathers who set and apply rules autocratically. Dan provided an example of how, in his interactions with his children, he has found creativity helps him maintain the authoritative stance:

I would have [in the past] just have had an argument with them. [This] is an example of the job is to get the kids to eat the sandwich. It's the preparation of the sandwich that makes all the difference. [Before I would have said], "Eat the sandwich, this is nourishing food, I spent a long time preparing this for you and you're going to eat this because it's good for you. Think of all the starving children out there." That's the way I was brought up (laughs). The other way is, "Do you want stars or teddy bears sandwiches? You have a choice." Both of these choices are acceptable to me as a father, you know he's winning by eating the sandwich he chooses and I'm winning here too.

Both men and women stressed how important it is to keep a child's perspective in mind when parenting. Awareness of developmental stages, as hinted in Bill's words, is one way these men have to build an awareness of the child's world. The strength of their belief and commitment to holding the child's perspective in view go beyond awareness of developmental stages. Carol, a woman in her mid-30s with two children, who works in the medical field, conveyed these ideas:

We look very closely at the why's and how they are feeling, and we both come up with a game plan based on that. We've had to change the game plan many times, because something will work or it won't work. I think that's real fundamental to the way we're rais[ing] our kids is trying to figure out what's making him tick? Why all of a sudden are we seeing this or that? . . . If I had married a person who didn't help me be more empathic, I would have continued along the path of being very much an authoritarian.

Carol talked of learning about empathy from her partner (Steve); learning to appreciate how a child might be experiencing a particular situation, not just what the child is capable of developmentally in a situation. Rodney talked about using his empathy—his ability to appreciate a child's world as different from an adult's experience—to allow his children certain small comforts. Rodney, a man in his early 40s with two children, who works full-time in the social services field, said,

My kids will come to me at bedtime and ask for their lights to be on, they'll come and ask for an extra snack or something like that. [Remembering] myself as a child, I would say well yea, that's okay because nighttime is very difficult [for kids] . . . so generally I'll let her (daughter) have her light on in her room, read a book until she falls asleep.

Phil's narrative introduces another perspective on entering a child's world. He, along with other men, talked about surrendering to a child's pace, allowing himself to slow down, not push his daughter to rush through life on an adult's schedule. He recognizes the potential discovery and simple wonder his daughter has in everyday experiences. Phil is in his early 40s with one young daughter and works as an executive in the commercial services industry. He said,

We'll do things at her (daughter's) pace on Saturday mornings. I spend a lot of mornings just going out with her and going at her pace. If she wants to stop and look at some store window for 5 to 10 minutes, I stop there and look at it for 5 or 10 minutes, because why should she always travel at our pace? I see parents everywhere, you know, yanking their kids along, like we gotta get going, and I don't want to get her overbooked into things once she gets a little older and starts doing clubs and all the rest, because I want her to have that sense of wonder and be able to drive things at her pace.

Charles, and other men, talked about another way to join with children in their world. They mentioned specifically participating with them in activities they enjoy. To do this, Charles knows he has to suspend his adult sense of what is fun, interesting. He narrative suggests he feels close to his children when he is able to do this, and that he feels enriched by their joy. Charles, a man in his mid-30s with two young children, who is a co-owner of a service industry business, said,

I always sort of try to get on their level almost, ask them what would be fun for them—just sit[ting] and watching Polka Dot Door is not a lot of fun for me, but they like it when I do it, so I do. Just trying to do stuff that they like to do and doing stuff on their level, I think they sort of get a kick out of [it].

CREATING AN ENVIRONMENT
FOR THE CHILD TO THRIVE

Men often talked about their awareness of the physical and emotional environment they helped create for their children. This was usually coupled with ideas about children's growth and what children need to realize self-confidence and feelings of self-worth. These men did not mention physical elements of the environment— the basics of shelter, food, and clothing were seemingly assured in their middle-class life-styles. They did stress, however, their participation, attention, caring, and guidance about basic values as crucial beams lighting their way in parenting their children. Going back to Charles's narrative, he concluded his talk about these guiding elements with a rhetorical question, suggesting he could not imagine it any other way:

> I think [the] most important thing they can have is a good sort of family environment. If you're going to start having kids, then I think you should be responsible for helping them . . . giving them that kind of environment to grow up in, I just believe that that's appropriate. . . . That's the way it should be. . . . I think it's good for developing confidence in kids—knowing who they are and where they come from, knowing they are part of something. The whole love and caring thing—that that's always there for them. I don't know, a basic sense of probably right and wrong, that's all kind of corny stuff, but I think it's good stuff for kids to learn, sort of basic principles and beliefs. How you should act, and if you don't have a good family setting, where are they going to learn it?

Part of creating an environment for children to thrive seems to be intentionally providing diverse opportunities for children to experiment, discover, and experience themselves as competent, participating, growing beings. Expanding their potential and their horizons of possibilities and appreciation for the world around them seemed to be an important part of how men saw their involvement with their children taking shape. Erik talked at length about intentionally acting as parents to create opportunities:

> We encourage them to do stuff. When we were setting our priorities on how we spend our money, our number-one priority, our covenant and number-one priority for the way we spend our money, is to educate our kids. It's the number-one thing, and what we lumped into education is not just academia, providing for university and whatnot, although we do that and it's costing a fortune, but we lump into education experiential stuff, and we justify expense under the guise of education. We don't even think about what it costs to do swimming lessons, T-ball, music, what else do they do—there's skating. . . . It doesn't matter what it costs. That's one thing we're trying to do, is give them a full experience.

The importance of spending time with their children was repeatedly mentioned in my conversations with these men. Erik continued his comments related to creating an environment for his children to thrive. He wrestled with distinctions between time and quality time, or considerations of time and expense. His ideas capture two notions: One, quality time does not necessarily mean spending money on creating experiential opportunities for children to be exposed to the world around them. He also said he values money spent on entertainment as a form of education. Two, he believes one can convey connection and caring by just being with the children at home or in activities that do not cost money.

> Just hang out with them. Spend time with them, that was one of the most influential things that I've ever heard about parenting. . . . So we spend, try and spend, I hate to use catch phrases, but you know quality time. That sense of a lot of time, quality time. I think if you try hard to make it, by doing special things like Amber (child)-and-Dad days or our Chris (child)-and-Mom days, that also comes under the guise of education too, because we usually end up spending a lot of money and we don't always have to—well that's not always true either. I'll take that back. Sometimes we spend money by going and doing things like museums or miniputting or movies, but there's other times when we just go to the park and fly a kite or throw around balls or play and so on.

Bill provided another perspective on the ideas men seem to have about spending time with their children. He, like other men, spoke of the importance of spending time with his children, mundane time in the daily flow of family life so that he gets to know them, their idiosyncrasies, their rhythms, and their individuality. In Bill's narrative (and others), I noted the potential for men to become highly attuned to their children by being in a position to care for them over significant periods of time. Bill's account suggests he feels fortunate to have had time to know his children in their complexity and in the simplicity of daily life:

> I don't think I would be near as good a father if I were working full-time. Especially what I was doing before, [commuting] and coming home at 6 or 7 o'clock at night. I wouldn't have the time, nor the energy to deal with them—be around them, watch what they were doing. I'm with them when they get up in the morning and I'm with them all day, and frequently with

them when they go to bed. And that's, that (pause), I consider myself
fortunate. . . . I know that, for example, Scott (child) gets very, very,
very—he's in a bad mood around dinner time. If he doesn't get fed, he
won't be very happy. As a matter of fact, he's very far from happy. . . . If
I weren't around nearly as often, I'm sure I wouldn't pick up on nearly as
much as I have.

Spending time with their children seems to represent opportunities
for the men to build connection. Spending time with their children
also seems to be especially appreciated as unpredictable opportunities
to influence the child's growth. Hearing men talk about hanging out
with their children, including their children in their daily comings and
goings, I began to appreciate what they were saying about the myriad
"teachable moments" involved fathers have with their children. Charles described his appreciation for how children can learn in any
moment, especially moments when adults are available to share their
experiences:

I think they learn a lot from play, and we always sort of are telling them
about exercise being good for them and playing is good exercise, it makes
you grow, it makes you strong and all that. So it's a really good thing to
play. . . . So I think aside from fun, I think they get, if we're with them,
they sort of get a sense we're into what we're doing and they learn, they
learn stuff, play is good. I guess everything for them is a learning
experience. That's one thing we've noticed. We're not trying to teach them
anything particularly, but just going around looking at stuff and saying,
"Oh there's this or that" and you know the next time we drive by and
Greg (child) will, 3 weeks later he goes—like we were driving to work
one day and they go what's that thing on top of the church? I said it's a
weather cock, and so we're driving by about 3 weeks later and Greg points
at it and goes "There's a weather cock" and stuff like that. So they really
seem to sponge everything in. So whether we're trying to or not, they're
always sort of sucking it up. Absorbing.

Men typically introduced ideas about setting limits and helping
their children learn difficult lessons. I think of these as significantly
related to creating an environment for children to thrive. When men
spoke about guiding and setting limits, they most often spoke of their
commitment to give their children guidance through a positive focus,
not punishment. They spoke of these ideals as central in their parent-

ing approach. An interchange between Steve and Carol initially brought this theme to my attention. Later, I heard other men speak of similar ideas, especially appreciating what their children do well, not dwelling on what they have done wrong.

Steve: Because it's not arbitrary, and it helps build their own concept of how to behave and how things work . . . we measure by the high marks they [kids] make not the low marks. I think when people evaluate the kids, they measure them down here [low marks]. It's just not fair. This is who they are up here [high mark]. They do screw up, they mess up [but that's not who they are]. . . . I say okay, what's that person's perspective, whether that person is your wife or your kid. Especially the kid. This is a little kid that's worn out—trying to learn language, and walking, and pencil holding all day. The kids are at their wits' end. If you can realize that, at least I've found that if I can imagine how it feels like to be them, it makes it easier for me to do the right things for them.

Carol: In terms of guiding children and disciplining them, we have avoided punishment and tried for consequences, and it's always been really challenging, I mean, in many instances, it's really challenging to figure, "What is the logical consequence?"

SELF-MONITORING

All the meanings I have made about these people's parenting philosophy could easily slip into glib rhetoric of everyone's ideals of good parenting. At first I was somewhat skeptical about what I thought I heard people saying about their guiding philosophies. I heard myself say to myself, "Of course, these people would describe themselves as good parents in this way, but do these men really live up to these ideals?" Later, I asked men to share examples of how they interact with their children. I began to hear about philosophy in practice and about times when they are aware they did not live up to their ideals. This brought my attention to another way these men live their philosophy—they monitor themselves, holding themselves accountable to themselves, to their children, as well as to their partner.

Jack described a preemptive monitoring, or anticipating what his ideas and reactions might be and making adjustments before he reacts in an undesired way. This is a monitoring of the self in action that suggests men will hold an awareness of the potential effect of their actions on their child while they are interacting with the child. In this way, men, such as Jack, try to match their behavior in the moment with their ideals in a conscious way. Jack is a man in his mid-40s with one child, a toddler; he decided to be the designated stay-at-home parent. He said:

> I give Jessica more thought in terms of teaching—like, "Oh I better not do that because she'll pick up this bad habit," or do something that I don't think would be appropriate.

Men mentioned their awareness that preemptive self-monitoring was not always present in their moment-to-moment behaviors. Dan's description of falling short of his ideal in a recent interaction with his son introduced another potential way to hold himself accountable to his principles and the child's experience. Dan's honesty, and the openness of other men describing similar situations, about how he behaved in this interaction convinced me that self-monitoring was a significant part of their philosophical guiding light:

> Recently Tom was playing with our record player, and I came and found him with the needle running round and round on the rubber pad, and I pushed him away from it and I called him an idiot, told him he was stupid, told him to get out of there. So after my 30-second tirade where he stood numbly by, I realized what I was doing and that he was a small person experimenting with this. (pause) Aaaaand so, you know I do quite a bit of backtracking with my children, saying, "Okay this is, it was wrong of me to say these things." He actually, he knows what comes after what, after I've exploded. I calmed down and I said, "Tom, this is really serious." He said, "It's all right, you'll come and apologize to me tonight." I thought, *You little bugger.* (laughs) Now, this is going too far because he's on to it, because I do go straight into the bad parenting pattern and then overreact, overshout, overpunish, you know. I threaten . . . I become very extreme and oppositional in my thinking and black-and-white mode, and then I calm down.

I found another piece that encouraged me to think of self-monitoring and holding oneself accountable to one's children and partner. Acknowledging mistakes to the child and vowing do it better next time struck me as another bright ray in men's guiding light.

> . . . and again Liz (partner) comes in and says, "Well he was just experimenting with it." She has this appalling woman's gift to see the truth. I go up and say to Tom, "I shouldn't have shouted at you" and [explain] where that comes from and that my reaction was wrong. I'll tell him it was still wrong to ruin the record player needle. It costs a lot of money to try and replace it, and that it's something he shouldn't be playing with and things he should check and that's an out-of-bounds thing. That's . . . it's hard work and it takes a lot of saying sorry and admitting you're wrong. But I've got to watch that, you know, 'cause if I start to teach him that whenever adults react strongly, they will retract later. This is not useful to him. (Dan)

REFLECTIONS

The meanings I have constructed from the descriptions men and women shared are, in my mind, tightly interwoven. I have presented them here as separate ideas and concepts for heuristic purposes. I do not think of them as separate and distinct, however. The illustrative quotes suggest connections between parents' goals and what they try to do in terms of building partnership, interacting from a stance of respect, co-creating opportunities, establishing a creative environment in which their children can thrive, taking and keeping the child's perspective, and monitoring their interactions for congruence with their beliefs. These men and women likely experience what I have called their guiding light as one beam, not fragments. These foundational beliefs seem to illuminate the general path through myriad complex interactions daily, weekly, monthly, and yearly. When that beam is shone intensely on any one interaction, however, it could reveal incongruities between beliefs and actions. The humble honesty I heard in the telling of the narratives convinced me that the incongruities would not destroy the integrity of the beam. The beam of the guiding light includes both a self-monitoring and a self-reflective ray that brings the incongruities into focus. These men spoke with self-awareness of their incongruities and their efforts to self-correct. Another part of that integrity seems to be a sense of creating and taking a stance of goodwill for their families.

Goodwill

In everyday life, we often hear someone described as a "person of goodwill." When pressed to specify what gives rise to this attribution, people try to offer examples of generosity, good works, contributions to others, prestige, or general benevolence. In the end, these examples are attempts to qualify or quantify intangibles. As intangibles, they are not readily discerned by the mind.

The idea of intangibles seemed to fit with my experience of meeting and talking with the 18 families in this study. My conversations with these men and women often left me with a feeling of knowing something, but not knowing what to attach to that knowing. I was left questioning, searching, asking myself what examples and excerpts I could offer to justify my knowing. I knew I was dealing more with impressionistic data than the research evidence I could provide in the tapes and transcripts. These questions, these feelings, led me to the idea of goodwill. Then I wondered, can a family be depicted as having goodwill? In making meaning of their stories, I finally concluded yes! I arrived at my answer after pondering whether the particles and waves of light I have tried to separate in the above discussions "Commitment to Parenting" and "Parenting Philosophy" adequately captured the ideas that went into my construction of the guiding light concept.

The impressionistic data I brought to this meaning-making were of several types: Observing the man, the woman, and their children interacting in their home environment at the opening of our conversations; segments of the conversation when I was talking to both the man and the woman in which I observed and felt the flow of ideas between them; listening for affective information behind their descriptions by tuning in to the expressive tones men and women used to convey their experience of living in this family; and reviewing the tapes and transcripts repeatedly to hear the grand story as well as the fragmented stories. I include as documented impressions my construction of goodwill, which says something about the unseen, unheard energy that holds the particles, the waves of light, together in the philosophical beam I have called guiding light.

The men's talk left me with a sense that they carry a belief and a commitment to live collectively. Their stories conveyed a sense of meaning-making about their family life in a way that cast them as being part of a larger whole. Hearing their stories, I came away with a sense of them saying, "We are all in this together" and "To keep us together it is imperative to work it out to everyone's best interest." This struck me as suggesting they did not see themselves as operating in their family along the lines of a "zero-sum proposition," or one wins and the other loses, that is so prevalent in the larger culture. Erik, for example, spoke at length about cooperating, co-constructing, and negotiating in his family. He concluded this segment of his narrative by suggesting that, if he approached his family with culturally sanctioned male privilege, he would miss precious opportunities to know himself and others through connection:

> I would miss out on the richness of human relationship. What makes human relationship rich and captivating is the dancing around, feeling each other out, and experiencing one another. If you're in an autocratic position, then you don't have the experience of anybody else, you just overwhelm everybody else.

Men also spoke of knowing that their beliefs, ideas, actions, and reactions affected others in the family. They spoke of learning that self-reflection and self-monitoring were imperative in this light. Returning to Bill's narrative, I found an example that stresses this idea:

> I know they copy that behavior, I've seen Scott do that. Imitate my behavior when I'm getting angry. I don't like it. I suppose my goal then is to not let him see that behavior again. It's not always successful, but I just don't like it and all because of what it really is in their reflection. Sometimes you look in the mirror and you don't like what you see. What bothers me also is that he's learning behavior that's not effective. I don't think it's effective anyway. I can't help it sometimes because we have emotions, and I don't care for it. I don't care for it myself and I don't care for it in him. I just don't think it's very effective. . . . I think that's one of the things that it's (parenting) taught me, because I didn't spend a whole lot of time in self-reflection before. I feel that if you're going to know other people, you should know yourself pretty well. If you want to understand other people, you should [get] a pretty good handle on what's going on with yourself.

Erik and Bill—and the other men—were suggesting that their participation and presence in intricate human relationships in a family

required them to demonstrate, in spirit and action, a sense of benevolence, trust, respect, and cooperative spirit at every turn. When they
fell short of that ideal, they felt they could rely on the benevolence of
their family members to allow them forgiveness and opportunities to
do it better next time. They did not see this as their right as a father
and husband, but as something they earned in their relationships.
Dan's narrative highlights ideas about relationships:

> It seems to me child care is phenomenally about relational skills, that
> getting food into children is not what child care is about—child care is
> about relationship with your children, and helping them build relation-
> ships with each other and with friends. You're a relationship manager.
> You're not in the business of getting them clothed or keeping the house
> clean, or making sure they eat nutritionally—these are ancillary activities
> that are important and significant—but they're secondary. It's much more
> important in the ball game, like I said with Tom, it was much more
> important that we had fun together than that he learned how to catch or
> throw. For me, it's important—the primary importance is to have fun
> together, that he and I are friends. I want to like my children; I want them
> to like me. I don't want to screw them up.

Dan, along with other the other men, mentioned that he didn't want
to screw up his children. His words suggest another aspect of goodwill:
carrying an embodied sense of responsibility to one's children and
partner. Charles conveyed how his sense of responsibility to his family
feels natural:

> [I feel] really responsible, or a sense of responsibility. Like financially and
> sort of just general responsibility of being in charge of these two [little]
> people—hoping that we do the right things and make choices that in the
> end will work out for them. I don't ever really miss not being able to run
> down to the [bar] and have a beer at 10:30 [at night] or doing something
> with Janice (partner). I mean sometimes we wish we could, but generally
> speaking, I don't feel like I've given anything up because of them. Well it
> really goes back to that sense of responsibility. The responsibility part of
> it [all]. . . . My focus is really on the domestic scene, that seems the way
> it should be to me.

Reflections

In my conversations with the men and women in these 18 families, people kept coming back to ideas about their philosophical foundations, articulating their beliefs, values, and ideals about family life. Men's narratives reveal a sophistication in their thinking about their potential influence as fathers, especially as involved fathers. Their talk was of seriously considering how they wanted to affect their children and their partners. They approach their family relationships with good intentions. I saw these men as having the integrity to make adjustments when they saw, or were alerted by others, that they had strayed off course. I came to appreciate that these men may be unique because, in our conversations, they kept coming back to their guiding light, stressing their deep-rooted philosophical commitment to be involved and aware fathers.

6

Tag-Team Parenting and the
Mechanisms of Sharing Parenting

As I listened to men and women talk about the routines they had created to manage the busyness of their daily lives, stories about taking turns being the parent who was "in charge" were common. The sense of a rich rhythm and a continuous flow of sharing parenting and covering parenting responsibilities on a daily basis was deeply embedded in these stories. Men's and women's narratives were generously sprinkled with talk of "taking shifts." Their talk of shifts began to carry new meanings for me. These women and men were using words like *team* and *tag team* and *spelling each other.* This language seemed quite distinctive. I decided to peer deeper into their narratives, exploring the nuances of why they believed their arrangements to handle the work-family interface worked for them. The language used in their descriptions of sharing parenting experiences led me to call this *tag-team parenting.* This chapter sets out important structures that organized and supported the perceived successful functioning of a parenting tag team. Tag-team parenting is a metaphor I heard about, in one aspect or another, in the narratives of each couple. As a metaphor, it is tightly packed with meanings. The task here is to unpack some of these meanings and illustrate some of the texture of how men and women understand and see themselves negotiating their conjoint juggling act.

What's in the Language?

I asked these people to clarify what they meant by words such as *team, tag team, spelling each other,* and *shifts.* Later, as I studied their transcripts, I reached for the dictionary to help me unpack the tightly held nuances hinted at in their descriptions.

Uncovering the common meanings of *team* serves as a springboard for understanding some of the subtle complexities hidden in these couples' depictions of a tag team. In common parlance, a team is often thought of as a group of persons associated together in work or activity. A team also connotes some notion of collaboration—or joint working toward a shared goal. The narratives suggest that, underlying what these men and women described as their parenting arrangements, is their stated commitment to a shared goal—generally, that most taken-for-granted notion of raising their children well (see Chapter 5, "Guiding Light"). I thought most parents might mention a similar general and shared goal. The question then became one of tracing lines of meaning that could suggest nuances of how they believe they create ways to share the realization of that sacred goal—raising their children well— actively. I looked for distinctions in the narratives that might clarify how these people thought they created structures to make this happen in ways they reported they found satisfactory, especially given that they were committed to sharing the activities and responsibilities between them. I came to question whether their parenting team was organized around ideas of hierarchy (i.e., designated team captain and cocaptain) or some other notions of nonhierarchical cooperation. If they co-created some relatively nonhierarchical pattern, I wondered what allowed this to work for them.

MATCHED TEAM: STRONG,
COMPETENT TEAM PLAYERS

Generally, both the men and the women described themselves in a nonhierarchical position relative to their partner when it came to parenthood. Their narratives depict both partners as equally strong team players. Being a strong team player, and believing your partner is also a strong team player, seemed crucial for making and maintaining an actively sharing parenting experience. Men's and women's narratives suggest they believed they were both active in the trenches of daily parenting. They both acknowledged each other's competence to handle all the responsibilities. They both talked about feeling comfortable having their partner actively involved in raising the children. Kelly, along with many others in my research, spoke with obvious joy when describing her experience of her partner's competence and participation in covering the child care responsibilities. Kelly, a woman in her mid-30s with one young daughter, works full-time in the management team of a social service agency. She said:

> As much as I have a tendency to sort of like things to be done a certain way—I mean I have sort of a way I like the house to be tidy and everything—I felt, well, in this case there are different ways of doing things. So right from the beginning, we've had different ways of doing things. . . . I think by the time Amy was born, I owed it to him to let him be as much of a parent as I am. There would be no [way]—I would have no right to hold onto the mother thing as being more important or more crucial than the father responsibility. . . . I think I always felt how important it is to him—plus he's just really good at it.

Valuing Differences

Like Kelly, these couples recognize that they each do some things differently. Both the woman and the man can cover the basic functions of parenting, but they may have different forms, or ways of getting the jobs done. In talking about managing parenthood's myriad responsibilities, both men and women acknowledged that they believe they have relative strengths and weaknesses in their repertoire of skills and specialties. They typically concluded that they value their differences. During a couple conversation, Rodney and Kate expressed their awareness of differences. Their story richly highlights their differences. They also seemed to want me to appreciate that, despite having times of feeling they are each doing too much, they ultimately feel a general level of satisfaction with their team work. Their narratives suggest that any burdensome feelings emanate from the scale of the demands on their time and energy, not from their partner's lack of cooperation and participation. Rodney and Kate are a couple in their early 30s with two children; both parents work full-time.

Rodney: Kate tends to find the big things [like] transporting the kids around, back and forth to school, and that kind of thing [as] being a priority for her. And I kind of tend to think of around here (the home) as my priority, making meals and cleaning up, doing dishes, chores, those types of things. . . . There are times when I think, or I expect, that she should be doing more than what I'm actually doing. Sometimes I get cheesed off about that, but I know she's out doing other things and I kind of think, "Well that's fine."

Kate: There are times when I really sit and think, or try to think things through. When I've listened to people talk about the differences between mothers and fathers. Most of the time, I think that we have things pretty, pretty even. Pretty balanced. But there are still times when I think that I carry the burden and it just ticks me off . . . but I don't even think I can identify a time when it's been Rodney who has been putting that [burden] back on me. . . . I tend to take on a lot of outside things for work. . . . We've also discovered that we never sort of reach the breaking point at the same time.

As with most couples, both Rodney and Kate mentioned the perceived edge of potential conflict contained in their awareness of their differences. It seemed they were talking about recognizing the need to walk a fine line between feeling burdened by all that they are doing in this partnership and appreciating what each other does to keep it going. Sometimes walking that fine line is more challenging than at other times. When these couples found themselves in the more challenging times, they said they were likely to have some minor conflicts. Both women and men were clear, however, that during these conflicts, they held onto their larger vision of family life and their commitment to each other to share in parenting. This vision and commitment seemed to allow them to trust that they would work through any conflict.

For example, Dan recalled a conversation when he believed he and his partner came to a face-to-face realization about their harsh individual realities of juggling all the demands while sharing their parenting. His narrative suggests the possibility that, by sharing their individual perceptions of how burdened each felt, they averted serious divisive conflict. By talking it out, they regained perspective on the unique challenges they had created by doing family life differently. Dan, who is with his children about 60% of his time, said:

> It's funny, you know, we talked about [our sharing] the other night—we talk about it now and then—we had a really big discussion a couple of months ago. Well I was getting really cheesed off because I was doing all this work, looking after the kids, cleaning the house, and I was really feeling, gosh Dan, you're a marvelous guy. You know, you're such a wonderful New-Age man, doing all this stuff, getting all these really mega points, brownie points doing all this stuff and enabling Liz to work full-time, and she should be really grateful. You know—she really owes me. And Liz was feeling—I'm working full-time, I'm never home with my kids, I'm doing, I'm out here in this workplace, battling away, doing this working, putting up with this pressure so that Dan can be home with the kids and do his thing in Stonevale. You know he really owes me. We both thought the other was so in debt, and it was a very funny conversation when it came out. . . . There are conflicts. It's not easy doing what we're doing because we're not running down anybody else's tracks. There are no channels for the fluid in our relationship to easily run, and we have to dig them as we go, and it does get difficult.

Dan's words, like the narratives of several other men and women, highlight the difficulty of juggling the multiple demands of family life and work outside the home for both partners. These difficulties are especially apparent as couples try to co-create a shared way of doing this while having no models, no clear guides as to how it can be done. They are co-creating the rules and patterns as they go along, as they encounter the daily flow and challenges in their family life.

Any time there are differences between people, there is the potential for conflict. In my conversations with the men and the women in these 18 families, I heard a lot about differences, but very little about conflict.

Again, these people went back to their basic beliefs about sharing the responsibilities and activities of family life. They remained grounded in their guiding philosophy. Their guiding philosophy seems to account for differences. People talked about how differences in their respective ways of doing things are quite apparent. Typically, in the next breath, they mentioned how they believe these differences are not a source of serious conflict. Some people in the sample even challenged my inquiry into negotiation about contributions to their tag team. An interchange between Steve and Carol in response to my question about negotiating responsibilities highlights their discomfort with the suggestion of conflict. Steve and Carol are a couple in their mid-30s with two young children. Steve works out of their home as a consultant to the computer industry, and Carol works in the medical services field.

> The only thing I question is what you (researcher) have in mind when you use the word negotiation. Somehow that word makes it sound like it's more—like maybe there's some struggle or some points that need to be agreed on that aren't initially agreed on, and I think for the most part, it all just kind of happens automatically. . . . We agree on the fundamentals.

This interchange suggests that these people do not perceive themselves as being on opposite sides of some negotiating table holding out for their own position. These men and women stressed, as demonstrated in Steve and Carol's interchange here, that they agree on the fundamentals (their guiding light) and work out the details cooperatively.

Being cooperative and collaborating to construct solutions to situations where apparent differences warrant reflection does not mean that problem-solving conversations are without affective content. People's narratives often include comments about their affective experiences of working with their partner's differences. These people can and do get irritated with each other at times. One woman, Daphne, made a point of expressing her affective state in some situations. Daphne and Patrick are both in their early 40s with two school-aged children; she works full-time as a medical technician while Patrick completes his degree.

Daphne: I don't really think that we have [power struggles], but I mean, that doesn't mean that I don't get mad at Patrick. . . .

I was really mad at him for wrecking the screen to get into the house, when I did have a key hidden in the garage, but he didn't remember that the key was in the garage. I was really irked about that. But I wouldn't say—we didn't have a power struggle over it. I mean, if we have disputes, it's over stupid things like that. Or, like if I do something like if I walk across the floor with my boots or something, he'll get mad or whatever.

Patrick: I think there are some things that, if I bugged you and bugged you and bugged you enough . . . if I just wore you down, you'd end up [doing what I wanted]. I know that could happen, but there's no reason to do that because I have the sense that, well all of us would pay the price down the road, so there's no need to do that. It's not worth it!

Daphne, like others, concluded that she believed her affective states were not damaging to the relationship or to their tag team. She hinted that she feels disagreements or arguments are not experienced as serious divisive conflicts because Patrick and Daphne are not dealing with fundamental issues—they both agree on the fundamentals. Patrick's narrative highlights another aspect of how conflict in these families does not threaten the basic stability of the tag team. His words suggest he operates from a perspective of considering how his position will affect the whole family, not just his individual interests.

SPELLING EACH OTHER

Turning to the dictionary to guide me further into possible interpretative meanings of the language people used to describe their team work, I found a tag team is a "team of two or more professional wrestlers who spell each other during a match" (*Webster's*, 1983, p. 1201). I don't much care for the masculine imagery and competitiveness conjured up by the wrestling aspect of this part of the metaphor, yet I see its potential fit. As the above narrative excerpts suggest, the sheer amount of juggling that each family faces can make their lives feel like a wrestling match; each person wrestles with the myriad demands on his or her time, energy, and personal resources. At times, couples' differences can also feel like a wrestling match about who's doing what, as the excerpts from both Rodney and Kate's and Dan's narratives suggest. Parents also talked about feeling like they were wrestling with their children—especially during episodes when attempting to get the child(ren) to do some chore or self-care routine that the child(ren) did not approach with particular eagerness.

Of interest in this definition is the notion of team members spelling each other. This fits with how these couples described their tag teams. Wrestlers on a tag team relieve each other—taking turns on the mat with the opponent—pooling the best efforts of each team member to accomplish the tasks at hand. The tag team is a cooperative effort to maximize the team's chances of taming the opposing forces. In using the language of a tag team in their narratives, both men and women often talked about their partner spelling them. Carol, like others, talked about the potential for both partners to experience the relief of being spelled:

> I think we pick up each other's slack a lot of times because, you know, one or the other of us may get overloaded, or just be at our wit's end, and the other one hasn't, maybe hasn't been dealing with the kids or the situation. So, you say, "Okay, it's time for me to take that over for a little while, or give the other person a break."

These men and women repeatedly suggested that they saw joint ownership of decisions and activities and joint responsibility for all aspects of managing family life as paramount in the successful tag team. I heard about how they thought they found myriad ways to operationalize their commitment in everyday life—to really "live it." In their talk about living it everyday, both partners mentioned times of spelling each other. The conversation between George and Teresa suggests the reciprocity of spelling each other so the partner can get a break or have a fresh perspective introduced into the event. George and Teresa are in their mid-30s with two children and a third expected soon. George's work in the construction trade is highly variable, whereas Teresa's work in the education system is quite regular.

Teresa: It's kinda whoever is closest to him, or if I did it last, he'll do it next.

George: Depending on what you're doing, or you know, sometimes, I'll just get tired of it and Teresa will take care of it.

Teresa: I don't have that option!

George: It depends. When she gets really mad, then sometimes, I think I gotta do something about this.

Teresa: Yea, you take the kids and let me have my space.

George: There's no real expected roles. It's always been that way. Jobs need to get done, somebody has to do it.

Both men and women expressed appreciation for the relief they said they felt when their partner came into an interaction as they were about to "lose it" with a child or no longer had the energy to be effective. Their perceptions of this experience of relief was set against the backdrop of "we're in this endeavor together"—their sense of their joint responsibility. Karen's narrative conveys this quite clearly. She stressed her appreciation about not having to experience parenthood or handle it alone as being a big relief. Karen is in her mid-30s, with three children between the ages of 7 and 3 years. She is the designated stay-at-home home parent during the day, and works part-time some evenings and weekends in retail sales.

> . . . just having somebody there who you can count on, who's as much involved as you are to sort of spot for you. You know you're not on 24 hours a day sort of thing. There are times when the kids are sick and up through the night, and you know that there's two of you who can do it . . . you just know that there's always somebody there.

While listening to their narratives about spelling each other, I was also listening for hints of the culturally dominant idea that men offer only temporary relief in parenting, which leaves the primary responsibility clearly in the woman's domain. Out of context, the conversation between George and Teresa (above) could suggest this dominant cultural idea. Yet, men were often most vocal about feeling offended when they encountered hints of such beliefs. Several men reacted very strongly when I asked about this idea. Todd's narrative, like those of the other men, conveys what I came to understand to mean he felt dismayed and angry. He seemed to highlight his sense of responsibility in caring for his children, not caring for his wife's children. In our conversation, he often came back to his idea of joint responsibility. Todd, a man in his early 30s, has three young sons. He works full-time in the construction trade.

Todd: I can't stand when guys say they're baby-sitting. That drive me nuts, they're not baby-sitting! They're you're own kids—you never, never baby-sit your own kids. Never! I can't—I can't—baby-sitting. You are not! You're looking after your own kids. Like, I can't believe people will say that.

Interviewer: I've had people tell me that they think it implies that it's the women's responsibility, not the man's.

Todd: No, pshaw! No, nuh uh. Why would they say that—that's not fair!

At the same time, women often spoke of a time in their family experience when they felt that their joint responsibility was indeed lopsided. At times, they spoke about feeling they were carrying the primary responsibility for child care. They suggested that this experience often began at the birth of their first child and was reinforced by nursing their infants. Liz's narrative captures these sentiments: "I had experienced being the primary care giver for 4 months since I was nursing." Women also spoke of getting to a point when they asked their partner to get more involved, and later experienced their partner's initiative in seeking adjustments in some aspects of their sharing. Kate, and others, talked about the flow and shifts in the experience of joint responsibility in her experience of working out the daily demands of shared family life. Kate and her husband have two children and both work full-time in social services. She said:

> I felt like I was sort of—demanding is too strong of a word, but (pause) I can't think of a better one. I think probably early on it was, "Look you know, I can't do this anymore and I need some help," whereas these last sort of changes that we have made have been more Rodney just saying, "You know, well, I don't think this is fair. I don't think its fair that you do all this, and this is what I'm going to do so that you're not getting to the point where you feel like you're burnt out anymore." Those changes are his.

TAKING TURNS: WHO'S IT NOW?

Kate's and others' narratives suggest another aspect of a tag team: Each team member has turns of being "it," of being the member who is exerting the physical, mental, and emotional energy of interacting with the children in routine and nonroutine daily events. I wondered how men might describe their turn at being it and not it. Jason's description of his perceived experience of being on the tag team of sharing parenting speaks to some important nuances of what being it carries. Jason, a man in his early 40s, has two children and works full-time as owner-executive of a successful business.

> If I'm totally responsible for Mike for a small segment of time, or a large segment of time, the feeling is different [than] when we're together with Mike . . . almost a freedom . . . a liberation. A freedom that I'm the one who's responsible. I know it sounds funny, because it sounds like it should be a burden, but in a sense, it's kind of a freedom that I'm not having to second guess what the right thing to do is. I'm just doing what I feel the right thing to do is. . . . [When Hillary is present,] I feel more inadequate as a parent. It feels like maybe if I felt liberated on one side, I feel inhibited [on the other side].

Jason's description suggests that there may be both a freedom and some constraints inherent in being it on a tag team. His narrative suggests that being it carries both privileges and power and burdens and powerlessness. I came to think about the dynamics in the following ways: While you are it, you have the privilege of being in the spotlight; your partner may be on the sidelines watching, anticipating how your turn might shape his or her turn coming up. In a sense, you are calling the moves, you are the reference point, you set the pace, you have some control or choice over how you are it, and you know your turn can affect your partner's turn. You are also in the position of keeping track of the flow of the interaction at hand—especially when interacting with children—and monitoring what might call in your team partner. Being it means anticipating moves, judging what moves, direction, or pace will prolong or shorten your turn as it. At the same time, being in the spotlight carries with it an awareness of others' gaze; others (including your partner) may watch how you carry out your turn as it. You also know that you cannot anticipate, judge, or strategize your moves with guaranteed success of relinquishing your turn when you feel you've had enough. When you are ready to shift turns, your partner may not be available or equally ready to come into the field. Sometimes, you just want your partner to come into the field, to say "Let me take over." Jason recalled a conversation with his partner, "Hillary was saying, 'What are you going to do about this? Can't you do something about this?' " that suggested she was wanting him to volunteer to be it in a situation. At other times, you want your partner to relinquish his or her turn and let you be it. Everett's narrative suggests his sense of a readiness to be it when he came home from work. Everett, a man in his late 30s, has two children. Both he and his partner work full-time; he works as a manager in the financial industry.

> She had this baby all day long during that [first] 3 months. I mean, I was the break at night. She was a good baby, which was a bonus, but it was kind of like my turn. I want her now, you know!

Everett's words echo the experience of several men I spoke with. Their narratives suggest they assume they will be, and want to be, it when they are home. They said they organize their work life so that they can be home with maximum participation in family life. Their apparent desire and willingness to be it left me wondering about times when either partner might choose not to be it—or "not it"—or refuses to be it. I wondered about the dynamics if both partners want to be it or not it at the same time. This possibility seems greatest when both parents are apparently available to be it (i.e., not at their jobs outside the home). Indeed, men and women spoke about times when they both felt "not up to being it," or both wanted to be the designated it in a situation.

Phil and Kelly talked about perceived experiences highlighting some of these dynamics. They, like other couples, shared stories that indicate that they feel there are times when both partners are in the same position of either wanting or not wanting to be it and needing to figure out who will be it. This excerpt highlights the not-it side:

> I think the main benefit is the relationship—that it gets everything done and we don't have to fight about it. There's no fight about it's your turn to do this, or she's your child, you watch her! There's not much resentment about being shouldered with the responsibility. I'm tired of being

the main ferrier right now, but its just circumstances, I mean, it just—this is the way it worked out that my job happens to be that close. It's ludicrous to think that he would travel all that extra distance to take her places when I'm right there . . . about right now is when I'm pretty worn out with it (partner's busy work schedule) because I feel like I'm carrying more of the emotional load too because he's tired. Like he's tired, but he's in a situation where he has to just keep his head down and keep doing it for another few weeks, I think most of the work is going to be done, out of the way for this big client [soon] . . . it's just that when he isn't as busy, the weekends are more open, he's just a lot more relaxed and a lot less distracted. . . . I think the reality is, when he's here, if you took a calendar and marked it out day by day, despite his schedule, he still bathes her and puts her to bed equally to when I do. And he still is here most mornings when she gets up. So, nothing much is changed for her . . . the law of averages of getting her to bed, and the time spent on weekends—sometimes it's a bit more tradey-offey. You know, I'll be with her and then he'll need to [be with her]—or he'll be with her and then he'll need to sleep, that kind of thing, but she still gets lots of time with him.

Kelly spoke about times when she perceived they both felt quite exhausted, each realizing their daughter needed their attention despite their states of mind. Her narrative suggests that couples may find themselves shifting around times to be not it—determined by some implicit assessment of which partner most needs to be not it. In their stories about these experiences, the notion of goodwill hovers in the background—this seemed to enable Kelly, the partner in the tag team who became it by default at times when Phil's work was extraordinarily demanding, to trust that her need to be not it would be honored in the future. She came back repeatedly to how even in busy work times, Phil organized his work time to continue his involvement with their daughter—especially around morning and evening routines.

What About Refusing to Take a Turn?

Coming back to the dynamics of taking turns being it in a tag team, I wondered about times when one partner might refuse to be it. In my conversations with these men and women, I did not hear about these times. I speculated that this dynamic may have been a possibility for them, but it was not elicited by my questioning. In fact, couples often noted the absence of significant power struggles between them, suggesting that they may feel the option of choosing not it at times eliminates the need to refuse to be it. Patrick and Daphne's narrative highlights how their ways of dealing with issues have shifted since they had children:

Patrick: I don't think we have a lot of power struggles—we don't have the time, I don't have the time, I don't have the desire, I don't have the need to get into a power struggle with Daphne. I probably used to before we had kids, but I don't think, I mean, I just think that there's probably come a time in our life where it's life experience and maturity—it's just not an issue. It's not an issue for me. . . . I know what she's good at. I know what she's best at, and she knows the same thing about me, so there's no big need to.

Daphne: I really can't say that we've really had any power struggles. Now, I know you're not going to believe me because the books don't say that (laughter), but I really don't think that we have, like, [power struggles].

I continued to wonder about the semantic differences among choosing, refusing, and default positions, as well as the perceived experiential differences in these stances given the general sense of goodwill and the commitment to sharing. The closest example of refusing to be it came from the accounting equity couples. Narratives about the historical dynamics between the man and the woman in these couples suggest that women may feel they have more potential to hold their partner explicitly accountable to their agreements about who will be it for specific times, tasks, and general splits in responsibilities. Jason's narrative provides an example that might suggest that his partner (Hillary) was refusing to spell him during one of his designated times to be it. His description of this interchange led me to think about her refusal as a special type of refusal, based on a prior agreement.

> I asked for a favor this morning—I asked for a favor, I asked, "Can I do this [have extra time away this evening]" and I get the answer, "You know that it's your turn, wait, you still have some make-up [time] from last week!"

What About Stepping In, Taking Over as It?

The routines and experiences people described in their tag-team narratives left me wondering about times when one partner might be tempted to step in, to take over being it when the other partner was taking a turn at being it. Women mentioned that they often feel a temptation to step in, and described how they made decisions to stay out.

Cheryl's narrative about a recent event caught my attention in this regard. Cheryl, a designated stay-at-home parent with three children, also works part-time starting up a retail business out of their home.

> I've been more conscious these past few months of really trying hard not to take over when I know he can handle the situation. One day I was in the shower and I heard one of the kids get hurt. Ned fell off a chair or something, and he wanted to come to where I was, and he stood outside the door pounding. Well, I was ready to get out of the shower and I thought, no, no, no, daddy can do it. I could hear Erik (partner) calming him down and giving him hugs and his cuddles and kissing wherever it hurt and doing everything that I would do, and I thought okay, I don't have to get out of the shower. I came out [later] and he felt really good that he'd been able to do it and he didn't have to call me, and I felt good that I'd been able to sit back and listen and hear that he did all of that without having to think, "Oh geez, I have to get out of the shower, get back in the shower, it's going to be cold"—and it was nice. There are different times as I've come along with each of the children that I've stood back and kind of watched and stepped—stepped right back out of the picture to let him do that. It's just reminding myself to do it. I have to remind myself that Erik's a capable adult and that I don't have to do everything for the children.

I also wondered about times when the partners saw themselves as both simultaneously it—working together rather than spelling each other. Both men and women talked about their weekend time as "family time"—time when they prize being together as a family. Their talk about these times, though quite general, creates an impression about seeing themselves as both being it; that they are both in the arena, ready and willing to be involved with their children as the situation unfolds.

Men's Hesitation to Become It

Men's narratives often resonated with tones of watching how they experienced their turn being it, and being aware of how their turn being it was viewed by their partner. Jason mentioned his sense of freedom when he was it, and expressed a sense of constraint or inhibition and inadequacy when he was not sure about being it in the presence of his partner. Sentiments similar to those were mentioned by other men. In this, men seemed to be suggesting that their tag-team arrangements allow them to experience more efficacy as a parent when they are not parenting right next to their partner. They said they then seem to be able to let go of concerns about comparison with their partner.

Men also talked about feeling initial doubts—doubting whether they would make a good job of being it, whether they were really up to being it. Their narratives suggest that they felt that these doubts seemed to hover in the background for some time, but would later give way to delight as the man discovered his capabilities and enjoyment of aspects of being it. Bill, a man in his mid-40s, stays at home with two young children. He said:

> The first 3 or 4 or 6 months were very frustrating. Very confusing, I suppose. I just wasn't prepared for the job, and didn't really realize what it entailed, and I think it took me that long to adjust. Now I like this, I know how to do it, and I know I do it fairly well, and I can relate [to it] really well too.

Tag-Team Parenting: Key Mechanisms to Making It Work

The men and women in this study described a variety of mechanisms or structures they rely on to hold their tag team in place in the face of everyday demands, challenges, and distractions. Three key mechanisms—agreements, specialization and interchangeability, and negotiation—serve as a concepts to organize the intricate workings between men and women as they cocreate sharing parenting. These mechanisms are viewed as necessary arrangements couples have put in place to keep their family and their tag team running day in and day out.

AGREEMENTS

Several types of agreements emerged that underpin and maintain successful sharing parenting arrangements. Foremost among the considerations of how to do sharing parenting is the commitment to "getting all aspects of family life covered" by one partner or the other, and in some cases by both partners. This is the notion of "somebody's got to be it." Given that these couples said they had already generally committed to a partnership model, they described how they thought the challenge then became one of decision making, problem solving, and managing the flow of everyday routine and novel situations. To a certain extent, their narratives contained ideas about how external circumstances (e.g., work schedules) and, at times, biologically based limitations such as breastfeeding, operated to constrain the degrees of freedom each individual and the couple collectively has to be available for participating in an event or situation.

Possible Patterns

The kinds of agreements and arrangements that these 18 couples said evolved or were negotiated span a multilayered spectrum. The first layer seems to be the most apparent—that is, explicit and concrete formal agreements as to who does what when; for example,

> He goes to work early before the children are up so he can come home early, usually well before dinner. A few nights a week, he walks in the door and I leave for my job. On Saturday, he is with the kids alone as I am out at work. Then we have the rest of the weekend as family time. (Karen)

Another type of agreement is characterized by evolving and revolving formal arrangements (or negotiating and problem solving as they go); for example,

> Recently our arrangement shifted. When we initially came to town, we job-shared and shared parenting. We both worked part-time and were at home part-time with the children. That way we could make sure at least one parent was always with the children. Because of what had been developing as far as funding our job goes, this year we changed our arrangement. Liz now works full-time, because she has potentially more influence, can potentially make a bigger impact in that job, and I work

part-time in another position that came up. Now, I'm home more with the children, and we have our youngest in child care a couple of days a week. (Dan)

Couples also spoke of ad hoc informal arrangements (it just happens as they go along):

It's sort of what's naturally happened for us . . . fortunately with my job, working at home as I do being self-employed, I know it's given me a chance to be flexible . . . you work on a project and then its done and there may be a time when there's no project on, during that time Carol may work or not and I'm with the kids most of the time. . . . We just ended up this way, mostly because that's what we wanted and we didn't have any circumstances that compelled us to do it some old-fashioned, unpleasant way. (Steve)

Finally, men and women mentioned yet another layer of ad hoc informal arrangements. These are responsive to the daily flow of work and family life:

I would say 2 or 3 evenings a week, one or the other of us is out from about 7:30 onwards at one sort of meeting or another. We've entered our eldest into a softball league, so that's one parent gone 2 evenings a week for an hour or so. (Dan)

Flexibility and Variety

Combining these various types of agreements seemed to allow couples to feel like they were effectively managing to cover different aspects of meeting the myriad demands and tasks of everyday family life flexibly. For instance, some narratives depict couples as having explicit, formal arrangements covering routine daily tasks, and evolving or revolving arrangements about who does these routine tasks on the weekends. The same couple may have an ad hoc arrangement regarding bath and bedtime routines. A couple may have a formal agreement about who does what household maintenance chores, and informal or ad hoc arrangements about who steps in when a child is having trouble getting some task accomplished. Of course, this could go the other way around too, with child care needs explicitly agreed on and house chores handled on an ad hoc basis.

Jack: We have, you know, our responsibilities are sort of split all week long—it isn't necessarily just, um Karen doing all the meals and stuff like that.

Karen: Except you don't do toilets! I do the household cleaning, I do.

Jack: Yea. And like with the kids, like tonight, they wanted me to take them up to bed. Other nights they want you to do it.

Decision Making

The mix of formal arrangements and informal arrangements for any given family seems to arise from a combination of decision-making strategies. First, intentional or planful decision making (e.g., "Our theory had been that we would job share and parent share"—Dan) was often called on when initially setting up the tag-team approach to parenthood. This strategy means that both the woman and the man talked explicitly about how they were going to share and manage the various calls on their time and energy. They set in place the structures for who was going to cover what, when.

Second, reflective revisiting and redirection following some problematic situation or event allows couples to make periodic adjustments in their sharing arrangements:

> I think when it comes to the division, its been we sort of go for a little bit and then things sort of even out, and then we sort of make some more changes, and then things sort of even out, and then we sort of make some more changes. (Kate)

Finally, reification of patterns evolving from the pragmatics of handling situations and events as they arise allows couples implicitly to claim areas through routines of handling what comes up.

> . . . it could be specialization, that if Hillary does that, well if she covers that part of it, that allows me not to develop in that same field, yet I could do something else. (Jason)

SPECIALIZATION AND INTERCHANGEABILITY

Both men's and women's narratives often highlight their perceived differences in individual preferences, their relative standards, or their expertise in certain areas of everyday family life. At first glance, what I conceptualized as the notions of specialization and interchangeability seemed somewhat contradictory. On closer scrutiny, I noticed that both men and women described the necessary coexistence of these two mechanisms. Specialization allows them to claim certain ways of being and separate handling of certain jobs in the family that acknowledge individual differences. In their narratives, the couples suggest that they did not expect themselves to be equal in the sense that they are indistinguishable from each other, but to manage a division of labor with an eye on fairness. At the same time, men's narratives often note that they believe their involvement in tag-team parenting requires certain degrees of interchangeability with their partner. Interchangeability, on the other hand, was talked about in terms of either the father or the mother covering the activities and responsibilities of parenting, but not necessarily covering them in a way that is an exact replica of how their partner would do things. In this, men and women talked about interchangeability in function, not in form.

Specialization

Specialization emerged as an interactive layer of determining influences for how couples believe they juggle who is available, capable, and willing to be it across the myriad aspects of parenting and managing the household. Specialization was talked about in terms of individual preferences, relative expertise, relative standards, and resource specialization. Specialization is a way these men and women see themselves coordinating their complementary skills and talents. It may also have the potential for people, both men and women, to lay claim to some not-it opportunities without challenging their sense of sharing parenting. Early in Steve and Carol's narrative, the issue of specialization and laying claim to a not-it domain came up:

Steve: It's just a lot harder for me to do certain things than it is for her, like finding matching clothes in the morning and all that good stuff.

Carol: Anything that's routine, it gets real hard for him to deal with, and then once it's routine for me, it doesn't really make sense for him to be messing with it cause it takes him three times longer.

In the narratives of some couples, men seemed quite aware of their tendency to specialize (or maximize) their participation in areas where they felt most comfortable based on their sense of being up to the task. Jack described an awareness that his sense of comfort sometimes directed his specialization when interacting with his three children:

> It's natural, I get involved in baseball and hockey and those kinds of things, and I guess if I was responsible for more of [my daughter's] play time, [I would feel less natural], it's probably because I didn't know anything of her side, [her] maybe getting involved in something other than base-ball. . . . She plays with us, all of those things because she's part of a family with two older brothers, . . . but I also feel like I don't want to leave her out, so it's challenging in that there should be some time with her.

Men's and women's narratives often include talk about their per-ceived specialization in certain areas in terms of feeling like they enjoy the activity, or they feel competent to handle the task, or they have relatively higher standards (or in some cases more or less tolerance) for a given situation, event, or domain. Karen, Jack's partner, de-scribed how her perception of his enjoyment of certain activities created some specialization in their respective interactions with their children:

> Well, Jack's a real goof with them . . . they wrestle, and he's just more open and goofy with them. Like I think, I don't know if all mothers [are like this], but I tend to be more, more sort of rules-and-regulations a little bit. And he's really interested in a lot of things, like they go out on walks and find bugs and snakes, and things like that. Kevin (son) really enjoys those kinds of things.

Although many men's narratives suggest their specialization in areas—such as active play, fantasy play, cajoling or teasing a child out of a mood, public outings—that could be considered gender stereo-typical, I found they often also mentioned preferences in areas that are not generally stereotypical—such as meal preparation, teaching daily-living skills to the child, shopping for the children, medical visits, and conflict negotiation between children. Several women and men spoke of the man being in charge of most of the household cleaning or meal preparation. Their narratives often seemed to depict his involvement as based on his skills and tolerances, and in the case of meal preparation, his relative skills and preferences for types of meals. Janice noted a difference in how she perceived she and her partner approached meal preparation. Her narrative mentioned her partner's use of this activity to get the children involved in both play and learning. Janice, a woman in her early 30s, stays home with their two young children and volunteers many hours of her time to a local public service agency. Her partner (Charles) works full-time in his own business. With regard to his specialization, she said,

> I do the Monday-to-Friday type dinners and that's, you know [my approach is], "You kids go play or something, mommy's just getting dinner ready," whereas Charles will spend Saturdays or Sundays cooking up big batches of things to freeze and he'll let them get involved. So they sort of have fun doing things, learning things, that to me are tasks.

Jason's described areas of preferred specialization reflect a broad base of connecting while taking his daughter to various appointments:

> I just connect at all different parts of life experience, even going to the dentist, the doctor . . . and shopping for Linda (daughter). I took Linda shopping and I enjoyed the happiness that she had and that she was learning to do it herself, and she felt real grown up doing it, that's what I enjoyed.

Interchangeability

Being interchangeable seems to mean, at least as far as covering all the bases, that either the man or the woman can handle any situation as it arises in the course of his or her time with the children. This is the notion that, in Rodney's words, "It's a matter of who's ever there does it kind of thing." The degree of interchangeability varies proportionally with the amount of time each parent spends alone with the child. Dan spoke of how his sense of being essentially interchangeable with his partner spans both his family life and his work world. He suggests that this is because he sees himself as spending about the same amount of time as his partner in both their endeavors. He said:

> It's very vague, and that flexibility and amorphousness of the kind of profession I'm in has made it possible. (pause) I think the fact that Liz and

I are in [the same profession] and have shared our work has made the
(pause) the openness to our interchangeability in earning and child care
much easier than it would be for many couples.

Aspects of interchangeability were quite apparent in the narratives
of other men. Despite their preferences, their perceived and experienced level of comfort or relative expertise, and their competence with
any of the myriad situations likely to come up while with their child,
these men felt they would rise to the occasion. They may not be it in
the same way their partner is, but they can carry the full responsibility
of being it—especially if their partner is not available to step into her
specialized area. Rob's narrative illustrates this idea. He believes he
gives nurturing to his children, but he also recognizes that he does so
differently than his wife might. He is in there doing it, but he does not
feel he has to replicate how his partner would handle the situation.
His narrative suggests he believes women and men do not have to
match the method and perhaps the mood of their partner's way; they
can express their uniqueness even when operating as being interchangeable with each other. Rob is in his early 40s with two children.
He left his job in the financial industry to have the freedom to be more
involved with his children. With regard to his ideas about specialization, he said,

> I was much more in the early days (pause), pretending isn't the word I
> want, um, attempting to be a mother, as opposed to being a father. I was
> attempting to be the mother figure when Donna wasn't here I think . . . I
> think a father's got a lot of (pause) nurturing to give, but it's certainly not
> a feminine [type] in my mind.

Several men in the study conveyed a sense of how important it was
for them to have had a chance to perform all the daily responsibilities
of parenthood. Men tended to see themselves as being essentially
interchangeable with their partners in every situation and interaction.
Steve said,

> . . . just sharing experiences that way, so we've both seen or heard most
> of the things that have happened to the kids. If something happens today
> that was interesting or exciting or sad or awful or whatever, the one who
> saw it tells the other, so it's not as though one of us has had a dispropor-
> tionate exposure to who the kids [are] and what really happens day-to-day.

You know what it's really like to be with the kids from 6 in the morning to 10 at night on a routine basis. I suppose that's one thing that gives us both a real common basis and makes it a lot easier then to decide what you do about a certain situation.

Other men's narratives suggest that they may see themselves as reserving their resourcefulness for occasions that obviously require it of them. An example of this comes early in Everett's story. He shared how his sense of needing to be interchangeable seemed to shift for him when his partner went back to school. Everett is in his late 30s and has two young children; both he and his partner work full-time; he works in the financial industry.

You know, I'll do what I have to do to make it work. . . . We don't have anything specific we do on the weekends when Jenny is away, but, I really enjoy it in that it really gives me some time with the kids. I mean, I think I'm very involved with my children, but I don't think that, um, when there's another spouse here, you know, it's just like—I don't think she does more—I'm not sure what I'm trying to get at here when I say this. I guess when it's just you, you know you're [the one who's] responsible. That's what it [is]—I guess that's what it comes down to. And I guess I really try to make it a positive thing then.

NEGOTIATION

Negotiating agreements on an ongoing basis seems to be the backbone of making tag-team parenting work in these people's everyday lives. Both men and women talked about the work of negotiating. They depicted negotiation as a crucial practice in maintaining their commitment to sharing parenting and active parenting with their partner. Men's narrative accounts suggest they accept that this requires them to lay aside the traditional cultural sanction for them to impose their will on their families. Instead, they adopt a co-creative stance so they can construct together their experiences and decisions. As Erik put it,

I must confess, it's a real pain in the ass sometimes working in a partnership, and I feel like sometimes, "Look, I'm the dad, you know. I'm the man, what I say goes." That would be easy. That would be a lot easier. It's a hell of a lot easier, easier than to work at it and to keep myself back and to negotiate that with Cheryl, you know, just trying to work this out together. It would be a heck of a lot easier to sort of get caught up in that other stuff, and it's pretty tempting sometimes. It's work! And that's it. It's pretty straightforward. . . . But I think it's a better way than being an autocrat. It's not that I don't feel that I can't because its not politically correct, or because I've learned somewhere that it's not appropriate, it's because I don't want to. I mean, it just wouldn't be comfortable!

Negotiation seems to require, as Erik implies, the explicit and subtle work of figuring out how each individual (in this case, a father and a mother) sees the situation in terms of his or her goals and resources, then somehow making decisions between them about how to handle this and connected situations satisfactorily. It seems to require a fair amount of talking.

Talk

Talk emerged as a core feature in the narrative accounts of both men and women in this study. They spoke about "talking it out," which I took to mean listening to each other with an ear tuned into their philosophical band of cooperation and commitment to sharing parenting. Steve and Carol's story provides an example of how talk is depicted in these couples' narratives:

Steve: We do a lot of talking about, "Well gee, what do you think about the way that has happened," or you read some book and you kind of talk about it, "Well gee, I don't like that—I do like that," but, for the most part, we pretty much see eye to eye in sort of abstract issues of philosophy and in specific details of implementation.

Carol: I think one difference in our dynamics as a couple, as compared to a lot of couples is . . . I think there's a lot of discussion, particularly about child rearing and what we want for our family, for our kids, for ourselves.

Over the range of domains and events that men and women are likely to encounter in everyday family life, some things have been talked about more and are the subject of more detailed negotiation. In other areas, both men and women said they are more likely to handle issues on an ad hoc basis. In my meaning-making of the negotiation accounts and how partners see talk facilitating their tag team,

I saw how, in the absence of negotiating formal arrangements or agreed-on rules, ad hoc decision making may prevail. In the narratives, ad hoc decision making is often characterized by a sense of ambiguity and minimal in-the-moment talk. In accounts of these circumstances, the lack of negotiation is most apparent. Both men and women talked about going along for a while in a taken-for-granted pattern until the arrangement or pattern became problematic for one or the other. I also heard about informal, on-the-spot deciding who's it now as being more likely to occur in the moment-to-moment flow of daily living— just handling the complex dynamic interchanges between parent and child—when both parents are present and apparently available. In their accounts of these everyday situations, men and women spoke about the absence of explicit negotiating and of the potential of falling into habits and patterns—habits and patterns that may or may not be congruent with their guiding philosophy. Couples talked about going back to the negotiating table periodically to redress these patterns. Karen talked about regrouping:

> So, it does tend to take, like Jack and I, we have these little regrouping things. It goes on for a while and then it falls apart. You just get all caught up, we've had a busy fall . . . if I think something can be better, or if I think something may not be going right, then I react . . . Jack tends to just coast and hope that it would get better . . . but then he also goes along with it [my reaction], so we work it out. It gets better, so that's really what the ultimate goal is [that we work it out together].

Reflections

Tag-team parenting is a constructed, metaphorical concept developed to capture aspects of sharing parenting. Couples arrive at these formal, informal, and ad hoc arrangements to juggle myriad responsibilities and activities of family life with work. In my mind, tag-team parenting also suggests an ongoing flow of sharing the responsibilities as couples encounter the demands of everyday living. These people see experiences in family life against the backdrop of their joint commitment to share fully in the parenting of their children and in handling the tasks of family maintenance. They spoke with a subtle acknowledgment that they are doing things differently than others around them, and certainly differently than they experienced in their own families of origin. Although they talked about doing it differently, my curiosity was also piqued by their talk about not being special or having found *the* solution for creating equity in their families. I experienced their talk as being full of awareness about how their arrangements are constantly challenged—both from external sources (e.g., changing work circumstances) and within their own family circle. Their accounts highlight their perception of the ongoing demands of daily life and needing to be ready to rise to the occasion to meet a spectrum of expected and unexpected challenges in any given moment.

For tag-team parenting to work effectively, both the woman and the man need to see themselves and their partner as a highly competent parent across a wide spectrum of activities, engagement, and responsibilities. Women's narrative accounts stress their feeling of trust in their partner's competence, although also acknowledging perceived differences in the ways they might think about and do various aspects of their parenting. Men expressed initial and intermittent concerns about their abilities and expertise, as well as realizing they had come to a point of feeling effective with their children and a well-matched, strong team player with their partner.

The men and women talked about seeing their own tendencies to specialize in certain areas of family life; they also acknowledged the pragmatic requirement of being interchangeable to certain degrees with their partner. The dialectic between specialization and interchangeability is resolved by the dynamics of tag-team parenting. Specialization is more likely when both parents are available to be it, and interchangeability is more likely when one or the other is clearly tagged it.

The complexity of everyday living is highlighted in the stories these men and women told, especially in their talk about how they see themselves figuring out who is it at any given point. These couples expressed their sense of a general satisfaction with how their tag-team parenting arrangements are working for them. Both men and women suggested at times that they wondered if it might be easier in some ways to go back to the traditional way of doing it. They were referring to models where the division of labor and family roles and responsibilities are more distinct between men and women. Typically, this was a fleeting thought; they spoke again and again from their foundational commitment to share parenting fully with their partner.

7

The Dance of Father Involvement

Men's and Women's Connected Experiences

Talking with many couples, I learned about more than the pragmatics of deciding on and carrying out complementary parenting roles, divided up somehow between women and men. I heard about more than a woman deciding, as a mother, that she would do the bedtime routine, for example, which then meant the man was free from that responsibility but was expected to clean up the play room, for example. There was more to this than that it was agreed on in some complementary fashion and bargaining for advantage. I detected, over the flow of many conversations, something more ephemeral. I sensed I was hearing, seeing, and feeling an intricate constructive process happening between mothers and fathers. Constructive in that it was laden with a sense of positive intent. Constructive also in that it was a collaboration to build a solid sharing parenting structure for their family. So when at times, in these conversations, one or both parents would comment about having come to a new understanding of their own and each other's perceived experience, I paid particular attention.

My experience was one of being in the midst of a co-constructive process. A *co-constructive process* is one where, in the interactions between two or more people, they construct together meanings from their individual experiences while being influenced by others. In a co-construction, the creation of new meanings and possible under-standings is a social process. The result is that the people involved arrive at understandings that neither might have expected from their individual perspectives. The co-constructive interaction in these interviews was primarily between the man and the woman, but as the researcher, I was also involved. I was both an active and a passive participant. When I invited comments, asked questions, and sought clarification I was quite active. When I listened to the flow of ideas and descriptions between them, I was more passively engaged in the construction, but I was none-theless also making meaning of their exchange. This co-constructive process served to cast light on, and later helped substantiate, my tacit understanding of how men and women are engaged in a changing dance of father involvement, with each having somewhat different experiences of that dance.

I also tried to hold a clear appreciation of complex systemic connec-tions among individual family members and between the family and the larger culture. The story bits people shared—for example, "I think what's so complicated about all of this is that parenting, you know, isn't in a vacuum. It's always being influenced by so many other issues and conflicts and changes. It's sort of an arena of things beyond what is" (Hillary)—helped me keep these intricate webs of connected meanings in focus.

I adopted a dance metaphor to help organize the meanings about these men's and women's experiences of creating father involvement. This chapter presents general ideas about their dance and highlights some individual differences between men's and women's experiences. In Chapter 8, "Sharing Parenting and the Reciprocal Revisioning of Fatherhood and Motherhood," I continue with the dance metaphor to look into differences among individual couple experiences of the flow of working out sharing parenting. There I draw distinctions between several patterns in couples' ways of dancing sharing parenting.

The Dance Metaphor

Dance, especially dancing with a partner, requires each dancer to have dance steps and a way of putting the steps together in the flow of the dance. Some dances are based on a sequenced pattern repeated over the course of the music. Other dances, especially improvisational dance, allow dancers to generate unique patterns as the music unfolds. In any type of dance, each dancer needs a readiness to dance and a repertoire of steps. The breadth and depth of a dancer's repertoire affect the type of dances he or she can engage in with a partner.

Parenting, like dancing, has certain basic steps, yet also has the potential to be uniquely expressive—even when two couples are performing the same dance. Dance is an activity of movement: It flows and changes. Parenting is also a flowing activity. Sharing parenting actively and fully seems to require that two people somehow coordinate their activities over the flowing unfolding of family life. Dance can also be quite magical to experience and observe. As a metaphor, dance has the potential to reveal some of the difficulties of tying down aspects of sharing parenting.

The sharing parenting dance seems to be a collection of dances that bridge known dance repertoires for both women and men. Because family life typically is rife with complex and often unpredictable situations, sharing parenting dancing also requires a potential for improvisation in individual and partnered repertoires. The dance of father involvement in sharing parenting seems to require alterations in how both men and women vision their individual experiences of fatherhood and motherhood. In finding ways to dance together, each partner seems to be finding new ways to use his or her practiced repertoire, while also acquiring new repertoire pieces. An individual's new repertoire may expand the potentials of dancing together. In dancing together, women and men are in a position to influence each other's repertoire and in a position of being influenced by their partner. In this, the individual's readiness to dance and his or her individual repertoire are both separate from and connected to the partner.

Readiness to Dance: Some Differences
Between Women and Men

> I was the oldest of four . . . I had to help out a lot. I was pretty much raised to get married, to be a mother and all that. (Hillary)

I'm the fifth child of 10 children in my family. We were a farm family. . . .
I do have a closer relationship with my mother than with my father. . . .
I remember helping my mother with the younger ones. (Everett)

I was an only child in my family, and when we had our first child, we were
the first in our group of friends to have kids. So I didn't have any prior
experience of being around babies or young kids, and didn't really know
how to take care of them. (Jason)

These narrative excerpts suggest that the individual women and
men in these families came to their parenting with varied notions
about how their previous experiences with infants and small children
might affect their readiness to parent day to day. Their ideas about
how to parent; their expectations about what they would do, think,
and feel as parents; and their repertoire of skills for handling the daily
maintenance tasks and relational-socializing interactions with their
children usually differed between the two people in the couple.

As Hillary's narrative statement suggests, women generally had had
some contact with babies and young children before marriage and
starting their own families. Women talked about feeling a basic level of
comfort in being with and caring for children. Women generally believed
they could figure out how to handle caring for their child as expected,
and even unexpected, situations unfolded.

For men, there was more variation in their readiness to parent. The
narrative explanations offered by Everett and Jason illustrate some
differences found among the men. Like Everett, about half the men
made a point of talking about having younger siblings, or nieces and
nephews, whom they had cared for on some occasions. Like the women,
these men spoke of generally feeling comfortable in being with their
children from the first birth. Jason's narrative about his experience is
different. Like about half the men, Jason made it clear that he had had
no previous experience in his family, or elsewhere, caring for infants or
young children. These men typically said they did not have younger
siblings or any prior experiences that gave them ready opportunities to
learn to care for young children. They usually mentioned feeling unsure
of themselves initially, and often watched how their partner handled
things, looking for clues to shape their approach with the child.

Surprisingly, despite differences in their starting points, moving
toward sharing parenting seemed to present these couples with similar

challenges. In their narrative accounts, all the couples spoke of some basic challenges in working out their sharing parenting experiences. People's talk of creating sharing parenting together often resonated themes of playing off each other as they discovered ways to coordinate their efforts to raise their children. The narratives from both women and men suggest that they felt they had experienced lots of trial-and-error episodes in the daily flow of parent-child interaction as well as parent-parent interaction. Men and women often spoke of feeling like they were resources to each other in finding ways to handle the constantly emerging challenges accompanying their child's developmental changes. For example, Scott said, ". . . just problem solving—'How the hell are we going to do this one?' Yea!—It's more that kind of stuff. We do a lot of talking about, 'Well, gee, what do you think about the way that has happened?' "

In comparing the language people used and the reciprocal interaction patterns described in their narrative accounts, I noticed that parenting demands of people a constant readiness to step on stage and dance. At times, when they step on stage, they can influence the selection of music to which they dance. At other times, they are required to dance to whatever music is playing. They may find they are stepping on stage alone or with their partner. They may already know the steps they can use with the music, or they may be required spontaneously to try something new. I wondered about what might keep them ready to dance on demand, whether solo or partnered, especially in the context of their commitment to share parenthood.

Solo and Partnered Dancing: Claiming Parts in the Parenting Repertoire

Culturally, we think of a right as "the power or privilege to which one is justly entitled" (*Webster's,* 1983, p.1015). Our culture sanctions certain rights to women and men, as mothers and fathers, respectively. When rights are culturally sanctioned, we may think of them as *entitlements.* For example, our cultural tendency to see the woman as the primary parent, even when the man is quite involved in daily parenting, might be considered an entitlement. It also occurred to me that mothers and fathers who are endeavoring to share parenting responsibilities and activities fully may have earned certain rights over certain domains in parenting. These rights then may become deeply embedded in the weave of their everyday lives. This led me to delve into the subtle dynamics between men and women that may reveal how each may assert rights to certain pieces in the involvement repertoire, relinquish rights on a particular part of the repertoire, and maintain an entitlement to certain parts of the repertoire.

Rodney and Kate each made reference early on to their experiences following the birth of their first child, which seemed central in their later parenting patterns. Following the flow in their descriptions led me to the conclusion that they were saying something about how changes in circumstances over time can challenge one to modify once-comfortable dance patterns. I came to appreciate how the change process presents both partners with opportunities to let go of practiced ways of dancing together and experiment with a new repertoire. My conversations with Kate and Rodney highlight some important dynamics connected with asserting, relinquishing, and maintaining rights in the partnered parenting dance.

Tracking Kate and Rodney's narrative interchange—in the context of more than 6 hours of talking with them, first with each individually and then as a couple—I came to appreciate a complex dynamic happening around how ideas shape individual moves around certain rights, and how each individual's stances (positioning around his or her ideas) can shape interactive possibilities. I began to think of these interactive dynamics in terms of reciprocal positions around rights to certain kinds of involvement.

Kate and Rodney talked about intricate moves between them as their dance repertoire evolved over time. I began to appreciate how initially Rodney intentionally asserted his right to have some uninterrupted time with their firstborn. Kate's narrative suggests that she perceived this as meaning she had relinquished some exclusive entitlement to time with the child. At the same time, Kate clearly claimed her entitlement around health issues early in the family's history, and maintained this for several years. Their responses to a recent medical emergency suggested that Kate perceived changes in Rodney's approach that could mean their patterns might shift. Kate seemed to relinquish her entitlement briefly, but later sought to reclaim that piece for her solo repertoire. She was moving to maintain her primary involvement in medical situations. She was acting out of both a culturally sanctioned right (entitlement) and a right they had subtly negotiated over several years of raising their children. They talked about these recent shifts in their dance:

Kate: Sara broke her leg. So Rodney picks her up from school because they can't get ahold of me. He brings her home, and you can't see anything, you know.

Rodney: We didn't know it was broken.

Kate: It was a closed break. They didn't know it was broken. . . . I was pretty proud of myself, for the first time I was like, Sara, just calm down. I was denying it all over the place. You're going to be just fine. Take it easy. I wasn't rushing her to the hospital and it was when we took her downstairs, carried her downstairs, we didn't let her walk on it—it was Rodney who said, "I don't know—I think maybe we should just take her [to the hospital]." That was kind of bizarre!

Rodney: Well, you can never be too careful, I guess.

Kate: And sure as shooting—and I said fine. Did I say this out loud, or did I just think it? I'm not sitting there with her for 2 hours for them to tell me that she's okay!

Rodney: I don't know. I ended up taking her to the doctor anyway. They did an x-ray and it was broken.

Kate: So that's kind of a first, because I usually do that kind of stuff, and not because I don't think you can't do it but 'cause I feel I need to . . . because I think he underreacts.

Rodney (whispering): She overreacts.

Kate: Like this Thursday Rodney was taking Sara to the doctor [for her leg]. I was saying, "Okay, she's got to have lots and lots of medicine in her, lots of pain killer in her."

Rodney: I have a high threshold for pain, so I figure everybody else should have a high threshold for pain. I mean, she's kind of explaining, "Give Sara a couple of doses of this before you go because they may have to move her leg again." The week before, they put some wedges in the cast and they had to move her leg to reset it. It was fairly painful, but she was explaining that she wanted this done again. She wasn't able to take her.

I was taking her, and I said, "Don't worry about her, you know. Just never mind, I'll take her." And she says, "Well, maybe I should take her," and I said "No! You don't have to take her, I'll take her!"

Kate: I even said to Sara, "Sara, do you want me to give you some medicine now? Make sure Daddy takes some medicine. You know, I'll put it in your bag. Make sure Daddy gives you medicine," and she said, "Well, why do I need medicine?" and I said, "Well, because your leg really hurt last time," she goes "Oh! it didn't hurt that much!" It was like, ahhhhh!!!

Kate and Rodney's description of this event highlights the importance of a couple's complex interactive dynamics surrounding each individual's respective involvement in the sharing parenting dance. Both Kate and Rodney have ideas about each other's style of dancing in certain situations—in this case, medical issues—that prime them for interacting in certain ways. On the basis of these ideas—Kate thinking Rodney underreacts and Rodney thinking Kate overreacts—their narrative accounts suggest they each perceive they repetitively interact with each other in patterned ways. Kate's narrative includes descriptions of how she steps in to take care of most medical situations with their kids, and Rodney defers to her in these situations. She maintains the entitlement of solo involvement, while he remains willing to relinquish any right, yielding most of the involvement in these situations to her. His relinquishing any right may also be a cultural entitlement for male noninvolvement.

When an event occurred that interrupted this pattern, it disturbed their interactive dynamics and created the potential for them to reorganize their dance pattern, to renegotiate entitlements and rights between them. In this narrative interchange, I noticed that Kate recognized initially how Rodney had taken a position of being more concerned than she was about their daughter's injury. I thought of him as expanding his repertoire to include more apparent concern for his daughter's health. Expressing more concern and acting on that concern could lead to his earning the right to be more involved in the family's medical care. In their description of the interaction over the next doctor's visit, Kate seemed to return to her idea that Rodney underreacts. Then I saw her as reclaiming her right to be the parent who handles the medical repertoire. Kate even went to the extent of reclaiming her right by instructing their daughter. I see her daughter's response as again alerting Kate that the pattern was potentially shifting more substantially—or a shift in repertoire that might be apparent across situations rather than a one-time aberration (or, more than Rodney just improvising to cover a particular circumstance). They could be in the beginning of a significant (though quite subtle) shift in the implicitly understood agreement on entitlements and rights about certain types of involvement, in this case medical care.

Kate and Rodney's story bit led me to focus in on the tales other couples told about sharing parenting. I went back to stories about their interactive, dynamic, learning process of how to be involved in a sharing parenting team. In this analysis, the focus is on the dynamic interplay around how partners generally determine the balancing in their involvement.

The idea of a dynamic interplay seems particularly important given that 1) both men and women speak of differences in their respective ways of doing things, 2) they acknowledge differences in their relative comfort with various skills and patterns of parent-child interactions that parenting demands, and 3) particularly, men and women garner the messages from our culture about fatherhood and motherhood. Individually and interactively, women and men are balancing their dance repertoires and blending rights to myriad aspects of involvement—that is, both being involved and not being involved in certain pieces of their parenthood repertoire. In the complex dance of involvement, there is the potential for both the woman and the man to assert solo rights to parts of the repertoire, maintain a right, or relinquish a right to be involved or not involved in a particular segment of their dance.

The choices each individual makes has implications for her or his partner. I began to think of the co-created dance of involvement as one in which each partner can facilitate and constrain ways around one's own and the partner's involvement. Though I think of this process as highly interactive and dynamic between women's and men's experiences in daily family life, I have chosen to separate men's and women's experiences here for the sake of clarity. I begin with women's experiences, because it was from women that I initially heard about these dynamics.

Women's Experiences in the
Dance of Father Involvement

I have a close woman friend, conversing with her as she's gone through something similar with her husband has made me aware of some of what we've been talking about in terms of what we as mothers have had to let go of to allow our husbands as fathers to step in, but I suppose it's still a relatively new line of thought [for me]. (Liz)

Like Liz, women often mentioned their awareness of letting go or relinquishing their solo entitlement to certain aspects of the family's parenting dance. Letting go means relinquishing parts of a practiced or cherished repertoire. It means changing involvement in certain interactions or responsibilities to create space for the partner to be involved.

Women's narrative descriptions of their process in relinquishing an entitlement to a particular way, or a domain of involvement, highlights both their intentionality and their hesitation. In women's stories, ideas about intentionality in letting go seem to reflect their awareness that their willingness to do or to take the lead in dancing could be experienced as curtailing their partner's opportunities to be involved in the parenting dance. Their hesitation to let go seems to reflect a complex struggle regarding the commitment to sharing parenting and the effort to trust that anyone else (even the partner) can provide the care they desire to provide.

I asked women to share what they thought helped them reconcile the tension between letting go and holding on—or relinquishing pieces of their motherhood repertoire and staking or maintaining claims on a motherhood repertoire. In listening to their narratives, I also gained some appreciation for ideas and feelings that may constrain women's willingness to share involvement. Women also shared some ideas about specific issues that seem to increase their reluctance to share involvement in some aspects of their family life. I came to appreciate the reciprocal potential of each influencing experience—that is, each issue identified as having a facilitative influence has a reciprocal aspect that can act in some constraining ways. Two aspects—feeling displaced and primary parent acculturation holdover— highlight the tension between facilitating and constraining influences on women's experiences.

FEELING DISPLACED

Women spoke at times about their dual awareness of how sharing parenting both relieved them of feeling all the responsibility and left them feeling displaced. Even when a woman wanted her partner to get more involved, when her partner actually got involved in aspects she had enjoyed as her solo domain, she said she felt somewhat displaced. This talk caught my attention. I wondered how a woman's feelings of being displaced might interact both to limit and to create space for her and her partner's involvement. When exploring this idea with women, I came to a better appreciation of how it perhaps had more potential to keep her involved in some spheres—even when she might know a desire for her partner do more of that work. Feeling displaced might mean that women may inadvertently hold on to some spheres of involvement, simultaneously requesting more involvement of their partner and potentially limiting his involvement. Hillary, a woman in her early 40s with two children, who is just finishing her graduate degree, spoke to this tension:

> I realize one thing that I've worked through to this point is the jealousy in that partly I'm giving, I'm making sure that she [my daughter] has what I didn't have [connection with her father], and that's painful for a mother always, no matter what the issue is, you know. But certainly, that's part of it and another is the kind of, you know, I rarely feel left out anymore, but I've gone through plenty of times and years where I felt like I had to do everything, or be in the middle of everything, and that takes a lot of effort to get past that, you know that [feeling that] I do everything better or—of course, I still think I do (laughing), but it doesn't mean that things have to be done that way. . . . Mostly now I'm both relieved and happy when I see him doing those things, being sometimes emotionally supportive, but there certainly have been times [when] I've felt less positive. I do think women are also . . . playing a big role in keeping things standard and the status quo despite the fact that it's against their desires and interests. I try to tackle that, but it takes perseverance.

PRIMARY PARENT ACCULTURATION HOLDOVER

Many times during my conversations with these women, I heard them mention something they felt guilty about but could not quite explain why that was. Like Kate, below, these women often mentioned a sense that they felt they should be the first line of contact for their children, but they also struggled with their awareness of feeling that their partner could also handle the situation at hand. These women both wanted to be called on and resented being called on first. What seemed to be even worse was a woman's perception that she was calling on herself first. It seemed women saw this as if it was implicitly a woman's responsibility as a mother to be there, to be involved. Hillary's comment about families not existing in a vacuum came back into my mind. Most of these women told me they were raised in families with a stay-at-home mother in a time when the prevailing ideology was that women bore most of the caring and nurturing responsibilities. These women also grew up in a culture where that ideology was being unveiled and challenged by feminists. Although some of the women commented directly on the influence of the women's movement on their own lives, they also seemed to struggle with just how much they felt, at a gut level, the pull to stay in a position of primary responsibility for their children's lives. They noted that they felt this gnawing feeling even though they had a living commitment to share parenting actively with their partners.

I began to think about how this gut-level feeling of responsibility might be reinforced. I heard women talk about their experience of bearing and birthing children as central in their sense of how these gut feelings came into their lives. This talk seemed to be about having earned a right to certain involvement. I also heard about their experience of mixed messages regarding motherhood found in our culture. I saw these women identifying their struggle to relinquish cultural entitlements associated with motherhood. These two powerful influences—the birth right and other cultural entitlements—might create an ever-present tension for women who are working at sharing the parenting dance with their husbands.

Kate's narrative account captures these ideas. She is a woman in her early 30s who has two children and works full-time.

Kate: [When Sara's leg was hurt at school], I had come home and I realized the school didn't have the main agency's number where the secretary knows where I am most of the time. So that's something I've corrected since then. A couple of issues I think. One, I felt guilty cause they couldn't reach me, and second, and it was closely followed by the second, of why are they calling me first anyway? They know he's always in one spot and they know that I'm all over the place, 'cause I've said that to the [school] secretary before. So those two things I think, but my first was, oh gosh, I should have been where they could get me!

Interviewer: Could you help me understand that first reaction a bit more?

Kate: I don't know if I can help you understand that because I don't think I understand that piece. I don't know why it's like that or where that's coming from, but I know it's there! . . . It's on a twofold [level] I think. One, that I think I should carry the burden . . . that probably goes back to well . . . maybe that's what I heard. Or society. But you see, in my family, Dad did a great deal of stuff, but my mother still to this day says things like, "Are you going to do this for Rodney, or are you going to [take care of the kid's needs]? Like, ahrughhhh! Like I should be doing it!

Kate spoke about her sense of wanting to do things differently, catching herself feeling pulled to be the parent of first contact, and going back to an awareness that if she shares parenting responsibilities, then there are times when she is not going to be there for her children. Her story bit highlights the potential for women to feel the holdover of cultural entitlements in their everyday lives and how this might serve, at times, to keep them involved to the exclusion of their partners.

Men's Experiences in the Dance of Father Involvement

If you were in a partnership with somebody, there's no way that you'd get away with doing 20% of the work and somebody else doing 80%, so I mean [we have] a partnership. When somebody's not feeling well, or somebody's down about things, you pick up the slack and you're a little stronger than what you were, or what your partner has to be. I mean, in a partnership everything is shared. It's not you do this and I do this, those type of [trade-off] things. You may want to sit down and say, "Well, this is the way we're going to split it here," but because somebody doesn't maybe live up to their end of the bargain doesn't mean that the other person can't pick up and do that and not make the person feel guilty or use that in an argument. (Rodney)

Rodney's narrative emphatically demonstrates his notion of what his partnership demands from him regarding involvement. Other men mentioned similar self-expectations. Their narrative accounts suggest they see themselves as being part of a partnership. A partnership, in their minds, requires them to be clearly involved, actively and fully. In asking men to talk about how they experience their involvement and the sharing they do with their partners, I began to pick up nuances about how involvement may get negotiated subtly. Men spoke of expecting themselves to share equally, in some fair way, the myriad demands made on them as one of the two adults in their family. They also noticed differences between themselves and their wives in what and how they experienced that shared involvement.

I began to listen to the men's narratives for hints of what might support their arranged pattern of asserting rights, maintaining rights, and relinquishing rights on pieces of the involvement repertoire in the dance of sharing parenting. Their descriptions hinted at less deliberateness in their moves to claim or relinquish particular pieces of the involvement repertoire than I heard from the women. At the same time, they spoke with awareness that they have an ongoing responsibility to themselves, to their partner, and to their children to make sure they do not slip into traditional patterns of always letting the women take the lead in family life. These traditional patterns are tied to cultural entitlements (which are also potentially burdensome) associated with motherhood. These men (in partnership with their wives) were working to undermine the influence of cultural entitlements in their own families.

I began to reread the transcripts for story bits that might suggest men's awareness of the tension between taking an active lead in staking out their own involvement repertoire, and deferring to their partner's lead about when, where, and how they are involved in the sharing parenting dance. This led me to think about what attitudes and behaviors might support men in taking an active lead in creating their own involvement.

In shaping ideas about men's preparedness to participate in the sharing parenting dance, I came to an understanding of some influences that may facilitate a readiness to dance and enable men to expand their repertoire. I came to appreciate the reciprocal potential of each of these ideas to work toward either facilitation or constraint. First, there is the possibility for men to take responsibility for their parenting skills. This seems, on balance, to work in facilitating ways. Next, there is a complex meaning cluster around how the acculturation of men as providers, disciplinarians, playmates, and displaced persons in the family that has the potential to work in constraining ways. In presenting these influences as separate from woman's experiences, I remind you, the reader, that I do not think of them as separate, but as having an interlinked effect on the family's relationship dynamics. For heuristic purposes, I present them separately here.

MEN TAKING RESPONSIBILITY FOR DEVELOPING THEIR PARENTING SKILLS

Men talked about feeling responsible for learning parenting skills. Although most men described how they felt they had learned a great deal about parenting from their partners, they also went to some lengths not to rely solely on their partners to teach them everything. Men's talk about their willingness to enter the unknown, to experiment and adjust their approach, seemed to be an important element in gaining some comfort with asserting a right to a broad repertoire of father involvement. I got the sense that these men felt they knew the subtle distinction between taking full responsibility for learning effective ways to parent, thus claiming their place on the sharing parenting team, and keeping women central by relying on them to teach the needed skills and information.

In these descriptions, as with Tom's below, other women figures are often a rich source of information and modeling skills and approaches. Although it is not noted in Tom's description here, several men talked about taking parenting classes and reading child care and child development books and magazines. Tom, in his early 40s, decided to leave his management job a few years back to become the designated stay-at-home parent when their second child was born. In this narrative excerpt, he refers to the tension between men learning from their partners and finding other ways of taking responsibility for acquiring the skills to parent effectively:

I've heard of men who sit while the kid cries, they sort of look at their wife, I've seen it! I've seen them say "Why is she crying?" "Oh! [I say] Why would she know?" (laughs) Why would she know why the baby's crying or why don't you get up and go look? [I do it] by experimentation. (Tom gets up to burp the baby he has been feeding a bottle throughout our conversation.) Old wives' tales, or when my mother-in-law comes here and stays with us for a few days, I watch her do something and I think Oh! Okay! This morning, sometimes he's a reluctant burper, and I've noticed sometimes I get up and kind of like [this way] he burps. What works. And its never 100%—I think that's why I'm clumsy at it, it's never 100%.

Another way men's talk seems to suggest their desire and willingness to take responsibility for asserting a right to father involvement emerged in their examples of times when, or situations where, they challenged their partner's position on certain things. This seemed to be a tricky area: Men talked about balancing their respect for their partner's experience, ideas, and knowledge about child care with their own ideas, experience, and knowledge. Men were willing to challenge their partners—clearly asserting a right rather than tentatively maintaining or relinquishing potential involvement in the face of her expertise—when they had strong ideas about the situation at hand. At other times, men said certain areas were just not important enough to cause parental conflict.

Jason's example suggests that he was firmly committed on the issue of his son's thumb sucking. To assert his right to involvement in this situation, he sought a doctor's opinion, and later challenged his wife's resistance to the program. In the end, Jason continued to pursue this as his parenting responsibility even though his wife was of a different opinion. Jason, in his early 40s, has two children and works full-time in his own business.

At our 5-year-old's check up with the doctor, I brought up thumb sucking as an issue, and the doctor said there are a lot of opinions, here's what I recommend. . . . Hillary was on the bandwagon with me for a while, trying to convince him not to suck his thumb, and I've kind of stayed on [wife disagrees that she was on the bandwagon or that this is an important issue for her] . . . [asking his wife] Why were you proceeding for a while after the 5-year-old check up to do what the doctor had recommended as one course of action and then backed off later? Well, anyway, I'm still working with Mike (son) to get him to stop his thumb sucking.

MEN'S ACCULTURATION HOLDOVERS

Often men noted how they believe their wives, at times, feel guilty about not being available for their children even if the father is there to be involved with them. Men recognized women's struggle to relinquish an entitlement associated with motherhood. In commenting on this, men often explained that they do not experience the same kind of guilt—they might experience guilt about other things, but not what they believe their wives feel. In asking them to tell me about things they might depict as different in their experience, I began to get a sense of how cultural entitlements associated with fatherhood might leave them with a sense of an "acculturation holdover" on issues of 1) providing for the family, 2) taking a disciplinary position, 3) being depicted as a playmate, and 4) feeling unplaced (or challenged to find a place). I began to speculate about how these entitlements might have been taken into self-identities. As such, these entitlements may interact to shape a man's experience of asserting or relinquishing rights to certain parts of the dance repertoire of sharing parenting.

Financial Providing

The first narrative excerpt suggests the tension men may feel between the cultural entitlement (responsibility) for providing for the family, and asserting a right to be with the family as an involved member of the sharing parenting team. Charles noted that he feels his perspective has changed to a long-term view. He feels the pressure of being the primary financial support for the family, and that worries him. He also noted that, although he has chosen to work in a situation where he does not have to put in long hours so that he does not miss his children's early years, occasionally he finds himself missing family time to handle the demands at work. He explained that he does this so his providing for the family remains secure in these difficult economic times. His experience suggests that there were times when he would relinquish his asserted right to daily involvement to secure long-term financial stability. I also got the sense that these men wanted me to value the importance of providing for their family as a way of being involved. Charles is in his mid-30s, has two preschool children, and is co-owner of a service industry business. His partner is the designated stay-at-home parent. He said:

I guess the responsibility that goes with that, if anything happened, all the eggs are in one basket in this situation, so you're always worried that you can keep things going, you're not really in total control of the situation. Everybody's effected by the economy, and the last few years have not been that positive in terms of the economy generally . . . that brings worries, late nights lying in bed thinking of things—responsibility as opposed to remember when you didn't have to worry about supporting a wife and kids, so it's just please God, let's make money. So it's more I guess long-term kind of thinking now as opposed to what's happening to-night. . . . If it gets busy, really busy, I'll have to stay and work, but I prefer not to do that, and most of the time I don't have to. It's really been a decision on my part not to miss it [miss out on family-time].

Discipline

Another aspect of men's acculturation holdover associated with entitlements to fatherhood is highlighted in Rob's narrative. His story bit contains several references to discipline. He and his partner, Donna, have created a highly interchangeable partnership in both their family life and their co-owned business. Yet, he feels that he takes more of the responsibility for setting the distinctions between right and wrong and setting limits on their two children's behavior. At the same time, he appreciates that his partner does discipline in her own way. He speculates that experiences of bearing and birthing children can challenge women in the area of disciplining and setting limits. He also seems to suggest that he is in the position of being somewhat more the disciplinarian because he feels his partner takes a softer touch.

I tend to be a little bit more of the disciplinarian. She does some disciplining when I'm not here, she disciplines them in a certain manner, but it tends to be [on] a softer basis with more outs for the child, I think. I think the male doesn't bring forth the child—doesn't bear the child, so that there is a potential to be a little less forgiving, or to be a little less susceptible to little pressures from individuals [children] and manipulations where the mother perhaps is.

Although several of the men shared Rob's experience, several others had an alternative story about differences between men and women regarding discipline. Some of the men saw their partners as more concerned with and involved in the discipline. This tended to be associated with families where they had designated the woman as the stay-at-home parent.

Play

On the other side of disciplining seems to be play. One of the most frequently stated differences between men and women—by both women and men—was how much men engage in active play with their children.

> [The] a song about parenthood—Moms are for maintenance and Dads are for fun—and I think that's true to some extent, although I do my share of maintenance. Anita (child) and I play games that Kelly (wife) and Anita don't. Like we have a, somebody said this word at day care, a roughneck [play]. You know, when you're roughhousing around. So it's something that she and I play; she has had me try and teach her mommy how to do that. We go up on the bed and hit each other with pillows and tackle each other and all this horsing around that Kelly doesn't do, and we'll wrestle more. It's that kind of physical contact. That kind of thing I did when I was a boy. (Phil)

Phil mentions how much his daughter enjoys his roughhousing—so much so, she has asked him to teach her mother how to play this way. He also seems to think it is important that I understand he does his share of the maintenance required in daily family life too. Earlier in our conversation, Phil mentioned how, in his morning routine with Anita, they have created a ritual, a game, around getting breakfast together. It seemed that Phil wanted to balance his entitlement to "fun" with his efforts to assert his rights in both serious and mundane domains.

These examples from everyday family life challenged me to think about how seeing men as playmates for their children could miss valuing the variety of involvement these men have in their families. I began to appreciate how active play can help children develop an appreciation for their physical capabilities, the potential learning from fantasy play, and learning about limits in situations. I also began to appreciate the obvious connection children make with the parent who plays with them. Later in our conversation, Phil noted how he also engages in quiet time, serious time with Anita, seemingly acknowledging the importance of a diverse and broad repertoire of ways to be involved and connected.

Men Finding Their Place

Men's narratives often conveyed their seeming awareness of how their involvement with their children was, at times, determined by the child's preferences and developmental stage. This realization seemed to help them deal with feeling, at times, that they could not find their place with the child and how awkward or hurtful this was. Sam's experience explicitly addressed the temptation to say "Forget it, I won't claim any more involvement" and feel quite justified in doing so. At the same time, his experience suggests that he has learned to persevere for the long term, to claim his involvement as a father, even if that involvement is overshadowed temporarily by the mother's importance in the child's life. He noted that it would have been too easy to miss out in the long run because the current situation was difficult. Sam, a 40-year-old with two children, works full-time as a management trainee. He said:

> Whether it's rejection or the love [from the kids] and how Meg [my wife] tells me it's good to return that affection. She has to tell me that. . . . [We've been through a tough period with our older daughter, Keltie.] Meg kept waiting and waiting and waiting for 4 or 5 months for Keltie to develop some sort of crush on me. I'll give an example, she always wanted her mom to be with her, and we were taking groceries out of the car and she refused to let me take her into the house. My gut reaction was, it pissed me off. My other reaction was I was determined not to run away. You know I kept trying. . . . It's fun now with Keltie, she tells me she loves me and I think she really means it.

Listening to how these men depicted their ways of being involved, I understood them to be suggesting that they do not expect themselves to give up father entitlements subtly learned through acculturation, but to develop them within a broader repertoire of actively fathering and sharing the parenting dance with their partners. These men spoke of expanding their repertoire of involvement by taking responsibility for learning and practicing new ways to be a father, as well as co-operating with their partners to choreograph a new dance.

Reflections

After talking with the men and women in these 18 couples, I saw clearly that the reshaping of fatherhood is not accomplished by men's efforts alone. The men and women in these couples are closely connected in a dance to reshape both fatherhood and motherhood. Certainly, the moves men make to involve themselves actively and fully in the daily life of their children are extremely important in this dance. Yet, the moves women are also making to step away from culturally sanctioned, if not subtly culturally dictated, rights and responsibilities for child care are also crucial in making a difference in their family life.

When deciding on a language to use to work with ideas about women and men claiming certain aspects of a parenthood repertoire, I hesitated. I do not particularly like the notion of right, yet I realize that some of what these couples are struggling with is a sense of how to figure out who will and can handle what parts of the multilayered, ever-changing demands of parenting. The concept of a right seems to contain the notion that one must demonstrate an ability to handle a certain situation. One needs to earn a full place in the dance troop by acquiring and practicing the full repertoire. The concept of rights also became attractive as I thought about the associated concept of entitlements. Restrepo (1995) alerted me to the subtle and sometimes insidious ways entitlements operate in families. Entitlements are most often culturally sanctioned and may imply privilege. Yet, in talking with these men and women, I came to realize that with privilege, there also comes the potential of a burdensome responsibility. Shedding the privilege (burden) can be tricky business, because it is often kept in place by structures outside everyday family life.

What struck me most clearly is the struggle both men and women face in challenging often unarticulated expectations embedded in cultural images of fatherhood and motherhood, and the entitlements associated with them. The subtlety of their intricately interwoven dance patterns often seems to obscure, even from their intentional monitoring, the insidious hidden influence of their acculturation. As I listened to women, in particular, I was aware how they struggle to effect changes in what they expect of themselves as parents, what they want for their husbands as fathers, and how they feel as they experiment with unsettling culturally entrenched patterns. Hillary's narrative excerpt introduces the issue of feeling jealous when her husband engages emotionally with their daughter. She struggles with reconciling how she both deeply wants this for her daughter and her partner, but she knows she faces a hidden loss of the previous exclusive connection her daughter's emotional world. Hillary was one of the most emphatic about wanting her husband to carry at least half of the emotional responsibility for parenting. Thus, I found it enthralling for her to speak so clearly about how she knows she has interacted, at times, to limit his involvement. Hillary's, and others', frank admissions that they might be giving men double messages (unintentionally, I believe) led me to rethink my reactions when I hear some men suggest they cannot figure out what women want them to be doing differently.

I now see that women and men are engaged in creative dances, improvising as they go along, each trying to figure out what one wants for oneself and one's partner as they reshape their possibilities of fatherhood and motherhood in their own families. In this dance, each woman and each man seems to be in the somewhat tricky position of figuring out her or his own vision of parenthood, and shaping that vision in connection with her or his partner's evolving vision. I was struck by how the men and women in these 18 couples seem to have tremendous energy to revisit continually their individual and collective visions; how they engage in ongoing exploration of their experiences, making adjustments and readjustments; and how they seemingly maintain a joy of dancing even though they work at it so purposefully and diligently.

8

Sharing Parenting and the
Reciprocal Revisioning of
Fatherhood and Motherhood

Exploring the mood and flow of the dance opens an appreciation of a dynamic, interactive process between dancers. In this chapter, I focus on ideas of multiple, reciprocal effects and revisioning possibilities for both men and women in families. These ideas came to me as I reflected on the possible wholeness to be found across all the narrative accounts, rather than what could be found in individual and couple accounts. Reviewing all the transcripts as complete texts, rather than the segmented pieces that result from thematic coding, I detected talk about engaging in a process of modifying and adapting one's ways of interacting. People talked of participating in an ongoing, active, experiential, working out of ways to have their family life work for them individually and interdependently. Thus, the ideas in this chapter are a complex construction of somewhat elusive processes. They are a combination of the processes of creating and living with visions of what may be possible, ongoing revising of what one does and believes, and interacting in an intricate social and relational domain of family life.

The idea of reciprocal revisioning captures the sense of living in a family environment laden with a constant presence of "shared, felt, shown by both sides, [or] mutually corresponding" (*Webster's,* 1983, p. 983) interactive effects of one's actions on others. In short, men and women affect each other in complex ways as they work out patterns of parenting in partnership. The process of revisioning captures some of the creative intentionality. *Revisioning* is a term borrowed from Terry Kupers (1993), though he does not define the term. Included in my definition is a complex conceptualization containing revising and visioning. The notion of revising implies an ongoing process; it is a process of "look[ing] over again to correct or improve; to make a new, amended or up-to-date version" (*Webster's,* 1983, p. 1010). A *revision process* is one of visioning, or seeing different ways, actively and intentionally creating visions of what may be possible. Once one has been inspired by a vision, one may make intentional efforts to create it in everyday life, and in the process discover yet other possible revisions in an ongoing evolution. Again, I turn to a dance metaphor as a heuristic tool.

Revisioning Patterns of Leading-Following

There are many ways for people to dance together. The same could be said about reciprocal revisioning sharing parenting. When observing others dancing, I often become so enthralled with the grace and artistry of the performance, that I lose sight of the untold hours invested in learning and practicing the intricate steps, the flow of the dance. I forget how each partner must know the steps, the sequences of steps as an individual dancer, as well as be ready for the unique way they may fit together and unfold in each partnership.

In watching dancers dance, I also lose sight of the traditional notion of leading-following. Watching a couple that has obviously danced the steps together many times, I cannot tell who is the leader or who is the follower. They seem to move together with the music—each in tune both with the music and with their partner's way of moving. Their steps appear to move together simultaneously. I cannot see him step back, followed by her stepping forward. I see a synchronous movement of back and forward. The dancers seem to be poised between their individual steps and the balance in their steps together. The music appears to dance them, rather than one partner dancing the other to the music. As an observer, if I was to see the early practice sessions, I might have a better appreciation for the off-beat steps, the missed steps, the process of finding the synchronized steps that are embedded, yet hidden, in this performance piece.

The reflexive process of making meaning about how these couples have co-created sharing parenting experiences often brought me back to these reflections about dance. Coming back again and again to reflect on the narrative accounts, I tried to capture a meaningful depiction of fatherhood's potentials. I sensed some meaning beyond simple ideas; something beyond what these men had simply told me about the expanding potentials of fatherhood. Reviewing the narrative accounts women and men shared, I noticed hints that both men and women were seemingly saying they felt affected by their partner's moves in the sharing parenting dance. They perceived their experiences as interconnected lives in ongoing motion, interacting to create possibilities for them to shape and reshape fatherhood and motherhood.

I kept in mind that I was likely hearing about the "performance quality" (or the "for public viewing" quality) of their sharing parenting. Yet, sometimes I noticed that they shared selected recollections about some of the less-than-performance-quality trial-and-error sequences that preceded their current experiences. I also remembered that each couple was at a different place in dancing together as parenting partners. I reminded myself that each couple also likely approached its co-construction process somewhat differently than any of the other couples in the study. Although recognizing their distinctiveness, I discovered a few broadly shared common patterns. I think of these patterns as *out of step, matched steps,* and *concordant steps.* These concepts are illustrated here through three descriptive and interpretive biographies.

OUT OF STEP

A few of the couples in the study told stories of beginning their relationships with fairly traditional gender patterns, and eventually making changes in response to changing circumstances or resulting from one partner wishing to live differently. For these couples, it struck me that their narrative accounts seemed to depict one partner—usually the woman—as beginning to take a more obvious lead in moving to another way of shaping family life. The changes women were making meant that both partners were experimenting with new ways of interacting with each other and with their children. She was clearly seen as taking steps that invited him to learn new ways of being a partner and father. The changes these women made were perceived to reverberate throughout their family system and call forth changes in the man's participation. For these couples, it seemed that both partners continued to feel some sense of being out of step with each other. They seemed aware of the potential to collide, or at least to step on one another's toes frequently.

The stories Jason and Hillary told, individually and as a couple, struck me as exemplifying this pattern. They have been working out their new pattern for about 5 years, yet still talk of being out of step with each other.

Jason and Hillary

At first, Hillary was unsure about taking their relationship in a new direction; she had fears that Jason would not follow her lead and she would be left as a single parent in the family dance. She said, "I used to be afraid to be angry or to want changes. I was afraid he'd leave me, and what would I do. I've kind of worked to the point where, well, if he left me, I'd survive." In taking early tentative steps toward a new way, Hillary chose to go back to school and sought the support of therapy. She also began to challenge their taken-for-granted patterns of parenting. Her tentativeness seemed to give way to more deliberate choreography, while Jason indicated his willingness to try out new ways to be involved more actively.

Though apparently willing to change, Jason spoke of feeling resentful initially. He experienced Hillary's request for changes in their parenting as criticism. He said, "I think I resented it at first. I fought it." He felt she was saying he was a bad father. Once he was able to hear Hillary's request as suggesting a revisioning and reorganizing of their way of sharing parenting responsibilities, he was able to appreciate that she valued him as a father, and began to follow her lead. In following her lead, Jason found he also needed to take more initiative to learn new ways to father his children. Hillary was not going to be ever present to show him how to be more involved.

Five years later, Hillary seems to continue to experience their partnership as one where she takes the lead and Jason follows. In taking the lead, Hillary often initiates something new. She may have to invite, request, or direct Jason repeatedly to match her lead before he seems to get into the new dance pattern. Jason often experiences being awkward, hesitant, or resistant in his following. He said, "It's frustrating, because I usually approach the situation not quite knowing what's going on." At the same time, he deeply values that Hillary has led him to this new vision of family life. He now seems to notice how he has begun to appreciate more fully having a different balance in his life. He seems to be increasingly finding ways to claim what he needs to do to maintain this balance between what he devotes to family and what he allows his work to demand of him. Jason said, "I've been real proud of myself. Now I know I want balance between the business side of life and the personal side of life. I want to be able to put all those things that are important to me in balance."

Hillary's overall feeling about these dynamics seems to be anger. She said, "Doing this, you know constantly pushing for years for this kind of parenting is—it exacts a price, constant anger!" She both resents finding herself carrying around frustration or anger and sees that it keeps her from letting up and risking backsliding into less conflict but more sole responsibility. Jason's overall feeling seems to be one of not being trusted that he has changed sufficiently for Hillary to ease into a more relaxed flow of sharing. At the same time, he often feels intimidated next to Hillary's parenting, because he feels mystified by Hillary's seemingly intuitive way of anticipating and knowing what the children need—especially emotionally—and responding to them.

Jason suggested that revisioning his way of being a father has largely been, and seems to continue to be, shaped by his perception of Hillary's strong desire to revision her experience of being the mother in this family. Hillary's narrative account strongly conveys how she is deliberately revisioning her ideas and experience of being mother. She believes her changes require Jason to change his involvement in daily activities, as well as in the more subtle aspects of feeling the responsibilities of the intricate and myriad calls to parent.

The accounts of their experiences contain several references to times when they were feeling out of step with each other. They were likely to experience conflict when negotiating shifts in their sharing parenting repertoires. Hillary was often the one who decided to try out new steps, exploring new possibilities for herself outside the family and demanding Jason take on more responsibility for the day-to-day parenting. As she stepped out into new areas, he was required to step into new aspects of the parenting repertoire. He spoke of feeling awkward at times, especially as he took on each new parenting responsibility.

I found myself thinking of their dance as one where she would lead into a new pattern and introduce a new rhythm, and he would attempt to follow awkwardly, perhaps tripping along for some time until he got the feel of the new rhythm, but by then she might be moving onto yet other new steps that required his adjustment. I saw this dance as, perhaps, the most reciprocally linked, with the sense of mutual correspondence taking some time to realize.

MATCHED STEPS

The couples I saw as revisioning parenthood through a process of matched steps talked about purposely exploring alternative possibilities for motherhood and fatherhood from the outset. Their narratives suggest that neither one saw it as the other leading them toward a shared experience. Rather, they were both participating in creating their visions of what they could experience as parents. For these couples, their dance seemed to be that of matching each other's changes, each taking turns at leading and following. Their talk often suggested that they were well aware of each other's preferred ways of engaging in their parenting activities and responsibilities. They have found patterns that accommodate and complement their differences.

Rodney and Kate

Rodney came to his parenting partnership with a clear desire and commitment to be involved from the outset. He spoke of those early days as a parent with delight and dedication. He wanted to be involved, and did not wait for his wife to show him the way. He took it on himself to ask the hospital nurses to show him how to bathe, diaper, wrap, and hold his daughter. Kate both wanted and expected Rodney to be involved. She welcomed his participation with their infant, and seemed to appreciate that he would need time alone with their daughter to begin creating his own unique relationship with her. She remembered "times when it was just him and the baby, it was just their time together. They now have a pretty solid and unique relationship." At the same time, Kate struggled with her own sense of wanting to have both the experience of being at home with their child and desiring the challenges and engagement she found in her career. She found the early years after the birth of their two children to be most challenging. She was juggling work demands and career satisfaction with her pangs of guilt at leaving her children, especially when their son was ill. Kate remembered "needing and wanting to be at work, but I needed to be with our son when he wasn't doing well. When I was at home, both kids would be very, very well physically. As soon as I started working again, they would get unwell." Rodney's positioning during those difficult years seemed to be one of supporting Kate as she moved in and out of the workforce, and being involved at home as much as his work schedule allowed. He continued through these years to take most of the responsibility for maintaining their home environment, a pattern that began early in their marriage. In a sense, they would share quite equitably when the children were well, then Kate would take the lead when they were ill.

Over the past few years, Rodney has taken the lead in making changes in the distribution of how they manage the routine and nonroutine demands of daily family life. Kate now feels like she is at times uninvolved—preferring to take time at home to relax alone while Rodney immerses himself in the children's interests and activities after school. They both have challenged each other on occasion to move deeper into the underlying meanings of how they share their responsibilities. Both Kate and Rodney invite talk about what it means to each of them to be doing the things they are doing in their family, each seemingly remaining open to experimenting with modifications and new ways. Kate continues to feel deeply the responsibility for her children's health, and maintains the lead here, though Rodney has made some subtle moves to change his positioning in that realm, to which Kate is gradually finding some room to shift her position.

Both Kate and Rodney seem to appreciate the times when their routine steps match each other's. They seem to experience a certain fluidity between them as one or the other begins to initiate changes that may lead them into a different pattern of sharing. Kate and Rodney seem to have reached a comfortable acceptance of their differences, and recognize how their individual strengths enhance the quality of parenting they share. Rodney said, "Generally we're happy and satisfied and having a lot of the same interests and exposing the kids to new things and giving them a choice on what they want to do—we're together on those things. I don't think about any sort of drawbacks." Kate seems to feel respected and supported in her parenting. She seems to enjoy the energy she takes to her work, energy she notes she might not have if Rodney did not participate as fully as he does. Rodney seems to appreciate the effect he sees he has on his children and the ways they influence him, enriching his experience of life. He seems to know he is healing his own wounds of childhood by doing fathering differently for himself, for Kate, and for his children. He said, "The rewards for me are basically being together as a unit and doing things together as a family. I didn't have that as a child. So maybe I'm getting some self-gratification through that I didn't get as a child."

Rodney's and Kate's narrative about their individual and collective revisioning of parenthood suggests they see each other as flexible, with each of them able to accommodate the other as they move through the challenges of daily family life. Both partners seem willing both to initiate changes and to respond to the other's initiation. They seem to feel they have room for and tolerance of each other's "specializations"—areas where one or the other takes a more obvious lead, while remaining open to influencing their partner and to being influenced by their partner even in areas of their own specialization.

Stories about the dynamic interactive patterns between the man and the woman in these couples seem to highlight a fluidity and tolerance of difference. I came away with the impression that if I were to watch them in a long performance piece, I might detect places where the woman led and other moments when the man was in the lead. When one leads, the partner seems to feel enough trust in the relationship that he or she follows the lead, at least for a while. This is not to imply that they dance through their sharing parenting without conflict or awkward times of transition. I came to understand from their narrative accounts that they might have some initial halting steps as they adjust to changing leads, yet the overall flow struck me as one of matching each other's steps. In their reciprocal dance, a fair degree of mutual correspondence seems to exist.

CONCORDANT STEPS

Concordant means consonance or agreement. It is related to *concord,* which can imply harmony, or a "simultaneous occurrence of two or more musical tones that produces an impression of agreeableness or resolution in the listener" (Webster's, 1983, p. 273). Because dance is often performed to music, I borrowed this musical concept; I realized some dance performances I had seen on stage created harmony in movement—a harmony in movement quite different from ballroom dancing or other forms of partnered dance.

A few couples shared narrative accounts that suggest that they are engaging in a different kind of dance. Rather than being partners engaged in ballroom-type dancing, they seem to be partners engaged in improvisational, modern-type dance. To dance effectively in an improvisational setting, each person expects self and partner to develop a full and effective repertoire of parenting responsibilities and skills. Each expressed a willingness and ability to parent fully. This seemed to mean they could be on the stage together or on stage alone.

Co-creating a sharing parenting pattern is uniquely choreographed interactively; each couple is linked in the parenting dance in a different kind of way. For these couples, the dance stage (or the responsibilities of parenting) is seen as a space where either one can perform. They both relate to the stage whether they are on stage dancing or not. I came to understand that their full presence in the sharing parenting dance could allow the audience to gain some appreciation of the individuality of each dancer and the overall coordination of their moves on the parenthood stage. One could form the impression that each has the willingness and ability to change his or her own repertoire, can adapt to changes in the other's repertoire, and can observe changes in their partner's repertoire without necessarily responding with changes in their own way.

Dan and Liz

Dan and Liz have each been in the position of being either the one who was more involved in the family side of their life or the one who was generating more than 50% of the family's income. They have also experienced a number of years when they off-shifted hours in their shared job to cover all their child care needs between them. Both Dan and Liz talk about the importance of their children having full experiences with each of them as parents and as working professionals.

Dan's experience of developing his parenting to its full potential has come gradually and intentionally. He said, "I enjoy the children more and more as times goes on. . . . It takes me quite a lot of effort to work out how to play with them. I have to learn it, but once I learn how to play with them, I enjoy it!" He sees himself as moving beyond ways of doing and thinking that are tried and true for men generally, and for him specifically, by letting his responsibilities as a parent and partner affect him, shape him as he shapes them. He seems to move between thinking and acting out of habitual ways and monitoring the effect of these ways on his children and Liz. He observes how other parents interact with their own children, especially a couple of women he particularly admires for their mothering. Dan asked,

> How do women know the rules of diversion instead of confrontation? How do women know all this stuff and men don't? . . . I think the model mother is a good resource for me. I often feel frustrated at how naturally competent mothers seem to be while I struggle. But they are still good models. I think "What would Bev [a friend of mine] do if she was in this situation?" and I try to think myself into that mode. Often it's just a matter of patience, and slowing down, and being less goal oriented.

He intentionally experiments with new ways of meeting the daily challenges of interacting with his children. He seems to have a deep desire to combine the tasks of parenting with a sense of connecting with his kids and a child's world while he is parenting. He seems to push himself to learn about relational ways of parenting, shedding his more comfortable goal focus that often works so well for him in his professional world. Dan also admires and supports Liz's way of parenting and being a mother, partner, individual, and professional. He seems to want to learn some things from her way and claim his own different way.

Liz's experience seems to be that of each of them being competent, effective parents in their own way, while each seems to be striving to develop further through their parenting and within their sharing parenting experiences. She misses being with her children at least 50% of the time, as a result of a recent change in their job-sharing situation. At the same time, she appreciates Dan's opportunity to be with them somewhat more now. Liz said, "I thought 'I'm going to miss some of those really exciting preschool years.' . . . I know that Dan can handle the kids just fine, and it won't be that I'll be sitting at work feeling absolutely torn and feeling only if I was home everything would be all right. I know he can provide the emotional nurture they need." She seems to admire ways that Dan interacts with the children, noticing that he is able to get them to do some things that are more difficult for her, while not necessarily choosing to interact in similar ways. Liz appreciates Dan's support of her career, and continues to contribute to his career when and where she can. She notices that she has developed some professional competencies that she previously observed in Dan. She said,

> I realized that it was probably not helpful in our work and not very healthy for our marriage for me to let him be the tough guy or even the bad cop sometimes and for me to be the soft one. But I also knew that I would have to change the way I was and take on some things that I would rather not.

Liz also seems to admire the ways Dan is choosing to develop personally and professionally, and encourages him as he moves down his own path.

Both Liz and Dan seem to appreciate the amount of personal resources each draws on in making their sharing parenting experiences work for them. They both noticed at times that they can loose sight of what the other is experiencing. In these times, they seem to take individual responsibility to open a discussion and to explore the potential to readjust their balance.

Dan seems to delight in experiencing his life opening up, cherishing the effect his children have on him, valuing how the challenges of sharing this responsibility contribute to his development as a full human being, and noticing how he is healing from the constraints and wounds he came through his own childhood carrying. He said, "So all sorts of things have altered for me, just the way I organize reality, I suppose. The significance of work is altered. I'm no longer hooked into deriving meaning and significance for my existence from my work."

Liz, too, seems to cherish her connection to her children, shaped as it is by sharing their becoming with her partner. She seems to value that her experience of motherhood is shaped within and by the challenges of working out their sharing, as well as maintaining her commitment to her professional calling. She seems to feel the grace each partner brings to their co-creative efforts, and sees them moving beyond what they initially thought possible in their early visions.

The narrative accounts told by couples co-creating sharing parenting in a dynamic, concordant way highlight how both men and women are moving back and forth, in and out, in their awareness of their separateness and connectedness. These people convey a clear, though complex, appreciation for how both affect each other's parenting dance. Each partner is depicted as equally committed both to one's own and one's partner's development of a broad and strong repertoire of parenting patterns. They each seem to value the idea that they can take full responsibility for all aspects of parenthood—being actively engaged with their children, being available to their children, and taking responsibility for all the obvious and subtle aspects of caring for their children and their family. These people spoke of a high tolerance for each other's differences in the ways instrumental and emotional responsibilities are expressed. They did not rely on complementary strengths or weaknesses in the parenting repertoire. Each person, as a parent, endeavored to develop a full and effective parenting repertoire. Yet, they seemed to appreciate how their full repertoire might reflect subtle differences in form. For example, many men noted that they nurture differently than their wives. They may rely on playful comforting of a hurt child, whereas they notice that their wives may use gentleness and demonstration of understanding. Their narrative accounts stress how they each feel highly valued for their ability to parent completely.

I came away from my conversations with these couples feeling a sense that they had generally stepped aside from the dependency-based notions of complementarity and symmetry in creating together their version of sharing parenting. It seemed to me these people were co-creating alternatives that call on each to expand his or her vision and experiences of being partners. Liz often used the terms *wholeness* and *interdependence* when talking about her recent experiences of the coparenting dance with Dan. She said, "I just think that the shifts have been towards more wholeness and interdependence rather than mutual dependence." She seemed to want me to understand clearly the distinction between their doing their parenting through mutual dependence on each other's moves and their doing it with an awareness of, yet somewhat independent of, each other's moves.

I came to construct an understanding of how these couples might be co-creating individual patterns within the family sphere in which each took responsibility for both their individual actions and the potential effect those actions could have on the other family members. I call this interaction pattern an *ecological co-creation* (i.e., one of informed, intentional individual choice in consideration of one's affect on the whole) as opposed to a *contingent dependent* kind of construction process (i.e., "I can do this if my partner agrees to do that"). In an ecological co-creation process, each partner counts on his or her own and the partner's abilities to parent effectively and to take responsibility for doing so. They seem to enter the sharing parenting dance with confidence that they have room to choreograph their steps based on competency in a full repertoire of dances. They seem to have the flexibility to move in a way that enhances the overall dance, whether they are in a solo piece or dancing with their partner. They do not wait for their partner to make a move in the dance to determine what moves they need to acquire or practice, but they also try to dance in a way that enhances the overall choreography with their partner. Such an interactional pattern seems to demonstrate concordance in their sharing parenting dynamic.

Reflections

Early in my conversations with the women in these couples, I began to gain an appreciation of how they not only perceived the effect on themselves but saw themselves as actively involved in shaping those effects and the partner's involvement. I began to appreciate how my focus on men could blind me to the separate and connected experiences of women. I wondered about what women experienced as their degrees of freedom to reshape their ideas, experiences, feelings, and meanings of motherhood. Then I started to question how women's changes had separate and connected meanings for men. I explored how men experienced their degrees of freedom to reshape their ideas, experiences, feelings, and meanings of fatherhood. I began to understand more fully how they were describing a process shaped out of an intricate weave of men and women both "doing" and "not doing" interactively.

The dance patterns of each couple seemed to be always on the verge of giving way to new possibilities. I got the sense that I would need to watch them dance frequently to gain an appreciation of how they might respond to each other and alter the flow of their dance as situations evolved. I had a glimpse of some nuances in their myriad steps and patterned moves, yet felt I could only partially and intermittently grab hold of central, though limited, aspects of the flow. The glimpse I was privileged to get, through the gracious sharing the narrative accounts, was abstracted and necessarily frozen in time. My understanding of the dynamic interactional process was pieced together from individual frames that I wanted to transform into a motion picture of their dance.

Conversations with these couples left me feeling both their delight and their struggle as men and women participated in the ongoing revision of sharing parenting. The stories men and women told are stories of interactively reshaping fatherhood and motherhood. As men change their ways of being a father, women are called to change their ways of being a mother. So too, as women change their ways in shaping the potential of motherhood for themselves, men are called to change their ways of shaping fatherhood's potentials. I gained a sense of the kind of tension each may feel between a known comfort in old ways—even in the discomfort of knowing the misfit with their vision of what could be—and discovering the potential in new ways—even through a transitory discomfort of not knowing how these new ways would shake down into a workable pattern.

I began to think of how change, for these people, seemed to be a blend of discontinuous shifts to new ways and evolutionary development of modified ways. It seemed there was always a sense of some continuity of old, adapted, or reorganized old and new patterns of fathering and mothering emerging that make up their sharing parenting experiences. I sensed that these people knew something about the potential to be continually in the process of becoming fathers and mothers, with different aspects of revising and revisioning the experienced with the as-yet-unexperienced possibilities. I constructed both an intuitive understanding and a grounded appreciation for the separate and reciprocal interactive and interpretive processes that seemed to be an ongoing aspect of the sharing parenting dance.

In formulating the conceptualization of leading-following patterns, I was challenged to think beyond hierarchical and sequential patterns. The narratives suggest that, in the fluidity of everyday living, these couples sense both patterns and randomness. I began to question if a leader-follower metaphor was appropriate to convey what I heard described in their narratives. Going back to the transcripts and tapping into my experience of sharing those conversations, I went back into my feeling perception of each couple. The couple conversations I had with selected families left me with an affective feeling about what it might be like for them to construct and live out daily their sharing parenting. I noticed that after some interview conversations, I came away feeling tense; after others, I came away feeling relaxed. I began to explore the patterns of my affective experiences. I noticed that when I felt tense with the couple, I felt they had shared their story bits with some restraint; to me, the co-constructive process seemed somewhat stilted and influenced more by one partner than the other. I noticed that when I felt relaxed on leaving, the couple had shared the story bits in a flowing interchange; the co-constructive process seemed open and deeply respectful of individual differences. These experiences led me back to the transcripts and tapes. I began to track what kinds of stories people told about their experiences of coming to their current pattern of sharing parenting. I noticed that those families who related story bits of the woman initiating changes or holding on to the privilege of spending more time as the designated stay-at-home parent were the families that I generally left my conversations with feeling tense. I noticed that those families who related story bits stressing the co-creative process were the families that I generally left feeling quite relaxed. Thus, I used my experience and the pattern I saw in their stories in constructing ideas about how leader-follower dynamics might unfold.

While engaged in face-to-face conversations with these families, and while sitting alone with the recorded tapes and typed transcripts of those conversations, I kept coming back to the words of several women and several men. I often heard women and men talk of feeling that there was something about being a woman or a man that was larger than their individual ideas and experience could explain. These words were spoken separately, yet touched on a similar dominant chord. The flow and intricacies of the interconnected stories they shared reminded me repeatedly of the penetrating influence of culture. The cultural backdrop seems to be an inescapable presence against which each individual's and couple's experience is played out and shaped.

My experience of these men and women increased my appreciation for the shifts that seem to be taking place in their interpretative dance of sharing parenting. Sharing parenting seems to invite both men and women to reshape their many-faceted identities as fathers and mothers.

PART III

Reflexive Commentary

R ather than take a strictly critical perspective, I purposely listened to people's narratives with interest in and sensitivity to ideas of resourcefulness. The types of narratives elicited were closely associated with this stance. These men's and women's accounts tend to stress resourcefulness and perceptions of positive experiences. Further, people likely chose to participate in this research because the contract explicitly pointed to an interest in their perceived success as men and women jointly sharing parenting responsibilities and activities.

The meaning-making presented in the previous chapters is cast in a similar vein; I maintained a stance of appreciating resourcefulness. The task in the next two chapters is to move toward interpretative implications and propositions about possible *alternative discourses*—or ideas that may otherwise be subjugated by predominant ideas located in academic research about men in families. Discussing alternative discourses, I also draw out some tensions that seem embedded within the generally successful stories people shared. Further, I venture beyond what the people shared in their narrative accounts by focusing on what things may be thought of as not said.

Before going forward, I must go back to refocus on a central aspect of the study that likely shapes the implications. I purposely set out to hear the narrative accounts of a select group of people. These 18 couples may be considered select—or a special subset of the general population—in at least three ways. First, their socioeconomic status or sociocultural background put them in a select group. In our culture, they are likely seen as well-educated, middle- to upper-middle class families of predominantly Anglo-Saxon descent. Second, these couples have generally been together for many years, and began having their children only after being together for several years and establishing a clear perspective on their family and career goals, as well as having rather stable jobs. They also had established themselves in their community before having children. Third, and perhaps most important, the research sample is select in its perceived and self-described position of selecting families in which the man is seen, by both partners, as fully and actively participating and involved in raising the children. Although a minority in our culture, these people offer significant ideas for academics, policy analysts and policymakers, family life educators, and clinicians working with couples and families to ponder.

The joint commitment to share fully in the parenting of their children and in handling the tasks of family maintenance, in particular, warrants further elaboration. Overall, the narrative accounts raise questions about this notion of being select. On some level, these people notice that others outside their family may look at them and make judgments and comparisons. As well, these couples seemingly make some comparison of their own families against others around them. In making comparisons between the local, private culture of their family life with the broader culture around them—both the local community and in the broad societal sense—they recognize that they may be viewed as select—or at least seen as "doing it differently." Yet, they rejected any suggestion on my part about being special or having found the solution for creating equity in families. Although I did not experience these people as political in the sense of organized, public advocacy regarding social change, they may be seen as quietly demonstrating different potentials. At the local level, their narrative accounts offer powerful examples of the potential to create new cultural ideas or alternative discourses about family life.

Reinforcing ideas about the potential of people's local narratives to gain public attention, despite their seeming reluctance to take their lives public in the "political" sense, I believe, is the way couples were referred to me for this research. Because I relied primarily on convenience referrals, these couples came to my attention because they were noticed by those in their community. The research couples, somewhat humbly I thought, also mentioned noticing that extended family, neighbors, and friends looked to them as trailblazers and models of ways men and women can create new potentials for sharing parenting. By participating in this research, they opened their private narratives to the public domain. This research also potentially extends their foray into the public domain; I am aware that the political profile of their narratives is potentially increased by the proactive stance I take. The meaning-making presented here could be interpreted as having prescribed them as examples or models for other people to fashion their parenting after. In addition, in some ways, the research narrative champions their success stories.

9

Sharing Parenting

Possibilities to Inform Alternative Discourses

What Makes Sharing Parenting Work?

The success and viability of sharing parenting families are based on many complex and interwoven beliefs and practices deeply embedded in everyday life. In discussing the resourcefulness and subtle implications of it here, I focus on their family philosophy, the practices of tag-team parenting, and the complex trade-offs involving stress reduction and conflict embedded in breaking socially sanctioned patterns of gender complementarity.

FAMILY PHILOSOPHY

Charting a family philosophy emerged as central to the success of sharing parenting. Simple "mom and apple pie" statements heard when most people talk about their families carried a profound meaning for sharing parenting couples. They related how their philosophy centers on a commitment to be the primary influences in their young children's lives and to be in full and active partnership in their parenting. These people place their commitment to family and child rearing above any other commitments in their busy lives. They want to minimize their use of day care for their children. This means they intentionally work to arrange family life and work outside the family in unique ways that rely on their abilities to collaborate as parents. In this, the families in my study were very similar to those in Schwartz's (1994) most recent look into peer marriage.

Narratives highlighting an explicit and thoroughly articulated parenting philosophy suggest that these people are dedicated to creating a child-centered and child-safe environment in their family. Creating a child-centered home means they exercise intentionality not only in creating the physical environment, but also in intangible areas of creating the feeling of trust, safety, and love. When asked to articulate how they did this, men and women often retreated to talking about taken-for-granted notions of "being there" for their children. Both women and men provided intricate examples of ways they attended to a hurt or joyful child. These narratives suggest that both men and women were, indeed, there for the child. Their dedication to shifting their work schedules is important evidence that they are making conscious and deliberate efforts to be with their children as guides and witnesses in their unfolding lives. Further, both men's and women's narratives stress respect for their child's integrity and growing life-space as the center piece of their philosophy. From this springs practices of balancing opportunities to enter the child's world in a co-creative spirit with times when they clearly step into the place of parental authority and responsibility. Creating and maintaining a child-centered family seem to mean the adults are willing to make intentional decisions to step away from personal fulfillment thought to be found in a career. It also often means carefully managing participation in cultural practices of material acquisition.

TAG-TEAM PARENTING PRACTICES

Often the sanctity of the commitment to family life is tested by pressures external to, though impinging on, the daily viability of the sharing parenting arrangements. Pressures in terms of the geographic location of work, work schedules, seasonal variation in work load, and children's outside activities present these men and women with opportunities to reconfirm the sanctity of their family commitment. The concept and practice of tag-team parenting includes a set of arrangements and agreements that allows couples to juggle the myriad responsibilities and activities of family life with just such work-life realities.

Tag-team parenting also suggests an ongoing flow of negotiating the sharing responsibilities and performance of activities required of parents. Relying on the mechanisms of a tag team means that both men and women have times of being the parent in the partnership who is in charge, or on duty, while the team partner is absent (usually out at work, but at times away from the family for other reasons, such as personal interests). Organizing their parenting like a tag team allows each partner to feel he or she can rely on the other to help carry the responsibility of caring for the children and managing daily family life. It also allows them to enlarge the pool of parenting resources needed to manage the busyness of juggling myriad competing demands for time, energy, and personal resources experienced in the family-work interface.

STRESS AND CONFLICT OF SHARING PARENTING: COMPLEX CONSIDERATIONS

Tag-team parenting works both to reduce stress and potentially to increase stress and conflict for parents. Tag-team arrangements help reduce the stress of carrying it all, managing it all, by providing some separation in the times and activities each parent is expected to cover. Tag-team parents build in on-off shifting, spelling each other, and another available perspective (the partner's informed and invested view) as ways of reducing individual and family stress. The potential increase in the level of stress or conflict between parents stems from two influences: the challenge to create space for each parent to have a claim on involvement, and differences in the styles each parent brings to parenting. Each person's investment and interest in parenting across myriad domains of parenthood need to be balanced with consideration for the partner's interest and investment. It seems unlikely that the parenting partners' preferences will be matched with perfect complementarity; thus, each partner is faced with balancing his or her own investment and preferences with those of the partner. There is a dynamic between "letting go" to create space for one's partner and "claiming" certain involvements for oneself. Working with differences challenges each partner to accept that the way things are handled will be out of one's full control regarding personal standards. Again, a kind of letting go is required to make this work.

Valuing Differences

Interestingly, I found it very difficult to get these couples to talk much about stress and conflict in their family life. They talked about differences, but not much about conflict. Talk about differences highlights what I see as its double-edged nature. Differences can be seen both as sources of potential conflict and as sources of alternative resourcefulness. Generally, these people related how they highly value their differences as sources of alternative resources, noting how their relative strengths and weaknesses augment the overall strength of their team. Their narrative accounts about times when one or the other or both felt burdened in their teamwork suggests that these times most often spring from the "ongoingness" and the sheer scale of the demands on time and energy, not from the partner's lack of cooperation and participation. The sophistication of their communication skills is also a key to keeping the conflict edge of differences from becoming stressful to the point of distress.

Communication and Negotiation

Talk and talking it out keeps a tag team viable over the course of shifting demands and changing circumstances inevitable in family life. Speculating on the relative absence in narrative accounts about distressing conflict, I see the power of both an explicitly articulated guiding philosophy and good communication skills as mixing together to move these couples through difficult periods. Further, similar to earlier findings (Haas, 1980, 1982; or see Lamb et al., 1987, for a review), these couples have been together for many years and generally waited some years before starting their families. According to their narrative accounts, their families were planned, with both parents having arrived at a place in their lives where they wanted to have children and were ready for parental commitment. Good communication and negotiation skills seem to underpin the couples' ability to come to this place in their relationships; these skills also enable them to work through their conflicts as they arise.

Specialization and Interchangeability

Tag-team parenting can potentially reduce tension between parents based on at least two factors related to specialization and interchangeability: First, the coexistence of specialization and interchangeability seems to allow both parents to have some things they prefer to do while maintaining a basic interchangeability in all functions. This may allow both parents to feel comfortable with differences and to trust that the parenting that happens when they are not on duty is, at the least, adequate. In most cases, both parents said they felt their partner was, by far, more than adequate at parenting across a wide spectrum of responsibilities and activities. These women and men view each other as competent parents individually and collectively. Second, tag-team parents have times when they are parenting alone. This may allow them to reduce the opportunities for conflict to arise in the context of both parents trying to be the active parent in the same situation.

Unique Sample Characteristics

The general absence of distressing conflict in these narrative accounts may be related to this select sample and the proactive design of the research. Couples may have been cued, by my original invitation to focus on their perceived success as sharing parenting couples, to minimize accounts of times when they felt distressed in conflict. Although I proceeded to ask questions about differences and their potential conflict, my declared stance of interest in their resourcefulness may have interacted in the co-constructed interview conversations to minimize talk about distressing conflict.

Obstacles to Sharing Parenting

Three major obstacles potentially constrain people from moving toward sharing parenting: rigidities in institutional structures and the implications for family flexibility required to make sharing parenting work for them; embedded cultural practices and attitudes that subtly

174 REFLEXIVE COMMENTARY

signal gender expectations; and gender entitlements culturally associated with family life.

INSTITUTIONAL CONSIDERATIONS

As reported in earlier research (Catalyst Staff, 1988; Lewis & O'Brien, 1987), institutional factors often operate to limit flexibility and alternatives to the traditional work-family interface structure. These limits are both explicit and subtle. The general inflexibility of employers' work structures and expectations limit people's ability to manage the work-family interface. Flexibility of scheduling is a major consideration for sharing parenting to work well for couples.

These couples are privileged to have a fair amount of work flexibility. This flexibility stems from particular work situations, such as owning one's business, working in a field that schedules nontraditional hours, or having one partner with sufficient earning power so that only one parenting partner needs to work to support a satisfactory lifestyle and standard of living. For those couples where at least one partner worked in a context that did not have much flexibility or required standard working hours, the mechanics of working out the tag-team shifts could be quite a challenge. I was somewhat surprised by the absence of discourse about subtle ways men and women may experience pressures in their work contexts that make working out the mechanics of scheduling difficult. I suspect the general, encompassing scope of my questions and interests may have obscured this kind of narrative. I wonder if a more focused study on the work-family interface with sharing parenting couples would reveal more of these of issues.

In addition to work contexts, institutions likely to be associated with children's activities (such as schools, day care, and recreational opportunities) also constrain men's comfort with active parenting. Narrative accounts frequently contained some mention of the continued subtle presumption that women are the first line of contact regarding the children. For example, experiencing the school sending notes home requesting that mom help out with a bake sale (as was one man's experience) challenges men to go public in their declaration of involvement or remain silent and quietly alienated. Further, these kinds of institutions schedule events in a manner that seems to disadvantage parents (both men and women) who want to participate in their children's activities but need flexible schedules to do so. For example, scheduling special school events only during the traditional school day often prevents working parents from attending, or it means only one parent can attend.

CULTURAL CONSIDERATIONS

American culture generally does not support families, specifically not families with nontraditional structures or those trying to create and sustain new patterns of sharing parenting. Neighbors, friends, extended family, and colleagues can be sources of very subtle criticism and lack of support. I find it interesting, however, how couples, particularly the men in these couples, told me they deal with these obstacles. In the initial research conversations, I was surprised at the ready dismissal of my interest in these issues. Men's narratives highlighted two strategies that defuse the potential for these subtle pressures to become obstacles. Men either take notice and dismiss subtle pressures as unimportant, or they withhold sharing information with people they judge will be generally nonsupportive.

Men often depicted themselves as individualists who see their involvement as their personal choice, negotiated within the privacy of family with their partner. I think of their stance on the external gaze as one that allows them to bracket the influence of critical opinion about men's involvement in family found in the larger culture. Such bracketing locates the basis of their involvement in the personal or private arena rather than within some larger cultural arena. Even men who mentioned the influence of the women's movement or the men's movement suggested that they retreat to an individualist position—they said they do not much care what others besides their partner think about how, what, when, and where they are involved. Their partner's response is what is important. I see this as personalizing the issue: a stance that may offer some explanation for the absence in the narratives of "P" political consciousness and public actions advocating social change.

GENDER ENTITLEMENTS

The narrative accounts of both men and women hint at the intricacies of the affective issues connected to shedding deeply acculturated images of motherhood. Women talked about purposely monitoring themselves around issues of entitlements to involvement, parenting expertise, and standards. Yet, the women also mentioned times when they caught themselves acting in ways that could be construed by their partners as asserting their right (or culturally sanctioned entitlement) to be the parent of first contact. Women mentioned how these times usually confronted them with the personal challenge to work through a gut feeling about their need to be involved. They often mentioned wrestling with some elusive sense of loss when they moved to change their pattern of involvement. Like Haas (1988), I see this as potentially closing space for men's involvement.

At the same time, men's narratives suggest times when they defer to their partner in a situation, not necessarily from a stance of not wanting to be involved, but from a stance of respecting their partner's desire to be involved. Similar to some earlier findings (see Benokratis, 1985, and Lamb, 1987, for reviews of these findings), men talked of feeling, in some situations, intimidated by the seeming naturalness of their partner's mothering. Men also mentioned their reluctance to diminish (potentially) women's feelings about their place as mothers in the children's lives. I see this as men accepting the status quo, which may ultimately close space for their further involvement. Although I did not ask directly, and though I did hear a few examples, I continue to be struck by the general absence in men's narrative accounts of fathers openly challenging their partners to scale back their involvement. If men were to be more assertive in this arena, I would consider such a move as men taking responsibility for creating their own space for active parenting involvement. Specifically asserting a desire or a right to be an involved father would also mean the man would be rejecting the culturally sanctioned privilege of noninvolvement or a disentitlement to more involvement.

Gender Politics of Sharing Parenting

In many subtle and complex ways, the politics of gender are embedded in the narratives of these men and women. Focusing on some of these here, I discuss questions of voice and choice, reshaping both fatherhood and motherhood, balancing between specialties and shared responsibilities, challenging deeply rooted gender practices, and valuing family work.

QUESTIONS OF VOICE AND CHOICE

The politics of gender—or the brokering of power between men and women—are, in my mind, based on notions of voice and choice rather than notions of equal status conferred in the public domain. Dominant discourse ideas about "legitimate" power in family relations are often cast in the light of status and the associated privileges to influence and choose. Such status is typically seen to be closely tied to access to, and decision-making authority over, economic resources.

In contrast, I see the notions of having a voice and a choice as broader concepts. Having a voice means having had the experience, or the perception it is possible and likely, that one's ideas and preferences count and will be heard and respected when spoken. Having a choice means having had the experience of having options to chose from, or believing that one has options. Both voice and choice are important concepts related to negotiation in the deep texture of a broad basket of family resources, including not only money and outside status, but time and energy resources, as well as affiliate resources.[1]

Notions of voice and choice present in these sharing parenting narratives emerge both as said and as not said acknowledgment of gender politics. The said was found in the actual words. I interpreted the not-said as either an implied sense of taken-for-granted beliefs, or things left unsaid because they were not part of the couples' awareness. Egalitarian ideas, found in both the said and not-said, guide the men in negotiations with their partners. Further, the women both said explicitly and implied they expect to be respected and to have their position considered equally, whether they make equal financial contributions to the family or not.

Interestingly, I found the accounts in the women-as-designated-stay-at-home parent couples to voice these ideals and perceived experiences emphatically. When I asked these women how this works, they generally suggested that they see themselves as having the choice not to put up with it being any other way. I took this to mean that they believed they had viable options, including raising the issue in the context of their commitment to an egalitarian relationship, changing their choice to be the designated stay-at-home parent, and perhaps leaving the partnership if the issue could not be resolved.

RESHAPING BOTH FATHERHOOD AND MOTHERHOOD

Another facet of the gender politics of sharing parenting is the changing nature of both fatherhood and motherhood. Contrary to what I take to be the mainline story in much feminist literature, women's narratives conveyed as much a sense of making adjustments in their expectations and practices of motherhood as I found in men's narratives. Both men's and women's accounts stressed the dynamics of working together to create visions and experiences of fatherhood and motherhood that are quite different from what they experienced growing up. At the same time, what was often left unsaid, though strongly implied, was the realization that they are immersed in a culture that both encourages different images of fatherhood and holds traditional motherhood images as the ideal.

Sharing parenting accounts challenged me to appreciate the possibility of reciprocal effects on both the man and the woman. Reciprocal effects have the potential to be mutually corresponding. Yet, contrary to dominant ideas about role complementarity determining potentials for change, reciprocal effects can be shared or felt by both sides without being strictly complementary. As men move to change their experience, expectations, and visioned potentials of fatherhood, motherhood's potentials are likely affected, though not necessarily in a directly complementary way. As women move to change their experience, expectations, and visioned potentials of motherhood, fatherhood's potentials are likely affected, though not in some known, predictable, or complementary way. Narratives about creating ways to respond to the effects that worked within their unique relationships cast these men and women as actively revisioning their images of both fatherhood and motherhood, unleashed to a great extent from dominant ideas and ideals of role complementarity and the culture of motherhood.

The complex, dynamic dance between men and women in sharing parenting families involves an ongoing working out of individual and interactive experiences and meanings. In a co-constructed experience, men and women participate in an ongoing, active, experiential working out of ways to have their family life work for them individually and collectively. Each family conveys a certain mood and flow in dancing sharing parenting. The mutually corresponding potential of reciprocal aspects in revisioning fatherhood and motherhood is most suggested in patterns of out-of-step and matched-step dancing. Couples dancing concordant steps told me about experiencing some steps as being in a mutually corresponding process. There were also steps that were more distinct and separated from each other; they felt their partner's changes but did not experience a mutually corresponding shift. The man acted to change his vision of fatherhood's potentials, and the woman acted to change her vision of motherhood's potentials, without necessarily needing or wanting or waiting for a complementary reciprocal move by the partner.

BALANCING SPECIALTIES AND SHARED RESPONSIBILITIES

For those moments and aspects of parenting when parents practice a specialty or efficiency-based division of labor, the dynamics of who claims and masters a particular part of the parenting repertoire affects the overall politics of sharing parenting over time, especially as they continue to work out the sharing repertoire between them. If one partner reserves a particular part of the parenting repertoire as a specialty to the exclusion of the other, over time, that claim may preclude the partner from participating fully (or at least from developing full competency in that part of the repertoire), and ultimately hamper the development of sufficient interchangeability to handle whatever situation arises. Asserting a new right to part of the partner's reserved repertoire may or may not be met with subtle reluctance by the partner to relinquish claim. These dynamics may be most apparent in times of disruption in the family's routines or developmental transitions over the life course. Studies into the subtle nuances of developing and claiming parts of the parenthood repertoire in sharing parenting families may shed further light on how gender politics might be different than that found in other families.

The complexity of gender politics in everyday living seemed to be highlighted as sharing parenting couples talked about how they figure out who's "it" at any given point. Although these couples expressed their general satisfaction with how their tag-team parenting arrangements were working for them, both men and women suggested at times that they wondered if it might be easier in some ways to go back to the traditional way of doing things. Yet, I found it quite intriguing that the narratives about how they negotiated the intricacies of their sharing seldom mentioned gender politics. Instead, people talked about knowing and respecting their own and their partner's preferences and competencies. In this, these narratives are similar to ideas found in Goodnow and Bowes's (1994) research. Additional analysis along the lines of the detailed study of household maintenance tasks might provide more understanding of this emerging alternative discourse about gender politics in sharing parenting families.

CHALLENGING DEEPLY ROOTED GENDER PRACTICES

Narratives about men's and women's respective acculturation suggest that gender socialization practices influence preparedness and willingness to claim and carry certain parts of the sharing parenting dance. Women's acculturation seems to nag at them to hold on to deeply felt, perhaps unconscious, expectations about motherhood. In this way, women are challenged to break through their acculturation when they want to share parenthood. They are challenged to let go of some of motherhood's responsibilities of feeling like the parent of first and last resort and, perhaps, the associated entitlement to set the standards for parenting and family life. Men's acculturation seems to challenge them to assert new claims on parts of the parenting repertoire, expanding their vision both to feel and to enact fully the fatherhood part of the sharing parenting dance.

Couples engaged in sharing parenting's dance of revisioning in a matched steps pattern told of experiences that resonate most clearly with gender politics found in discourses about men's reluctance to participate fully in family life. Below this resonance, however, I see a challenge to that discourse. The discourse suggests that women are ready and willing to have their partners involved, if only the men would step more fully into the dance. Although women are leading their partners in this dance, they often discover their own reluctance to welcome them as full partners. The letting go theme found in these narrative accounts suggests that it is more challenging to women, and often more rife with feelings of loss, than dominant discourses would lead one to believe. This finding further substantiates and updates speculations made by Pleck (1985) and others (Baruch & Barnett, 1986a, 1986b; Gilbert, Holshan, & Manning, 1981; Haas, 1978, 1980; Yogev, 1981) about women's reluctance to share what has traditionally been their domain.

The reconceptualization suggesting that revisioning both motherhood and fatherhood pushes our appreciation of the subtleties in a family's gender politics farther than suggested in currently popular academic discourses. Men's narratives convey their deeply felt responsibility for the care of their children. Although they acknowledge that the culture grants them the option of choosing how much involvement they want (Backett, 1982; Daly, 1993a, 1993b), they do not personally feel that they have a choice not to be fully involved. Women express, at a gut level, the felt connection to their children, and recognize that the culture grants them the option of privileging their connection over their partner's. In respect for their partner, these women let go of that privilege.

VALUING FAMILY WORK

Another facet of gender politics is associated with the private and public definition of family work. What I find intriguing in these narrative accounts is the consideration about how people define family work. In contrast to a dominant theme in much academic analysis of family life, these narratives seldom suggest that people define their time and involvement in family activities as work. Men and women did not portray themselves as slaves of the "second shift" (Hochschild, 1989). Narrative accounts about the demands on their personal resources and time abound, but women and men (particularly) talk of this as a very different kind of work. They convey their belief that family work is something they take a different kind of personal satisfaction from, especially taking a very long perspective on the opportunity to participate in the raising of another human being.

The exception was found in the narratives of the men and women who were the designated stay-at-home parent. Speculating on the implications of this, I ran up against the "P" politics of defining family work. There is a long feminist tradition arguing for the activities in the private family domain to be defined and valued as work. This kind of discourse is reflected in the narratives of women and men who are designated stay-at-home parents. Further, I find it interesting that the women often hinted at—and Collette explicitly captured it in labeling herself a "domestic goddess"—their feeling that their work contribution is undervalued in the public domain. The men also mentioned similar perceptions about the outside value of their private work. In contrast to the women, who seemingly felt it necessary to call attention to what they believed the status should be, the men seemed to adopt a rugged individualist stance and conveyed a sense of "I don't care if you think its valuable or not, I do!" These differences tell me something about gender politics and the private discourse in the context of the larger cultural discourse. Men who do family work are generally seen as special, as heroes in some sense of breaking down cultural stereotypes, but women who choose to do the same work are often dismissed as merely traditional. Although men and women in sharing parenting couples may, at some level, escape the confines of the larger gender politic, the politics of valuing family and the work that is performed privately therein remain a significant sociocultural issue.

Note

1. Similar to some feminists (e.g., Miller, 1976), I see affiliate resources as relational behaviors, such as holding an awareness of and sensitivity to others in the family, acting out of an awareness of the holistic effect on others of one's chosen actions, and extending oneself to care for others.

10

Revisiting Dominant Discourses and Final Reflections

Implications of Taking a Different View

I began this research endeavor with ideas about men in families shaped out of my exposure to dominant academic, media, cultural, and everyday discourses. After exploring these sharing parenting narratives, I arrived back at important initial questions: What might be considered beyond dominant discourses and from whose perspective? What are some of the implications of taking a different view to studying men in families? This chapter returns to those questions. Informed by the understandings gained from the study couples, I take a critical look here into some aspects of dominant academic discourses, specifically exploring the deficit model and comparative model discourses; discourse about the division of labor in families; ideas about men as individualistic and competitive compared to women's tendency to be relational; and finally, cultural discourses about the value of family. As well, there is some reflective discussion on dichotomous ways of thinking about men in families.

Beyond the Dominant Discourse?

If one sees these academic discourses, as I did, as generally critical about men's attitudes toward the family side of life, their style of parenting, and the amount they participate in the myriad aspects of daily family life, then I believe these couples might concur with my assessment that they stand largely outside several main themes in dominant academic discourses. If one moves to the more subtle aspects of academic discourses about men in families, then the questions become much more complex and more difficult to answer. Considering the nuances and complexities of the research evidence found in both academic discourses and these narrative accounts, these couples might concur that they stand within, and offer some important alternatives to, the dominant themes found in academic discourses. In the final analysis, the question of "beyond" may be too simplistic. If ideas about being beyond include the notion of expanding the possibilities for men and women to co-create parenthood in various nonprescriptive ways, however, then these narratives are at the cutting edge of presenting a counterdiscourse.

DEFICIT MODEL AND COMPARATIVE MODEL DISCOURSES

Much of the extant academic literature rests on either a deficit model (Hawkins & Dollahite, 1997a) or a comparative model for studying men in families. These perspectives are too narrow to understand the complexities and nuances of how and what men can, and indeed do, contribute to family life. The power of conceptualizing men as partners in parenting tag teams expands the potential to appreciate men's contributions.

Deficit Model Discourses

The men and women in this study did not talk about the tag-team aspect of sharing parenting in terms echoing deficit model themes so often featured in the academic discourses. Men were seen by their partners as highly competent parents. They were seen as performing and experiencing many aspects of parenthood's responsibilities differently from women. Different did not translate into deficient.

It seems crucial to pay attention to the subtle dynamics men and women face, personally and interpersonally, as they juggle the work-family interface, and to try to do so without recreating stereotypical gender inequities. This may be possible to do even while acknowledging the cultural tendency to let the woman's way of being a parent be the lens through which the man's participation is seen. Introducing a conceptualization of ongoing revisioning of individual and couple expectations, aimed at releasing both women and men from this view, opens discussion of an alternative understanding of how men contribute to family life. Men often do things differently than women, yet that difference need not imply that the men's way is in some way deficient. As researchers, we need to find multiple lenses to view fatherhood; lenses that value the contributions fathers bring to the complex shifting terrain of raising children.

Comparative Model Discourses

The conceptualization of tag-team parenting potentially facilitates the breaking down of monolithic tendencies to see motherhood as the template for the new father. These narrative accounts challenge the appropriateness of using a comparison with women when studying fatherhood. A research model that explicitly or implicitly sets up a woman-determined standard, with men working (or not) toward measuring up and being judged as falling short, is an inadequate lens.

Academic discourses maintaining an implicit "woman sets the standard" comparative model for assessing the relative contributions women and men make perpetuate a hidden cult of motherhood. Such a standard obscures the complexities of what it takes for both women and men to make contributions to what might be considered a good partnership in parenting. If the praxis of a feminist agenda is to be pushed further, one must go beyond strict notions of who does what and how; researchers may want to broaden their conceptualizations to encompass the complexities of specialization and interchangeability, while allowing for women and men to value differences between them.

I certainly heard talk about the woman being perceived as doing some things better than her partner. I also heard about the man being perceived as doing other things better. Couples did not depict their experience as valuing more highly the things the woman did better, nor did they portray their standards as invariably privileging her way. Both women and men were depicted as very competent parents across a wide spectrum of activities, engagements, and responsibilities. This does not mean that both were equally good at everything they did as parents. There is a tendency for both women and men to specialize in certain areas of family life; at the same time, there is the pragmatic requirement of being interchangeable to certain degrees. The dialectic between specialization and interchangeability is resolved not by comparing and judging men with and against women, but by the dynamics of tag-team parenting. Specialization is more likely when both parents are present, and interchangeability is more likely when one or the other is designated on duty. Thus, the working dynamics of tag-team parenting facilitate breaking down barriers to men's involvement in all aspects of family life.

Expanding Conceptualizations: A New Language Is Needed

The language of women and men being interchangeable is situated in these couples' narrative accounts. This language describes what their sharing demands of them as tag-team partners. As such, it challenges dominant discourse notions found in both deficit and comparative models of men's contributions to family life. The tag-team metaphor suggests that men and women can find ways to organize their coverage of all aspects of parenting without privileging expressive-instrumental specializations for women and men, respectively (Parsons & Bales, 1955). I see the language of "specialities" and "reserved specialties" as further challenging dominant discourse notions of androgyny and absolute equality in men's and women's experience. Narrative accounts about working with differences, not on the basis of gender stereotypes or gender-matched equality, stress the potential of enhancing the overall quality of family life by each partner feeling competent and special in some aspects of his or her contribution, while sharing broadly across many areas of child care and general family life.

DIVISION OF LABOR DISCOURSE

Gender Equality: A Quantitative Focus on Who Does What

The diversity of shared family work patterns found in these narrative accounts further challenges monolithic ideas about gender equality

(Eichler, 1983). This challenge is especially pertinent to notions found in some feminist-inspired literature about equitability in a gender division of labor. That literature often focuses on counting the amount of time who spends doing what. It measures men's and women's differential contributions along relatively accessible notions of who is doing what "jobs" in the family, not according to the meanings men and women ascribe to their individual and collective contributions.

The diversity of styles found in these sharing parenting families expands the idea of a couple designing a pattern that uniquely accommodates their personal aspirations to share family life, and allows for individual differences and preferences. Couples see this sharing as including both tangible and intangible family work. The day-in and day-out activities of keeping each person's body and soul together while keeping a household running, managing child care needs, and working outside the home are a complex weave of tangible activities and intangible aspects of life.

Intangible aspects are very difficult to quantify, but should not be overlooked. Each family works with different meanings about what each person contributes, rather than paying attention to the relative time each spends on specific tasks. This emphasis is more akin to Goodnow and Bowes's (1994) findings than the previous quantity and quality emphasis in much of the family research literature. Creativity and success in finding ways to organize and coordinate family life and family work rely on each partner's full investment in the family's well-being, not on traditional or stereotypic ideas about who does what and how based on gender. This means that each partner is valued for unique contributions to and participation in juggling myriad calls on his or her time, energy, and personal resources.

Specialization-Based Efficiency

Academic discourses about division of labor in family work are strongly influenced by ideas of efficiencies realized through specialization; ideas that are foundational to efficient use of resources in economics. These couples' narratives invited me to rethink these ideas, especially their transferability to family decision making. Decision making in families may not be based purely on an efficiency model. When people move beyond strict notions of the efficiency to be gained through a specialization-based division-of-labor decision matrix, especially gender-based specialization, how might we understand their arrangements?

The narratives of these men and women convey a notion of cooperating to divide responsibilities between partners to manage the busyness of daily life, while relying on a foundational spirit of sharing. This spirit of sharing leads to a practice of nondivision; in practice, each partner can and will cover whatever needs to be done to keep everyone going as a collective family unit. This then means that each parenting partner needs to develop a very broad repertoire of skills and responsibilities. Although the narratives suggest that a division of labor based in specialization facilitates streamlining some tasks and decisions, it seems too limiting as a general practice for the effective implementation of a full sharing model. These couples recognize that efficiency-based specialization ultimately has the potential to jeopardize the viability of their sharing.

Adopting a long-term perspective seems to allow these couples to avoid the risks of too much specialization and the strict separation of responsibilities associated with a division-of-labor model. The long-term perspective rests on the foundation of goodwill; this is what supports the potential to realize equitability over a long-term perspective. Operating with goodwill seems to allow these couples to appreciate that there will be many shifts in their family patterns over time, so they need to take a fluid and flexible approach. Goodwill encompasses the expectation that they will continue to recreate patterns of sharing that work for them. Thus, taking goodwill to the long-term perspective allows people to move away from feeling trapped in current patterns. The conceptualization of goodwill in sharing parenting couples includes a sense of trust that taking a long-term perspective in a here-and-now interchange will not result in a sense of an inequitable solution and sharing over time. These men and women see themselves as having created a family milieu that is somehow beyond the tangibles researchers often identify. The concept of creating and living with goodwill speaks to the intangible quality of sharing parenting experiences.

Alternative Language

These narratives challenged me to think beyond notions of gendered labor, specialization-based division-of-labor, and stable and static family configurations. The narratives about experiences in creating a shared family life subtly undermine dominant discourses implying that there is a universal "best way" for men and women to work out alternatives to traditional gendered division of family labors. I was challenged to find a language that might convey important subtleties revealed in the sharing patterns. The narratives were rich with men's and women's appreciation for the unique possibilities open to them to share family life. These possibilities seemed well beyond the constrictive ideas of traditional family structures that imply that family work is indeed women's work (Mandell & Duffy, 1988). Language in the extant academic literature, even the feminist literature, is very limiting. Dominant academic language largely remains within the traditional-nontraditional discourse. For example, notions of a traditional family with a stay-at-home mother and role-reversal families, where the man is presumably doing the woman's role, maintain ideas about the family being the women's primary realm of responsibility.

In contrast, the language these men and women use conveys a breaking away from the strictures of distinct gender roles, privileged women's standards for family life, and comparative assessments of different gendered parenting styles found in dominant academic discourses. The language of designated stay-at-home parent, whether male or female, is situated in the narratives and conveys a commitment to a choice for both men and women in designing ways of contributing to family life. The choices are mutually influencing and reinforcing, as well as breaking through culturally sanctioned jurisdictional issues regarding parenthood. The choices go beyond what Backett (1982) refers to as women's presumed involvement obligation and men's privilege of choice. In contrast, a woman's choice as to how much involvement both she and her partner have in rearing their children is necessarily tied to the man's commitment to get and remain involved. At the same time, a man's choice and commitment to be involved is necessarily tied to the woman appreciating the legitimacy of his right to be involved. Haas (1980, 1982) reports similar interpretations. Combined, this current study and Haas's earlier work subtly challenge Backett's (1982) clear distinction in woman's entitlement and, by implication, men's disentitlement (Restrepo, 1995) to be involved parents.

The language of designating a stay-at-home parent or an in-charge parent, notions found in these couples' narratives, clearly goes beyond dominant discourses. This language calls attention to the possibility that both men and women can make decisions, based on the particulars and pragmatics of their unique family experiences and situation, to designate a parent to cover the home base while the other is engaged in the outside domain. This distinction may be very subtle, yet it seems crucial for moving the discourse of men and women sharing family life forward.

INDIVIDUALISTIC/COMPETITIVE AND
COLLECTIVE/RELATIONAL DISCOURSES

Early academic discourses about family dynamics highlighted, to a great extent, ideas about women specializing in expressive-relational-nurturant functions and men specializing in instrumental functions. These ideas are subtly perpetuated by the tendency to focus only on the tangible qualities of family life and, thus, may continue to be dominant in the research. Though feminist writers (e.g., Miller, 1976) have championed the value of women's contributions to family (and society) stemming from an ethic of care, much research on men in families continues to focus primarily on tangible instrumental contributions. My reading of the narrative accounts of these 18 couples prompted me to entertain a new line of thinking.

Both Men and Women Interacting
From an Ethic of Care

Men and women emphasized their commitments to live collectively. They often stressed their belief that family life requires them to act out of a clear awareness of being part of a larger whole—a larger whole that exceeds the sum of its individual parts. I see this as a rejection of two dominant ideas about family life, particularly about men in families. First, these ideas run counter to notions of men carrying a mostly individualistic mind-set of placing themselves and their needs and accomplishments above others without considering their effect on others. Men's narratives suggest that they may also operate out of relational considerations in relationships that matter significantly. The context of the family may elicit relational strategies as opposed to competitive strategies thought to prevail in their work context. The work world relies on distant and often competitive or dominant language. The world of family life likely thrives when communication is more consistent with the ethic of care. Both men and women hinted that, at times, they found switching their communication style when they walked in the door to their home at the end of a work day to be a challenge.

For example, men's ability to take and practice a relational stance is reflected, I believe, in their narrative accounts about adopting a "teachable moment" style for their parenting. This strategy conveys the importance men place on connecting with their children as individuals and building a relationship with them through daily connection. This is further reflected in narratives about taking a teachable moment perspective to times when they need to challenge or set the child on a different course. Their narratives suggest that they reject the controlling practices of punishment, humiliation, and/or subtle forms of rejection as appropriate parenting stances.

Another example is found in men's narratives about admitting times when they realized their behavior is in violation of their basic ethic of care. They then saw it as their own responsibility to take action for correcting the situation. In their accounts, they did not expect their partners or children to be their "corrective mirrors"; these men said they expected themselves to know and feel when they had acted in violation of their beliefs and, indeed, in violation of the best interest of the child. In contrast to Lamb's (1987) and La Rossa's (1988) observations about men lagging behind in this important area of sharing child rearing with their female partners, the self-monitoring suggested here reflects a deep texture of responsibility these men feel they take in raising their children.

Both Men and Women Practice a Collective Consciousness

Men's and women's narratives about holistic living (i.e., with relational awareness and the understanding that the whole is greater than the sum of its parts as guiding considerations) are, in my mind, a rejection of larger cultural notions—or dominant discourse—of a zero-sum proposition for gender relations in families. These men say they do not approach negotiations and decision making with an attitude of competition wherein one member gains at the expense of the others. They prefer synergistic notions of cooperating, negotiating with each other such that the total effect is greater than individual ideas. These couples may be privileged in taking this stance. Their narratives generally acknowledge that they feel they have options and choices (personal and economic) about how they see their individual lives fitting into and balancing against the family's collective well-being.

FAMILY MAN DISCOURSE

La Rossa (1988) notes an asynchrony between the culture of fatherhood and the conduct of fatherhood—or what he believes is the danger of seeing the media's idealized images of the new father as reflecting what men are actually doing in families. He suggests that research looking at the conduct of fatherhood does not bear out the hopeful images of the current culture. This research, combined with finding from Haas (1988) and others (see Hawkins & Dollahite, 1997b), suggests that some men are conducting their fatherhood in ways that are in sync with positive images of the new father. In contrast to La Rossa (1988), I see this research as offering aspects of an alternative discourse and breaking down monolithic depictions of men being either a good dad or a bad dad (Furstenberg, 1988).

The narratives I studied are complex. The stories men and women told about the paths they traveled to get to their current pattern of sharing parenting wound around and through several lines in the dominant discourses. Yet, I see these men and women as arriving at a place allowing them to work with each other to co-create a discourse counter to what might be expected given their individual histories and the social culture in North America.

An Alternative to Women Demanding That Men Change Discourses

The relationship histories I heard both resonate with and challenge notions of women demanding men's participation in the face of men's reluctance to get involved. The stories that resonated with dominant ideas were those where some men experienced initial hesitation based on uncertainty about how they would be effective and safe fathers if they got more involved. Issues of effectiveness and safety were most apparent in the stories of men who were portrayed as suffering at the hands of an abusive father (and in a couple of cases an abusive mother). Other men talked about experiencing initial reluctance when their wives initiated changes, mainly feeling they were being criticized or thought of as a "bad father." These men related how they found ways to leave their reluctance behind. They recounted how they felt moved to change once they appreciated that they could be valued even more highly by their partners and their children if they got more involved in the daily routines of child care and family work. They then became full and willing partners in the construction of sharing parenting.

Several other men apparently did not experience any hesitation. These are the stories that clearly challenge dominant discourses about women demanding change of reluctant men. Many of the men in these families told me about how they came to their construction of sharing parenting quite willingly, not needing particular encouragement from, or demands by, their female partners. These men felt they wanted to be involved fathers from the outset of their family. Indeed, these men spoke of marrying women whom they knew could and would embrace their active involvement as fathers.

Father Involvement: A Question
of Deliberate Choice

The paths these people took toward sharing parenting challenge the dominant image of men in another area, the image of men typically becoming fully involved as stay-at-home parents by default (Gerson, 1993; Radin, 1988; Radin & Russell, 1983). This discourse suggests that in the face of unanticipated circumstances (e.g., unemployment or the absence or loss of one's partner through divorce or death), men get involved because they have no other options. In contrast, all the narrative accounts from the men in this study highlight the desire and commitment to be actively involved in their children's lives. Further, these narratives highlight the satisfaction men feel with their involvement. Like the men in Haas's (1988) work, the men presented their involvement in terms of making choices clearly from a place of their felt desire to be deeply personally affected (i.e., awaking sides of life such as emotions and deep loving that they had earlier envied in women), not out of a default response. When circumstances (such as financial trade-offs between day care and their relative earnings, or the birth of their baby in the middle of the mother's medical training) spurred changes in their family life, these men felt like they had a choice to move toward more apparent involvement or not. A few men related how they chose to become the designated stay-at-home parent; others recounted how they chose to juggle parenting shifts and work shifts with their partner.

Challenging Discourse About
Intergenerational Transfer of Violence

Narratives from men who grew up in abusive families challenge dominant social learning ideas about intergenerational transfer of violence (Okun, 1986). Although perhaps not the typical scenario coming out of such an environment, these narratives suggest alternative possibilities, especially if these men had some exposure to a more validating, caring, and protected environment at some point in their lives. The models these men grew up with did not give them the ready resources to parent effectively, but, according to their narratives, they have not repeated the violent patterns of their childhood. They talked about forging a different path for themselves and for their partner and children. Similar to Canfield's (1997) overcomer men, these men spoke of missing out in childhood and vowing to find another way to parent. They acknowledged that they were in some way healing from childhood wounds (Osherson, 1986) by experiencing the greater potentials of parenting actively in a sharing parenting family.

CULTURAL DISCOURSES ABOUT
THE VALUE OF FAMILY

Cultural discourses about the value of family are quite confusing. Cultural discourses both value and subtly devalue the centrality of family. I hear politicians putting family life at the forefront of election campaigns, but see social policy taking piecemeal approaches to addressing issues of the well-being of families in society (cf. Canada Committee for the International Year of the Family, 1994; Hertz, 1997). At the same time, family policy initiatives are typically considered in terms of their monetary potential to increase the country's wealth in terms of gross national product (GNP), while production in families (family maintenance, not to mention the intangible aspects of nurturing human beings) is not valued in calculations of GNP.

The research conversations with these 18 couples left me with a tantalizing sense that they challenge dominant discourses about financial decision making in families. Rather than operating from a principle of making decisions to maximize family income, these people seem to see financial considerations as part of a larger decision matrix. They intentionally make choices to value family time and connection in their personal lives highly, relative to the monetary value of their labor and capital. They do so against high odds.

Differential Trade-Offs for Men and Women

The dominant sociocultural backdrop of a capitalistic economic system—even modified by some socially liberal policies—rewards paid work while generally devaluing family work (Hartman, 1984). Both women's and men's narratives hint at struggling with constructing private lives in the face of differential trade-offs each is making. Our culture offers greater obvious rewards to women who have moved into the paid workforce, whereas men face hidden (or intangible) personal and interpersonal rewards for moving to take greater presence and participation in the daily workings of family life (Gerson, 1993). This facet of dominant cultural discourses makes women's changes obvious in their workforce participation—their money earning power outside the family—yet the accompanying changes they are making with their partners on the home front remain invisible.

The other side of this coin is that the changes men are making in their paid work outside the home may be invisible because they manage the trade-offs quite privately (e.g., rearranging work hours through flextime and individually negotiated schedules, or managing their career ambitions in a way that keeps them off the fast track of success), while their contributions to family may be spotlighted. The changes men make on the home front are frequently viewed as special by women onlookers and as odd or threatening by male onlookers.

Part of the inverse invisibility regarding the changes both women and men are making seems to be connected to the public gaze being focused on tangible indicators. It is easier to focus our gaze on what has shifted between men and women regarding who does what tasks and who spends what time devoted to family life. Although these tangible indicators are important, the focus on them has the potential to blindside the subtle changes in attitudes and feelings both women and men may be making in sharing the myriad responsibilities of family life.

Intentionally Choosing Family Commitments over Materialism

Narratives about valuing a child-centered family, and associated decisions to put children first, mean these men and women make intentional living a way of life. This means they face challenges and distractions from the outside culture (including work demands) with creativity. They creatively manage their work-family trade-offs to keep their foundational ideology alive. They talked about lifestyle decisions (such as moving to a more affordable neighborhood so that one parent could stay home with the children) that unleashed them from the bigger-is-always-better and accumulation-of-material-goods-shows-success themes dominant in a materialistic consumer culture. These decisions often mean that each parent has times when he or she is not there with the kids—or not in the position of being the first line of contact. Both men and women mentioned their comfort in knowing they had made a family decision that at least maximized the child's experience of having one parent there as the first point of contact daily.

BEYOND DICHOTOMOUS WAYS OF THINKING

Questions addressed in much of the academic literature, especially early interest in men as fathers, are cast in terms of the potential to generalize from central tendencies found in a population. The interest in central tendencies can lead to thinking in typical and, in contrast, atypical terms. Overfocusing on these distinctions can lead to dichotomous ways of thinking about and studying families. Prevalent questions in research have centered on the effect of a father's presence or absence, as if there were no significance in the type of presence or the amount of presence and no differences connected to the reasons for father absence; whether fathers have an effect on the child's development or not, rather than exploring the effects different kinds of involvement might lead to; whether he is nurturing or not, as opposed to looking at the different ways he might express nurturing; whether he experienced his transition to parenthood as a crisis or not, rather than exploring the different ways men adjust to this major transition in their lives; whether he feels more or less comfortable with his involvement in family than he feels in his provider role, as opposed to questions about how both roles in his life were experienced; and whether his involvement in parenting increases marital stress or not, rather than looking at ways men and women manage the stress of more complicated family life after having children. Although some recent research has begun to ask different kinds of questions, men's and women's narratives about sharing parenting suggest that complex dynamics need to be taken into account when we study men's involvement in parenting.

Provider Role

Asking questions that implicitly presume that men rank their provider role against other family responsibilities seems like searching for a trivial dichotomy. As in Cohen's (1987, 1993) work, narratives about the provider role suggest it does not exist apart from, but is an integral part of, family life. The meanings associated with my study suggest further that this is the case for both men and women. Men's and women's contributions in the form of providing for the economic viability of the family are valued as coexisting with their direct interfaces with the children and managing other family maintenance routines. Like women, men do not want to have to chose between family and work in the sense of placing them in some hierarchical relationship to each other. They see these aspects of their lives as very intertwined. Understanding provider responsibilities needs to be cast against a broad perspective of interconnected responsibilities, rather than on a restricted sense of dichotomous choices. Further, we need to understand the constraints in both men's and women's choices as they juggle their provider responsibilities among competing demands for time and personal and family resources. Typically, work schedules and other parameters of work can place severe constraints on both men's and women's flexibility to juggle the work-family interface.

Personal Resources

The question of where men invest their energy has been an area of study for some researchers interested in what may constrain men's involvement in family life. Lamb (1987) reviews literature suggesting that the energy demanded at work can place a significant constraint on men's involvement in child care. Much of the research in this area may be influenced by assumptions associated with the scarcity model of resource allocation prevalent in economic thinking about fixed resources. The form of previous research questions may implicitly perpetuate a propensity to see this issue as an either-or proposition; that is, men have only a given amount of energy, and either they invest most of it in their work (a pragmatic decision perhaps associated with constraints imposed by their provider responsibilities), or they invest it in the family. Adopting different assumptions (e.g., the availability of certain personal resources may not be fixed) and asking different kinds of questions may allow us to shift away from dichotomous ways of thinking about men in families.

First, this is not just a men's issue. Women's narratives echo those of men. Both men and women feel their work has the potential to, and often does, drain energy they would prefer to take to family. Both women and men also feel that the energy they give their family is, for the most part, different from what is demanded of them at work. They said it is different in that they feel the relational aspects, and the interdependence of family members, are much more significant. This is a sense of feeling family is closely connected to their core identity and, thus, allows them to call on energy reserves even when they feel depleted by work. Family interactions often reinvigorate these people. Family interactions often give them a sense of joy in connection that they do not experience at work. Thus, it seems, family life can both create energy and use people's energy.

Second, men also talked about a difficult balancing between family and work on some occasions. A few men suggested that when they chose work commitments over family time and responsibilities, they trusted and relied on the long-term nature of their family relationships. They made choices, at times, to privilege time at work over family, believing that securing the family's economic viability warranted their choice, especially in the current unstable employment context. At other times, men mentioned they had to be cautious about privileging work demands because the seeming immediacy of work could always take priority. Men see balancing between family and work as a big-picture issue. The big picture pushes them to go beyond simple decisions about enough and not enough family involvement on a daily basis. Men's accounts suggest that they trust their long-term commitment to family. They trust that their philosophy about being there for their children will sustain them and their partners through times when outside commitments prevail. I see this type of commitment as moving beyond dichotomous thinking about the immediate balancing between enough and not enough personal resources for family involvement and work.

Developmental Effects

In accord with Belsky and his colleagues (Belsky, 1979; Belsky & Volling, 1987; Belsky, Youngbalde, Rovine, & Volling, 1991), these men's and women's narratives indicate that a dichotomous perspective on fathers' involvement is an inadequate focus of study. Dichotomous thinking is more likely to stem from a unidirectional focus (i.e., does father involvement effect child development or not) than from a systemic perspective considering the complex multidirectional possibilities in family interaction and communication. A unidirectional perspective studying father-child interactions isolated from family interactions can lead to limiting thinking about developmental effects. Because men's interactions with their children do not occur in a vacuum, narrow questions about father-child interactions simplify the scope of inquiry into how father involvement affects the development of the child.

Multidirectional effects were very apparent in the narratives of men and women involved in sharing parenting. Men talked about being affected by their children as much as they feel they affect their children's development (bidirectionality), and by their interactions with their partner over parenting issues and general family negotiations (multidirectionality). Women's narratives also note these multidirectional influences on their sense of the child's development and their own sense of changing in adulthood. Understanding the interactive dynamics of sharing parenting can extend our understanding of father effects beyond simple perspectives on a father's potential influence on a child's development. To study these effects in detail adequately, a systemic and ecological perspective, including the multiple interactive possibilities across and between all family members, is warranted. Further, my reading of narrative accounts from both men and women indicates that these effects span terrain in the emotional, instrumental, and communication arenas.

Final Reflections

Initially, my ideas about men's active involvement in family life held both hope and despair. My hope sprang from observing (directly or indirectly) some men's increasing presence in the daily activities of child rearing. I saw men in public caring for infants and young children. I observed men comforting, guiding, disciplining, watching in wonder as their child discovered something new to her or his world. I noticed how seeing men caring for children in such public places as the grocery store, the park, the bank, the playground, restaurants, and music concerts held a certain sense of special curiosity for me. This awareness led to feeling some despair. I asked, "Why should I even notice men caring for children? I don't have the same degree of curiosity when I see women caring for children in these same venues." I stumbled on the realization that I harbored ideas about how involved fathers are somehow special. What does our culture expect of men anyway? I wondered if the cultural discourse about fatherhood sanctioned minimal involvement, with hero status if men go beyond providing financially for the next generation. This is a despairing thought. This led me to think about how the men themselves experience their involvement. I wondered how this balancing between hope and despair would fare if I listened to the stories of men who actually value being involved in the daily care and rearing of their children. The research conversations and analytical process are now behind me (at least temporarily), with the balance being tipped on the hopeful side.

I am convinced that not only is it possible for men to get actively involved in parenting the next generation, it is an experience that carries the potential to allow both men and women to construct new possibilities for fatherhood and motherhood. These men and women are actively constructing, ideologically and pragmatically, ways for both the mother and the father to be equally valued for their involvement and the contributions they each make to raising their children. In choosing to create and live the daily reality of sharing parenting, these men and women subtly undermine the power of stereotypical gender roles to determine how they will manage the myriad activities, decisions, and responsibilities of parenting young children. They are forging paths that work for them at this point in their family life, with little apparent concern for how they are doing it differently than other families around them. In this understanding, I came to appreciate the importance of valuing plurality, the diversity of ways people can create and manage sharing parenting, as opposed to searching for some monolithic family structure ideally suited to men and women sharing parenting.

Realizing that men and women in these families do not hold their arrangements up to some external standard of gender equity is closely associated with valuing the diversity of ways men and women can make sharing parenting work for their families. It seems significant that each family has negotiated a unique pattern of sharing who does what in their family, yet each couple reported that they feel their arrangement is based on achieving equity between them. Equity does not seem to be a measure that can be externally imposed and judged, especially some simplistic equity notion based on the proportional time each parent spends in various activities. Equity seems to be both a foundational value and an interactive experience spanning myriad activities and shifting responsibilities. Expanding our notions of how people negotiate equity in their parenting team to include attention to the unique meanings each partner gives to their various involvements would go a long way toward deepening our understanding of how men and women break down gender politics in families.

I was left to ponder the limiting depictions of men's involvement in family life associated with prominent conceptualizations found in academic literature. I struggled to pierce the veil of dichotomous thinking and reductionistic labeling, especially as it concerns role complementarity and gendered division of labor. These ideas seem so embedded in our view of family structure and family dynamics that I kept coming back to questions of what allowed these men and women to get beyond organizing their family life based on these principles. Their firm commitment to share has necessitated that they develop highly interchangeable skills, while at the same time allowing each partner to handle the responsibilities of family life with unique individual style. Men and women were valued for both their differences and their similarities. The idea of being interchangeable in function but not in form may carry important potentials to consider if we want to value both men's and women's contributions to family life without implicitly holding up one way, associated with the woman or the man, as the better way, and then judging any differences as deficient in some sense. In this arena, family science has a way to go to uproot hidden assumptions privileging women's ways of parenting in our discourses about men and women in families.

Reshaping fatherhood through the social construction of sharing parenting touches all realms of men's lives. The reshaping of fatherhood also reaches deep into all realms of women's lives. Both men and women have the potential to enrich their lives by venturing into new realms of relating to each other and to their children. For both men and women, the emotional experience of participating in the growing child's life is inspiring and challenging beyond all expectations. In this awareness, the men and women were similar, yet they were notably different in what they anticipated they would experience. Women seemed to know that they would be transformed through experiences of parenting a child. Men discovered unexpectedly, by the doing of it actively, they were transformed through the experiences of parenting a child. Both men and women appreciated that they had an involved partner with whom to share this life-changing experience.

I cannot help but wonder what I might learn about sharing parenting if I were to revisit these families when their children are beginning families of their own. I wonder what the next generation of parents will expect of themselves. Will they resort to antimodel expectations in reaction to having such involved fathers and mothers, wanting to have more clear separation between mothers and fathers? I hope not! Is the shift in this one generation of children's experience enough to remove most of the holdovers from embedded cultural practices that sanction different involvements and experiences for women and men? I suspect not. I suspect that the sons and daughters of these men and women will continue to face some residual expectations to do certain things according to cultural gender scripts. Yet, it is a hopeful sign that some men and women are actively challenging those scripts in their families, and offer alternative visions to the next generation.

Appendix A
Methodology

Recent research has begun to focus on the deep texture of men's experience in families. The research to date does not directly yield a grounded understanding of the why or how of fathers' full participation in sharing parenting, however. I was interested in bringing men's own stories of their experience to our understanding of men's participation in parenting. I was particularly interested in the lived experience and meaning-making of men who are actively sharing the parenting of their children with their partners.

I used the processes of qualitative inquiry to tap into complex constructions of the participants' worlds. Qualitative methodology opens the research inquiry to an explication of how people make sense of their life experiences (Denzin, 1994; Marshall & Rossman, 1989; McCracken, 1988; Moustakas, 1990; Strauss, 1987; Strauss & Corbin, 1990). Denzin's (1994) review of qualitative methodologies highlights the range in researchers' recognition of intersubjectivity in the research endeavor. He urges researchers to address explicitly the interactive exchange of ideas and meanings between researcher and coresearcher (research participant). Research conversations with participants are meaning-making exchanges (Denzin, 1994). This meaning-making exchange involves a process of the researcher listening to participants' narratives and clarifying with participants so that the subjective understanding the researcher is formulating captures the participants' experiences. This means the researcher needs to practice *transparency*—or the practice of clarifying how the meanings presented in the research product were constructed intersubjectively between the researcher and the participant. It also means the researcher clarifies whose meanings are being privileged in the research story. These central ideas and practices match the tenets of my social constructionist paradigm.

Qualitative Research Design

THE FOUNDATION OF THE RESEARCH DESIGN: GROUNDED THEORY

My search for a qualitative research process appropriate to study men and women who are fully sharing parenting began with the open and emergent design of grounded theory (Glaser & Strauss, 1967; Strauss, 1987; Strauss & Corbin, 1990) and the long qualitative interview (Marshall & Rossman, 1989; McCracken, 1988). Grounded theory approaches are particularly appropriate for the study of phenomena, action/process, and interactional questions, as well as biographical questions (Glaser & Strauss, 1967; Strauss & Corbin, 1990). The use of a long, qualitative interview offers the power to reach "into the life-world of the individual, [and] to see the content and pattern of daily experience" (McCracken, 1988, p. 9), while enriching our understanding of how human action is mediated by culture. In this research, I was asking men and women to share biographical stories. In hearing their stories, I was also listening for the meaning they made from their interactions and experiences of sharing parenting. I was interested in their individual and family histories, as well as their experiences and processes that allowed sharing parenting to work for them.

Incorporating Social Constructionist Ideas in a Grounded Theory Study

As I began interviewing couples, as well as the individual men and women in these families, I began to recognize more fully some post-positivist strains in the interpretive claims of Strauss and associates' grounded theory (Denzin, 1994). Most notably, I recognized the tendency to suggest that interpretations may approximate reality when different researchers, employing a similar set of conditions, the same theoretical perspective, and the same research protocol, are "able to reproduce the same theoretical explanations of a given phenomenon" (Denzin, 1994, p. 508). Wanting an updated research practice, I turned to the constructionist ideas and practices of Lincoln and Guba (1985) and Denzin (1989a, 1989b). Lincoln and Guba tend to be more explicit about the value-laden nature of all research. They emphasize the interpretive process that underpins research results or constructed theory. Further, they explicitly acknowledge the interactive relationship that exists between the researcher and research participants (or the observer and the observed). Their constructionist approach maintains a serious "commitment to methods and procedures that will increase a text's credibility, transferability, dependability, and confirmability" (Denzin, 1994, p. 508). In this, they adhere to the "canons of good science" (Denzin, 1994, p. 508), while allowing for an open and emergent design.

In working with the emergent design of this study, I eventually incorporated ideas and analytical approaches from life story narratives (Riessman, 1993), interpretive interactionism (Denzin, 1989a, 1989b, 1994), and heuristic research (Moustakas, 1990). All these approaches are positioned in a constructionist paradigm and offer perspectives to sharpen the interpretive process. The ideas and practices outlined by Denzin (1989a, 1989b, 1994) enable the researcher to be more explicit about a central role in the interpretive process.

Modifying my approach by incorporating ideas and practices found in naturalistic inquiry (Lincoln & Guba, 1985) and interpretive biography (Denzin, 1994), I created what Charmaz (1993) suggests is a sound social constructionist approach for a grounded theory study. In the meaning-making endeavor of a grounded theory study, the social constructionist researcher presents constructed concepts thought to be located in and generated from the narrative accounts of people's lives as they live day in and day out (Denzin, 1994; Lincoln & Guba, 1985). Within the framework of qualitative research, all these approaches share several central practices, in particular, the reflexive process of induction, deduction, and verification of concepts; the aim to identify, develop, and relate concepts; and ongoing and evolving data collection and data analysis (Charmaz, 1993; Denzin, 1989a, 1989b, 1994; Moustakas, 1990; Riessman, 1993; Strauss, 1987; Strauss & Corbin, 1990).

METHODOLOGICAL PRACTICES

Theoretical Sampling

The long qualitative interview was the primary approach to data collection (Denzin, 1989a, 1989b; Marshall & Rossman, 1989; McCracken, 1988; Moustakas, 1990; Riessman, 1993). Data analysis involves "successively evolving interpretations" (Strauss, 1987, p. 10) and the practice of theoretical sampling (Denzin, 1994; Lincoln & Guba, 1985; Strauss, 1987; Strauss & Corbin, 1990). *Theoretical sampling* is the practice of identifying themes (hypothesized patterns) and concepts in the data, asking where instances of these phenomena may be found, and then collecting further data for verification (or not) of their relevance (Glaser & Strauss, 1967; Strauss, 1987; Strauss & Corbin, 1990).

Theoretical saturation is an important research concept associated with theoretical sampling practices. *Saturation* refers to the notion that interviewing participants has reached the point where further interviews will not generate significantly different views or information relevant to the theoretical category being explored. When a researcher determines that saturation has been reached, he or she is convinced that concept development is already dense, and the relationships between concepts are established and confirmed (Strauss & Corbin, 1990). In this research, I tracked several themes across all couples. The rules of thumb I used to decide if I had sufficient data for a particular category were 1) a majority of the participants' narratives contained coded text in the category, and 2) the most recent interviews did not add or clarify nuances in any particular category.

Criteria for Participant Selection

Theoretical sampling involves sampling incidents, not persons (Strauss & Corbin, 1990). But it is in the lives of people that these incidents are grounded (Strauss & Corbin, 1990), so the issue of which people are studied becomes central to the qualitative endeavor. Theoretical sampling also requires that a diversity of perspectives be brought to the research question (Strauss, 1987; Strauss & Corbin, 1990). Thus, strategic selection of research participants is important (Strauss & Corbin, 1990).

The selection criteria for research participants involved a deliberate search for families in which men have an identifiable investment in being fully involved and active in the day-in and day-out responsibilities and activities of family life and child care. I was interested in the experiences of both men and women in these families, thus I sought only participant families in which both partners would be willing to talk with me about their individual and collective experiences.

In selecting families for this research, I identified three selection criteria and imposed certain limitations on sample diversity. 1) Both the man and the woman agreed that he was an active and fully participating father in everyday family life. The determination of what "active and fully participating father" meant was left to each couple. In the initial conversations, I asked questions about the extent of the man's participation in common everyday family routines (e.g., meal preparation, the child's hygiene, time spent in directly handling the child's daily care and development, and in-house maintenance) to satisfy my general sense of the extent of his involvement. 2) They had at least one child between the ages of 2 and 6 years old. 3) They were a first family of these biological children. These three selection criteria were designed to draw on some common experiences thought to be associated with families of young children.

Carter and McGoldrick (1988) identify "accepting new members into the system" (p. 15) as the primary task for families with young children. In attempting to include families that were likely to be experiencing generally similar developmental tasks, I chose both an upper limit (up to but not including children who have entered adolescence) and a lower limit (including children who have reached their second birthday). Preadolescent and younger children still require after-school care and significant adult supervision and involvement in daily routines. I chose a lower limit of 2 years after considering the importance of allowing some time for the parents to have established a basic pattern of sharing the high demands of caring for young children. If either (or both) the mother or father took parental leave following the birth of their child, they would likely have returned to work by the time the child was 2 years old and would have likely established routines of child care.

Convenience Referrals for
Participant Selection

Eighteen families participated in this research. The men and women in these 18 couples shared their family life stories from their individual and couple perspectives. Their narratives, told in unfolding, interactive conversations with me (as researcher), became the grounding data for research interpretation.

The men and women in an additional four families agreed to act as consultants to me in the interpretive process. These men and women are people in my network of colleagues and friends. They were the initial source of my interest in sharing parenting couples. They are people who opened their homes and their family lives to me as a friend. They are people with whom I had many opportunities to observe interactions before I began to contact couples for this research. As I created initial questions and designed the early parameters for this study of sharing parenting couples, these people listened to my ideas and offered their perspectives, which helped refine my questions and selection criteria. For the most part, these four couples meet the selection criteria I eventually adopted. As well, they resemble the general characteristics, both demographic and in their self-descriptions of family life charac-teristics. For reasons of respecting the boundaries of friendship, we eventually decided they would not formally participate as primary informants. I did not formally interview these couples, nor did I analyze their stories. They agreed to continue their participation by acting as consultants throughout the formulation of interpretative conceptualiza-tions. They agreed to listen to my ideas, to help me challenge my assumptions, and to offer their perspectives on what I thought I was hearing from the participant couples.

As consultants, these families were also the source of the first referrals to primary participants. Three of the four consultant couples contacted at least one other family they knew and gave them my project descrip-tion. The referred family then made its own choice to participate or not;

contacting me by telephone if they chose to self-refer. Four participant families came into the study via this route.

After initial contact with these first referrals, I asked couples if they would pass along the project description to another family. Two self-referrals resulted from this snowball procedure. At the same time, I circulated project descriptions to several people in my extended network of colleagues and friends. They in turn passed them along to other families. Six self-referrals resulted from this process. Another six families came into the study in response to a notice included in a parents' newsletter of a local preschool program.

Strategic Participant Selection and Theoretical Saturation

Several other families were suggested for participation. The decision not to contact these additional couples was based on the purposive element of the selection process. I was purposefully looking for a selection of participant couples representing different ways of combining family responsibilities with work outside the home. After talking to the referral source, I thought the combination of the man and woman sharing work and family responsibilities represented by these additional couples was already well represented in my sample.

Furthermore, I determined that my conversations with these 18 families had already given me access to a significant depth and breadth of experience to reach theoretical saturation. McCracken (1988) justifies the potential appropriateness of a small number of informants by noting the purpose of qualitative research as being to look into the "complicated character, organization, and logic of [local] culture" (p. 17), rather than to generalize to the larger population or to determine distribution and frequency of some phenomena.

DATA COLLECTION AND INTERVIEW PROCESS

Marshall and Rossman (1989) argue that the long qualitative interview is typically more like a conversation than an interrogation. Accordingly, I adopted an informal conversational style, using a general interview guide as a prompt to cover the same areas of interest with each person (Marshall & Rossman, 1989; McCracken, 1988; Moustakas, 1990; Patton, 1990).

Obtaining High-Quality Data

McCracken (1988) notes that the key to obtaining high-quality data is adopting a stance as an unobtrusive researcher. Being unobtrusive means that the researcher allows the informant to tell his or her own story. Thus, the researcher must create an atmosphere of trust and openness. Both trust and openness are thought to facilitate the full development of the person's narrative account of her or his experiences. Obtaining a fully developed narrative account, rich with detail, explanations, and meanings, is the initial basis for establishing a credible research product.

Establishing Trust and
Openness: Interview Practices

I believed I could demonstrate my trustworthiness to the parents by interacting with their children in a respectful, interested, playful manner that involved them in my research and provided a relatively nonthreatening introduction to the recording equipment. I usually arranged my meeting with each couple during a part of their day when their children would be present. When I entered their home, I made a point of getting down to the children's level (physically crouching so they could speak to me face to face), and engaged each child in some talk about himself or herself. I then proceeded to show the children my recording equipment and let them talk into the tape, then rewound it so they could hear themselves as recorded. In deciding to begin with this procedure, I was aware the parents would be watching my interaction, and likely making initial judgments about my trustworthiness. I took as long as seemed necessary for the children to satisfy their curiosity and move to looking to their parents for direction as to what was next.

In outlining what I thought might be the process, I described how I would conduct myself in the conversation. I let them know that I would be asking them as a couple to describe what their routines were and how they came to organize their family life in this way. I would follow their descriptions and ask clarifying questions to develop some detail in the picture I was capturing of their experience. I would then ask to speak with each of them individually; they could decide who would go first. I also invited them to feel comfortable with directing the conversation to areas they thought I should know about. Each person was assured that she or he need not answer any questions that did not feel appropriate or comfortable.

The Interview Process

I used two orienting questions. First, I asked people to describe a day and a week in the life of their family. In this way, I heard about who does what and how routine and nonroutine situations are handled. Second, I asked them to help me understand how they, individually and as a couple, came to organize their family life in this way. Typically, I followed the first orienting question with some general clarifying questions. After a general answer to the second question, I began to follow the weave of their story more closely. I asked them to expand on points, to help me make connections to things they had already said, or to tell me how the described situations affected them, their partner, and their children. These conversations became a guided coconstruction, wherein I both followed their lead and led in certain directions of primary interest to this study.

I conducted these guided conversations in the spirit of being informed by their expertise. Recognizing the power and privilege of my position as the researcher, I endeavored to establish, as far as possible, a spirit of egalitarian rapport between myself and informants. I recognized that their sharing could entail risks in terms of being time-consuming, endangering privacy, and demanding intellectual and emotional energy (McCracken, 1988). I viewed the sharing of their lives with me as a privilege of my being in the researcher role. I tried to convey these sentiments both directly in my introductory description and by my conduct throughout the interview conversation. To this end, I was keenly aware of trying to establish rapport, especially in the early segments of all my conversations with the couples and the individuals. I purposely positioned myself to convey my sincere interest in their experience and my respect for their unique story. To accomplish this, I used joining skills learned in my clinical practice to paraphrase and reflect back to them what I was beginning to understand about their experience before I would ask a question of clarification or redirection. Also, I would frequently pause and check out what meaning I was making by reflecting back what I was thinking and asking them if I was capturing their experience. I purposely used open language—such as "I wonder about . . ." or "I am curious about . . ."—that I hoped would encourage them to feel my attentiveness to their experience and meaning.

For each of the 18 families in the informant pool, I had the opportunity to speak with the couple and with each partner individually about their experiences. Following my initial conversations with these families, I selected 6 families for a second conversation. I selected these 6 families on the basis of initial analysis that they could be representative exemplars of some key themes. In these second conversations, the couple was asked to speak with me further about collective and individual experiences of phenomena they spoke about in my first meetings with them. Conversations lasted 2 to 3 hours, and allowed me the opportunity to have a more substantial experience of co-constructions and their understandings as a couple. These second conversations enriched the data, allowing my analysis to penetrate deeper into the intricacies of interaction and meanings these men and women created by sharing parenting fully.

Documentation of the Conversations

All my conversations with the research participants were audiotaped. A professional transcriber provided verbatim transcripts. Her transcriptions were conversational, and captured various tones and obvious idioms of speech. These annotations added, in many cases, subtle meaning to the spoken words. Annotations include conversational pauses, obvious affective tones (e.g., laughter, tears), and flow (especially when transcribing couple conversations). I proofed all transcriptions against the tapes and, where obvious, added my own interpretative notation of accompanying affective tone. These annotated texts became the data I analyzed for themes.

At the end of the initial conversations, all informants agreed to share basic demographic descriptions of their families. Basic demographic data include family income; education level; age; age at marriage (or beginning this bonded relationship); length of marriage (relationship); number, ages, and sex of children; and current family form. These data were included as background information and were not used for any quantitative analysis.

PARTICIPANT CHARACTERISTICS

The people who volunteered to participate in this research seemed to be highly motivated to share their personal and family stories. They were a self-selected group of couples who responded to the project description after being contacted by someone in their network of family, friends, colleagues, child care providers, and neighbors. The project description explicitly mentioned my interest in men's experience of creating highly involved roles for themselves in family life. It also explicitly stated that I was looking to them to make a contribution toward building a clearer understanding of the joys and challenges men and women face in creating new possibilities for men in families. When they contacted me to find out more about the research, I asked them what interest they had in participation. I often heard statements suggesting that they felt they had a sense that their family was somewhat different from the general population. I also heard people suggest that they felt motivated to share their generally positive experiences of sharing parenting with others.

Table A.1 summarizes some socioeconomic characteristics of the informant families. Fifteen informant families live in various communities in southwestern Ontario (Canada); three informant families live in southern California. The thematic analysis of similarities and differences across participant families did not reveal significant differences based on different geographical contexts.

The 18 couples who shared their stories could be considered a fairly homogeneous group. On the most general level, they share the characteristics of educated, white, middle-class North Americans. Most couples owned their home, and did not talk about serious threats to their economic viability, such as underemployment, unemployment, or poverty. Their narratives are rich with the sense of choice about their lifestyle. They also share characteristics of having been together as a couple for a fairly long time, as well as having established their couple relationship over several years before having children. Generally, their narrative accounts place them as having lived in their current community for many years, with several couples living close to at least one set of

TABLE A.1   Research Participant Characteristics

	Men	Women
Average age (years)	38	36
Education		
High school	22%	11%
College	5%	44%
B.A./B.S.	38%	17%
M.A./Ph.D./M.D.	34%	28%
Profession		
Senior management	22%	6%
Management	18%	6%
Professional/Semi-professional	28%	44%
Skilled trades	11%	6%
Retail/service industry	4%	6%
Students	—	15%
Designated stay-at-home parent	17%	17%

Family Income Range = $10,000-$140,000
Approximate Average = $50,000

Number of Children in Family
1 child   2 families
2 children   11 families
3 children   5 families

their children's grandparents. With the exception of one man, these couples are in their first marital relationship. (Although several couples reported having lived together previously, at the time of my research, all the couples reported being married.) The 18 couples represented several different configurations of family structure: 3 couples were dual earners, 3 couples job shared, in 4 families the woman worked part-time and the man worked full-time, in 2 families the man worked part-time and the woman worked full-time, there were 3 stay-at-home fathers and 3 stay-at-home mothers.

DATA ANALYSIS: THE
MEANING-MAKING PROCESS

The qualitative long interview generates textual data that are later subjected to analytical scrutiny by the researcher. The analytical process in a social constructionist study is interpretive. I used two approaches in the meaning-making process—the bottom-up analytical strategy of social constructionist grounded theory (Charmaz, 1993; Strauss & Corbin, 1990) and the reflexive holistic strategy of heuristic research (Moustakas, 1990).

The first analytical steps were located in the tradition of social constructionist grounded theory. After each interview, I reviewed the text by listening to the audiotape while reading the transcript, underlining emphasized words and making initial coding notes in the margins. The initial data analysis involved highlighting words in the text and identifying what I took to be the main theme (or themes) in the text segment. With each informant text, the data analysis involved both "successively evolving interpretations" (Strauss, 1987, p. 10) and theoretical sampling (Strauss, 1987; Strauss & Corbin, 1990).

Theoretical Sampling Practices

I practiced a modified method of theoretical sampling. The modification entailed how I positioned my follow-up and continuing articulation of developing themes. As I interpreted each text, I kept a running list of interpretive themes and evolving hypotheses. Then, in my interview conversation with the next informant family, rather than starting with questions around themes already developed (Strauss & Corbin, 1990), I started with an open invitation to listen to their unique narrative. I proceeded with my approach to follow their unique narrative closely. I also kept an ear tuned to notes of the themes I had already developed. If I heard similar themes, I would seek further clarification and understanding. If I did not hear notes of similar themes, I continued to follow the unique story of the particular people I was interviewing. Although allowing their story to take a shape that reflected their unique experience, I would at some point near the end of the interview take the opportunity to ask a question about other themes I was developing. I would introduce these areas by noting that there were some ideas I had heard about in conversations with other families, and I wondered if they would be willing to give me their perspective. If the hypothesized pattern (theme) did not resonate with their experience and meaning-making, I would not pursue it further. By using this approach, I believe I was both open to searching each text for unique themes in the informant's constructed worlds and employing constant comparative analysis of themes across a diversity of individual texts (Strauss, 1987; Strauss & Corbin 1990).

Heuristic Inquiry Practices

The process Moustakas (1990) calls *heuristic inquiry* describes my second analytical approach. This analytical strategy was both concurrent with and sequential to the selective coding and open axial coding of constructionist grounded theory (Charmaz, 1993; Strauss, 1987). Moustakas outlines six intertwined aspects of an interpretive research process: initial engagement, immersion, incubation, illumination, explication, and creative synthesis. In this process, Moustakas is explicit about the crucial place of tacit knowledge and the contribution intuition makes to the interpretive endeavor. His six layers of interpretive process recognize the ongoing presence of intuition in bridging tacit knowledge and explicit knowledge. I am aware of my reliance on both tacit knowledge and intuition in the meaning-making process. In the interview, I would follow people's story bits (partial stories), trusting my intuition to guide me in pursuing the current direction further, checking out the meanings shaped as I listened, and leading the conversation in new directions. Both knowledges were also operating as I approached the bottom-up analytical work of open and axial coding the textual data for meaning.

It was in the reflexive holistic analytical work—or the heuristic process—that I was most aware of using myself—my tacit knowledge and intuition—as an interpretive instrument. The heuristic approach to meaning-making values the portrayal of "wholes," not only the descriptive analytical bits of thematic analysis (Moustakas, 1990). As I listened, and listened again, to the audiotapes, and read, and reread several times, the transcribed texts of the story bits, I began to shape, in an intricate weave, a larger story of these people's experiences of sharing parenting.

LEGITIMATION PRACTICES

Qualitative researchers often refer to legitimation practices rather than the concepts of reliability and validity commonly associated with quantitative studies. Strategically designing and employing legitimation practices adds to the credibility of the qualitative methodology (Denzin,

1989a, 1989b; Lincoln & Guba, 1985). Such practices are meant to substantiate the legitimacy of the research. Lincoln and Guba (1985) suggest that qualitative research meet the criteria of trustworthiness that includes credibility, transferability, dependability, and confirmability. Verisimilitude (Denzin, 1989a, 1989b) is the notion that because all narratives are constructed fictions, the "truth" of the story is based on whether or not the story is believable to the listener or reader. The following research practices served to create trustworthiness and verisimilitude. All these practices are suggested in qualitative methodology texts (Denzin, 1989a, 1989b; Glaser & Strauss, 1967; Lincoln & Guba, 1985; Strauss, 1987; Strauss & Corbin, 1990) as important ways to create trustworthiness.

Persistent Observation

I introduced a practice of *persistent observation* (Lincoln & Guba, 1985, p. 304) by conducting all the interviews myself and maintaining the same objectives and manner of interviewing. I intentionally asked each research participant questions in the same general areas in an attempt to develop a depth of understanding and an appreciation for the salience of the pervasive qualities involved. These areas included their accounts of their family-of-origin history, the creation of their current sharing parenting practices, their individual perception of how sharing parenting affects them individually and their partner, their perception of what makes their sharing arrangement work for their family, and their perception of cultural practices that either facilitate or hamper working out sharing parenting in their family.

Strategic Selection of Referrals

Although using a convenience referral process to gain access to researcher participants, I endeavored to access families representing a diversity of family experiences and structure. For example, I purposely selected referred families where both parents worked full-time, one parent worked full-time or the other worked part-time, and families with stay-at-home mothers and stay-at-home fathers. Families came from both large urban centers and smaller communities. To increase further the number of perspectives accessed, I interviewed individual men and women, the couple at least briefly, and, for a subset, I also had an extensive interview with the couple together.

Field Notes and Analytic Memos

After interviews and when coding transcripts, I kept notes about ideas that caught my attention. I kept a running list of meaning bits and themes I was developing in my coding of the transcripts. When I clustered ideas into themes, I developed descriptive detail of the overarching meaning and speculations of the interconnections and interactive dynamics. My analytical process here was concurrent with further interviewing in which I would purposefully ask questions to check out my hypotheses and the analytic meanings I was developing. I also had frequent conversations with couples in my consultant group, where I asked them to reflect on the ideas and meanings I was piecing together.

Member Checking

I imported a practice learned in my clinical work to my research interviews. It is a technique for *in-the-moment hypothesis testing* that involves reflecting back to the speaker what I think I am hearing, commenting on the meaning I am making in the process, and asking the speaker to comment on the accuracy of the meanings I have made. This is an informal member checking practice. I also practiced member checking (Lincoln & Guba, 1985) formally when I submitted my constructions of interpretative biographical material to each of the five couples featured as exemplars. I asked these participants to comment on the congruence of my meaning-making with their self-perceptions— or their local knowledges. Each of the exemplar couples found my interpretive account of their stories to be good reflections of their narratives. I also widened the lens on the analytic frame by including other academic colleagues in the credibility checking process. I intentionally checked the credibility of the themes emerging in the meaning-making process with colleagues in a qualitative research support group (Lincoln & Guba, 1985).

Discussing analytic themes and conceptualizations with the consultant group was another form of member checking. At times, I took formulating ideas to couples in the consultant group. I met with each couple (separately, not as a group) for a discussion of what they thought about these interpretative constructions. I found their reflections helped clarify ideas in four areas in particular: 1) my initial research focus and orienting questions, 2) the ideas that came together in Chapter 4, "A Diversity of Paths," 3) the "special"/"not special" cultural bind for men and women, and 4) the acculturation influences impinging on women's desire to share parenting's responsibilities (Chapter 8, "Sharing Parenting and the Reciprocal Revisioning of Fatherhood and Motherhood").

Implications of These Legitimation Practices

Any one of these legitimation practices alone would not likely be sufficient to warrant a claim of trustworthiness or believability (verisimilitude). In combination, these four practices (persistent observation, strategic selection of referrals, filed notes and analytic memos, and member checking), along with extensive external review by academic colleagues not associated with the project, contributed to my confidence in the trustworthiness of the research story. These practices (especially member checking) and the feedback from the external reviewers suggest that the research story offered is believable, at least to the extent that it is told here. Though details are likely missing that would enhance the deep textured connection with other men and women endeavoring to practice sharing parenting, the basic outline of the patterns and dynamics capture some possibilities shared by these 18 families.

Some Limitations of the Research Design

I was most interested in taking a fresh look at men who are highly involved in the day-in and day-out parenting of their children in active partnership with women. A qualitative research design was well suited to this end, because it opened the inquiry to a peek at the deep texture of men's and women's experiences. The focus on a relatively small number of couples who are collaborating to share parenting actively does limit wholesale generalizations. What may be more important to consider, however, are some subtle constraints embedded in the meaning-making process.

The long qualitative interview challenges the researcher to remain connected to his or her initial research curiosities, while remaining open to the nuances of interest and focus of the research participants. My open-ended conversations often remained focused on the cognitive domain of experience, perhaps losing rich detail of the behavioral patterns and responses embedded in the interactive working out of parenting repertoires. In the future, I might incorporate more questions that specifically explore behavioral examples of sharing parenting and then invite explication of their meanings.

I discovered, in the process of interviewing and analyzing, that people often found it difficult to focus, retrospectively, on specific examples of times when they may have experienced conflict (differences between her way and his way) that disrupted their sense of ease in sharing parenting. To elicit these aspects, I might have created some prompting vignettes and asked people to reflect on similar experiences in their family lives. Alternatively, designing the study to include observational data in the natural environment of their home life could enrich the data by providing in situ examples that the couple could then reflect on and interpret with the researcher.

I purposely decided to allow research participants to self-define the level and pattern of the man's participation in the responsibilities and activities of parenting that they considered fully and actively involved. In choosing not to impose researcher-determined definitions of full and active involvement, I limited my ability to comment on the extent to which "equality" between the man and the woman has been attained in some sense that may satisfy feminist scholars. Taking the diversity of sharing patterns revealed in this study into consideration, further study might generate lists of routine and nonroutine parenting activities, and explicitly document the involvement of both women and men in each area. Then the couple could be asked to reflect on its particular patterns and to comment on the sense of equality or inequality, as well as on what factors may mediate what seem to the researcher as apparent inequalities. Such a design modification could enhance understanding of men's and women's experience of equity in family life.

Upon finishing this piece of research, I am filled with further curiosities. I am excited to make some of these refinements in research design. I look forward to going back into the field, engaging men and women in further inquiry into the intricacies of sharing child care and child rearing. I will need to be both more focused and more limiting in my research questions if I hope to explore deeper the texture of negotiation, conflict, resolution styles, and patterns that underlie the collaborative success of couples sharing parenting. I can see the benefit of taking a proactive focus on this area of research, and will likely continue to invite men and women to share their expertise as well as their successes. Creative approaches are required to engage people in sharing their experiences of the successes, while inviting them to share the personal and interpersonal challenges they face as they share parenting in its many frustrating, exhausting, and exhilarating moments.

Appendix B
Research Informants:
Descriptive Biographical Snapshots

Interchangeable Parenting Partners

DAN AND LIZ

Dan and Liz are in their late 30s, with three children 8, 5, and 3 years old. Both Dan and Liz work in the human services field. They have worked together closely over most of their 15-year marriage. Until recently, Dan and Liz job shared, both working half-time in the same job and shifting their paid work hours to handle all the child care and housework within the confines of their family (i.e., they did not "hire out" any of this family work). Recently, Dan shifted to a part-time job, and Liz took full responsibility for the job they had been sharing. Dan is now home with the children about 60% of the time; Liz uses some flex-time to cover 1 afternoon and 1 morning at home with the children. They now have their youngest child in day care 2 mornings a week. They both participate in household maintenance, though Dan has been doing more of these tasks lately.

Steve and Carol are in their mid-30s, with two children 8 and 6 years old. They have been married for 19 years. Steve works freelance in the computer industry, and Carol works in the medical field. Over the 19 years of their marriage, they have both worked full-time and combinations of full-time and part-time. They juggle their work commitments to eliminate the need to have their children in day care. When Steve has a contract job, Carol cuts back to part-time or casual relief work. When Steve is between contracts, Carol increases her hours to full-time. Steve typically works out of an office in their home, so even when he is working on a contract, he is able to stay very involved with the daily child care routine. When he is between contracts, he takes over more of the daily living and household care routines.

ROB AND DONNA

Rob and Donna are in their early 40s, with two children 5 and 3 years old. Rob and Donna have been together for 15 years, and they co-own a service industry business in a busy downtown location. Rob previously worked long hours in the financial industry, and Donna ran their business. Before their second child was born, Rob left his job to have more freedom to be involved in family life. Rob spoke of being ready to leave the fast-paced job to have more time for his family, and the change was precipitated by complications in Donna's second pregnancy. In the first couple of years after leaving the financial industry, Rob was the at-home parent more often than Donna. This has shifted, to where they were quite evenly shifting between the business and home, to more recently, where Donna has had a preference to be home more. Both Rob and Donna are involved in the daily living and home care tasks and responsibilities.

Parenting Partners With Reserved Specialties

RODNEY AND KATE

Rodney and Kate are in their early 30s, with two children 7 and 5 years old. They have been married for 11 years. Rodney and Kate both work in the social services field, and have recently begun to work in different departments for the same employer. When their children were younger, Kate moved between full-time work and periods of staying at home with the children. Rodney's work schedule is less flexible than Kate's during the 10 months when their children are in school, but he has the summer months off with the children. Kate's work schedule is flexible throughout the year. The flexibility often means she works evenings, plus she has contracts for extra work that is all evening work. Rodney and Kate prefer to minimize their use of day care for the children, and use their different work flexibilities to manage this. Rodney does the household cleaning and maintenance routines. Kate does the cooking when she is home; Rodney does it on those nights she is working. Kate reserves the children's health and medical care as her domain.

PHIL AND KELLY

Phil is in his early 40s and Kelly is in her mid-30s, with one child 3 years old. They have been married for 8 years. Phil is an executive in a service company. Kelly is a mid-level manager in a social services agency. Both currently work full-time, and both have some flexibility scheduling their work. Phil is able to work at home occasionally, including putting in a couple of hours in the mornings before their daughter gets up, and he covers the morning routine daily. Kelly works some evenings and weekends, with the freedom to take other "in-lieu" time off. Phil does all the cooking, and Kelly does more of the daily and weekly house cleaning. They have their child in private home day care and preschool, with Kelly doing most of the shuttling between home and day care. Kelly currently prefers to manage her career as secondary to Phil's. She made this decision considering relative earning power at this point in her career, but more important, she wishes to have a second child and wants a flexible, temporary job. They decided that earning power is an area of family life he would specialize in, at least at this point in their careers.

GEORGE AND TERESA

Both George and Teresa are in their mid-30s, with two children, 8 and 2 years old, and a third expected soon. They have been married for 11 years. George works in the trades, and Teresa is a teacher. George's work is variable, depending heavily on the economic swings in the construction industry. Teresa's work is stable. She has used her summers off to upgrade her credentials. Because George's work is unpredictable, they maintain their day care arrangement even when George is off work. This is so they do not lose the spots at their preferred sitters. George is more involved with the children and household responsibilities when his work is minimal to intermittent, which has been most of the time in recent years. He has used this flexibility in the past several summers to take over most of the daily child care in support of Teresa's return to school for special training. When his work demand is high, George maintains his involvement with the children by taking the evening bath and bedtime rituals. He especially enjoys reading with their elder son. George is also very involved in teaching through daily living opportunities and having hobbies and learning adventures with their children, especially with their older son. Teresa reserves her specialty in the area of preparing family meals. George is less talented in this area than he is in child care, so she trades this for an evening break when he puts the kids to bed.

Accounting Equity Parenting Partners

JASON AND HILLARY

Jason and Hillary are both in their early 40s, with two children 12 and 4 years old. Married for 20 years, they have been through a couple of configurations of working out their family life. Jason is an owner-executive of a successful business, and Hillary is finishing her doctoral education and works a few hours a week in her professional practice. Before their second child was born, Jason and Hillary renegotiated their parenting arrangement to allow Hillary to go back to school and to reinvolve Jason in the daily family routines. They also employed a housekeeper to relieve them of most of the household maintenance and provide some child care. Jason and Hillary negotiate their schedules on a weekly or biweekly basis to juggle both their work and caring for the children. Hillary has a more fluid schedule than Jason, but Jason has found that he can build in flexibility if he plans well. Both Jason and Hillary alternate cooking and have agreed-on tasks they do on a routine basis (e.g., making school lunches; driving children to school; taking children to lessons; evening child care, including dinner, bath, and bedtime routines). Often, Jason and Hillary negotiate their weekend schedules to allow Hillary to spend extra time on her studies. Jason and Hillary use this ongoing negotiating to keep an eye on "fairness," with both aware of keeping track of what each is doing on a routine and nonroutine basis.

PATRICK AND DAPHNE

Patrick and Daphne are both 40, have been married for 15 years, and have two children 9 and 6 years old. Patrick has been working toward his doctoral degree for the past few years, and has worked part-time contracts occasionally during this time. Daphne works full-time on a flex-time schedule as a medical technician. She also has returned to school in the past year to upgrade her credentials. Since Patrick has been in school, he has been available to be at home before and after school for their two children. He does the cooking on evenings when Daphne works, and does more of the routine household cleaning and tidying than his partner. Daphne's work schedule consists of 4 long days and 3 days off. On her off days, she does the cooking, and clears time for Patrick to concentrate on his studies. Although Daphne clears time for Patrick's studies, she also keeps on eye on not losing him to his studies. She often reminds him to come out and be with the family.

EVERETT AND JENNY

Everett is in his late 30s and Jenny is in her mid-30s, with two children 6 and 4 years old. They have been married for 9 years. Everett is in middle management in the financial industry. Jenny is a case manager in the social services field. Both Everett and Jenny work full-time, which means they have their children in private home day care at a neighbor's house before and after school. Jenny recently returned to school part-time on weekends to upgrade her credentials. Historically, Everett and Jenny shared the evening routines of child care and cooking, as well as the weekend home maintenance routines. Since Jenny has gone back to school at a university out of town, Everett has begun to carry all the child care and home maintenance on weekends, as well as do more of the food preparation and evening routines on weekdays. Jenny usually monitors how things are done when Everett does the household maintenance chores. Everett seems to maintain an awareness of what he is doing that he didn't have to do before.

RICK AND KAREN

Rick is 40 and Karen is in her mid-30s. They have been married for 13 years and have three children, 7, 5, and 3 years old. Rick works in manufacturing. Karen works part-time, some evenings and Saturdays, in the retail sector. Karen worked full-time until the birth of their second child; she then chose to stay home with the children until they were older. Rick's commuting has him out of the house in the early morning, but he is home in time for Karen to go to work 2 or 3 evenings a week. Karen does most of the house cleaning during the week. Rick and Karen both cook; Rick does the dinners on nights when Karen works, as well as sharing and often solo preparation of meals on nights when she does not work. Rick is very involved with the children in the evenings—even when Karen is not working—playing; doing homework, sports, and lessons; and handling the bath and bedtime routines. Karen keeps an eye on how much Rick is involved, and requests further involvement when she feels she is doing too much.

Man as the Designated Stay-at-Home Parent

JACK AND DENISE

Jack is in his mid-40s and Denise is in her late 20s. Together for 5 years, they have one child, 2 years old, and are expecting their second child. Jack is primarily engaged at home with their child, while Denise finishes her education in a medical specialty. Jack also runs a co-owned business from their home. Jack has taken over most of the daily living and household maintenance routines, as well as the daily child care since their first child was born. Denise has continued to be involved in the child care in the evenings and on weekends, especially on Saturdays, when Jack is more engaged with the business. Denise has identified a couple of home maintenance tasks that she does routinely. She also prefers to do the bath and bedtime routine after having playtime and involvement with feeding their daughter dinner, but when demands at school are high, she lets Jack cover these responsibilities.

BILL AND HELEN

Both Bill and Helen are in their mid-40s. They have been together for 12 years and have two children, 6 and 4 years old. Bill left his commercial sales job when their second child was 3 months old and Helen returned to her middle-management service industry job. Bill is the parent at home most of the time, though he recently began to work part-time a few evenings a week and on some Saturdays. Bill does most of the cooking and keeps the house clean and tidy on a daily basis. Helen does some household jobs on the weekends, if she is not doing other things with the children.

TOM AND SABINE

Tom and Sabine are in their early 40s and have three children, 7 years, 3 years, and 1 month old. They have been together for almost 15 years. Tom decided to leave his management job in the leisure industry and stay home with the children just before their second child was born. Sabine recently finished school and opened a professional practice, after deciding to change careers several years ago. Tom does the major child care and household maintenance tasks on a routine basis. He also participates in their eldest child's school programs and coordinates the services that come in for their special-needs child (second born). Tom and Sabine decided to bottle-feed their newborn so Tom could continue to be the primary care giver on a daily basis. Sabine is involved with the children when she is home in the evenings and on weekends.

Woman as the Designated Stay-at-Home Parent

TODD AND COLLETTE

Todd and Collette are in their early 30s. Married for 7 years, they have three children, 6, 4, and 2 years old. Todd works in the trades; Collette describes herself as a "domestic goddess" who chose to remain at home with their young children. Collette covers most of the caring for the children and coordinating their activities during the day. Todd is involved in both the morning and the evening routines. He gets the children up and feeds them breakfast while Collette gets dressed in the morning. He is involved in the evenings at dinner, family time after dinner, and getting the children bathed and put to bed. They both participate in bedtime stories. Collette handles most of the household maintenance tasks and the routine cooking of meals, but Todd often assists with meals and does the vacuuming weekly. His involvement in the evenings has increased recently, partly as a result of Collette letting him know she needed his participation and his kids needed him around. Collette also notes that Todd makes sure she has some hours to herself on weekends, when he takes over with the children.

SAM AND MEG

Together for 9 years, Sam is in his early 40s and Meg is in her early 30s. They have two children, 3½ and 2 years old, and are expecting their third. Sam commutes to his job as a management trainee in a financial services company. Meg chose to stay home with their young children after working at various creative jobs. Sam leaves for work before the children are up and returns at dinner time. Both Sam and Meg notes that he is the better cook, but his recent job change meant they changed their patterns of meal preparation. Sam enjoys reconnecting with his children when he comes home, and often takes over the bedtime routines so Meg can get a break. Meg and Sam do family shopping together on weekends, and Meg may plan some activity that takes her out of the family for a time on weekends; Sam takes over the kids' routines then. Meg also leaves the children with Sam when she has weekends away with women friends. Sam and Meg mention that the current situation is not ideal; Sam is looking for work closer to home so he can get reinvolved in the family routines. He doesn't like being away from the children for so many hours a day.

CHARLES AND JANICE

Both in their mid-30s, Charles and Janice have been together for 11 years. They have two children, 5 and 3 years old. When their second child was born, they decided that it was not ideal, or financially feasible, to have Janice return to her job. She had not been particularly invested in the job, and knew she could remain engaged in some volunteer work she enjoyed. Charles is co-owner of a consultant business, and has considerable flexibility in his work schedule. When his work is particularly demanding, he insists on coming home for a couple of hours in the evening to be with the family before he puts in extra hours at the office. Charles has regular weekend routines with the children, often taking them out of the house for several hours. Janice uses this time for herself or to finish some household tasks that are too difficult to accomplish when the children are with her. Charles is involved with the children in the evenings, often spending several hours with them in activities they enjoy before bedtime. Janice is out several evenings a month with volunteer commitments; Charles takes over the kids' routines happily on these nights. Charles does some of the cooking, often making several meals on weekends that they freeze and eat later. Janice comments how this makes her week easier.

SHAWN AND BETSY

Shawn and Betsy have been married for 12 years. They have three children, 8, 4, and 2 years old. Betsy notes how privileged she feels to be able to chose to be home while their children are young. She maintains a casual, part-time clerical job. She often spends 8 to 10 hours a week working at home, and delivers the finished work to her employer. Shawn works in industry as a middle manager in the operations end of the business. Shawn shifts his work hours, leaving early before the children are up so he can be home earlier in the evenings to maximize his time with the children before bed. Shawn is active with the children's evening play and putting them to bed. He takes over the evening responsibilities so Betsy can get her contract work done without interruption. Betsy covers most of the meal preparation and indoor household maintenance tasks. They both enjoy the family time they have on weekends.

ERIK AND CHERYL

Married 10 years, Erik and Cheryl have three children, 6½, 5, and 2½ years old. Erik is in his mid-30s and Cheryl is in her early 30s. Cheryl left her clerical job when their first child was born; she provides private home day care before and after school for a neighborhood family, and has recently taken on a part-time retail sales job out of her home. Erik works full-time on a self-determined, flexible schedule in the human service field. Erik manages his work schedule to be home for an extended time in the mornings o help get the children up, fed, and ready for their day. He is out a couple of evenings each week, and has the children alone one or two nights a week when Cheryl is out with her new business. Erik and Cheryl share in meal preparation; Cheryl takes most of the responsibility for indoor household maintenance.

References

Atkinson, A. M. (1987). Fathers' participation and evaluation of family day care. *Family Relations, 36,* 146-151.

Backett, K. (1982). *Mothers and fathers.* New York: St. Martin's.

Barnett, R. C., & Baruch, G. K. (1987). Determinants of father's participation in family work. *Journal of Marriage and the Family, 49,* 29-40.

Barnett, R. C., & Baruch, G. K. (1988). Correlates of father's participation in family work. In P. Bronstein & C. P. Cowan (Eds.), *Fatherhood today* (pp. 66-78). New York: John Wiley.

Baruch, G. K., & Barnett, R. C. (1986a). Consequences of fathers' participation in family work: Parents' role strain and well-being. *Journal of Personality and Social Psychology, 51,* 983-992.

Baruch, G. K., & Barnett, R. C. (1986b). Father's participation in family work and children's sex-role attitudes. *Child Development, 57,* 1210-1223.

Belsky, J. (1979). Mother-father-infant interaction: A naturalistic observational study. *Developmental Psychology, 15,* 601-607.

Belsky, J., & Volling, B. (1987). Mothering, fathering and marital interaction in the family triad during infancy. In P. Berman & F. Pederson (Eds.), *Men's transitions to parenthood* (pp. 37-63). Hillsdale, NJ: Lawrence Erlbaum.

Belsky, J., Youngblade, L., Rovine, M., & Volling, B. (1991). Patterns of marital change and parent-child interaction. *Journal of Marriage and the Family, 53,* 487-498.

Benokraitis, N. (1985). Fathers in the dual-earner family. In S. M. Hanson & F. W. Bozett (Eds.), *Dimensions of fatherhood* (pp. 243-268). Beverly Hills, CA: Sage.

Bernard, J. (1981). The good-provider role: Its rise and fall. *American Psychologist, 36,* 1-12.

Biller, H. H. (1993). *Fathers and families: Paternal factors in child development.* Westport, CT: Auburn House.

Blair, S. L., & Lichter, D. T. (1991). Measuring the division of household labor. *Journal of Family Issues, 12*(1), 91-113.

Blakenhorn, D. (1995). *Fatherless America: Confronting our most urgent social problems*. New York: Basic Books.

Bloom-Feshbach, J. (1981). Historical perspectives on the father's role. In M. E. Lamb (Ed.), *The role of the father in child development* (pp. 71-112). New York: John Wiley.

Bronstein, P. (1988). Marital and parenting roles in transition: An overview. In P. Bronstein & C. P. Cowan (Eds.), *Fatherhood today* (pp. 3-9). New York: John Wiley.

Canada Committee for the International Year of the Family. (1994). *The state of the family in Canada 1994*. Toronto: Angus Reid Group.

Canfield, K. R. (1997, May). *Effecting fathers: Origins, issues and notivations*. Plenary presentation at the first annual Conference on Fathering and Its Effects on Children, Mothers and Fathers, Toronto.

Carling-Fisher, C. S., & Tiedje, L. B. (1990). The impact of maternal employment characteristics on fathers' participation in child care. *Family Relations, 39*, 20-26.

Carter, B., & McGoldrick, M. (1988). Overview: The changing family life-cycle—A framework for therapy. In B. Carter & M. McGoldrick (Eds.), *The changing family life-cycle: A framework for family therapy* (pp. 3-28). New York: Gardiner.

Catalyst Staff. (1988). Workplace policies: New options for fathers. In P. Bronstein & C. P. Cowan (Eds.), *Fatherhood today* (pp. 323-340). New York: John Wiley.

Charmaz, K. (1993, May). *Studying lived experience through grounded theory: Realist and constructivist methods*. Paper presented at Studying Human Lived Experience: Symbolic Interaction and Ethnographic Research conference, Waterloo, Ontario.

Clarke-Stewart, K. A. (1978). And daddy makes three: The father's impact on mother and young child. *Child Development, 49*, 466-478.

Cohen, T. F. (1987). Remaking men: Men's experiences becoming and being husbands and fathers and their implications for reconceptualizing men's lives. *Journal of Family Issues, 8*, 57-77.

Cohen, T. F. (1991). Speaking with men: Applications of a feminist methodology to the study of men's lives. *Men's Studies Review, 8*, 4-13.

Cohen, T. F. (1993). What do fathers provide? Reconsidering the economic and nurturant dimensions of men as parents. In J. C. Hood (Ed.), *Men, work, and family* (pp. 1-22). Thousand Oaks, CA: Sage.

Coltrane, S. (1988). Father-child relationships and the status of women: A cross-cultural study. *American Journal of Sociology, 93*, 1060-1095.

Coverman, S., & Sheley, J. F. (1986). Change in men's housework and child-care time, 1965-1975. *Journal of Marriage and the Family, 48*, 413-422.

Cowan, C. P. (1988). Working with men becoming fathers: The impact of a couples group intervention. In P. Bronstein & C. P. Cowan (Eds.), *Fatherhood today* (pp. 276-298). New York: John Wiley.

Cowan, C. P., & Bronstein, P. (1988). Father's role in the family: Implications for research, intervention and change. In P. Bronstein & C. P. Cowan (Eds.), *Fatherhood today* (pp. 341-347). New York: John Wiley.

Cowan, P. (1988). Becoming a father. In P. Bronstein & C. P. Cowan (Eds.), *Fatherhood today* (pp. 13-35). New York: John Wiley.

Crouter, A. C., Perry-Jenkins, M., Huston, T. L., & McHale, S. M. (1987). Processes underlying father involvement in dual-earner and single-earner families. *Developmental Psychology, 23*, 431-440.

Daly, K. (1993a). Reshaping fatherhood: Finding the models. *Journal of Family Issues,* *14,* 510-530.

Daly, K. (1993b). Through the eyes of others: Reconstructing the meaning of fatherhood. In T. Haddad & L. Lam (Eds.), *Reconstructing Canadian men and masculinity* (pp. 203-221). Toronto: Canadian Scholars Press.

Daniels, P., & Weingarten, K. (1988). The fatherhood click: The timing of parenthood in men's lives. In P. Bronstein & C. P. Cowan (Eds.), *Fatherhood today* (pp. 36-53). New York: John Wiley.

Day, R. R., & Mackey, W. C. (1989). An alternate standard for evaluating American fathers. *Journal of Family Issues, 10,* 401-408.

Denzin, N. (1989a). *Interpretive biographies.* Newbury Park, CA: Sage.

Denzin, N. (1989b). *Interpretive interactionism.* Newbury Park, CA: Sage.

Denzin, N. (1994). The art and politics of interpretation. In N. Denzin & Y. S. Lincoln (Eds.), *Handbook of qualitative research* (pp. 500-515). Thousand Oaks, CA: Sage.

Doherty, W. J. (1991). Beyond reactivity and the deficit model of manhood: A commentary on articles by Napier, Pittman, and Gottman. *Journal of Marital and Family Therapy, 17,* 29-32.

Dollahite, D. C., Hawkins, A. J., & Brotherson, S. E. (1997). Fatherwork: A conceptual ethic of fathering as generative work. In A. J. Hawkins & D. C. Dollahite (Eds.), *Generative fathering: Beyond deficit perspectives* (pp. 17-35). Thousand Oaks, CA: Sage.

Dollahite, D. C., Hawkins, A. J., Brotherson, S. E., & Jensen, S. R. (1994, November). *Using fathers' narrative accounts to encourage generative fathering.* Paper presented at National Council of Family Relations annual conference, Minneapolis, MN.

Eichler, M. (1983). *Families in Canada today: Recent changes and their policy consequences.* Toronto: Gage.

Furstenberg, F. F., Jr. (1988). Good dads-bad dads: Two faces of fatherhood. In A. Cherlin (Ed.), *The changing American family and public policy* (pp. 193-217). Washington, DC: Urban Institute.

Garbarino, J. (1994, November). *Plenary address.* Presented at the National Council of Family Relations annual conference, Minneapolis, MN.

Gergen, K. J. (1985). The social constructionist movement in modern psychology. *American Psychologist, 40,* 266-275.

Gershuny, J., & Robinson, J. P. (1988). Historical changes in the household division of labor. *Demography, 25,* 537-552.

Gerson, K. (1993). *No man's land: Men's changing commitments to family and work.* New York: Basic Books.

Gilbert, L. A., Holahan, C. K., & Manning, L. (1981). Coping with conflict between professional and maternal roles. *Family Relations, 30,* 419-426.

Giveans, D. L., & Robinson, M. K. (1985). Fathers and the pre-school age child. In S. K. Hanson & F. W. Bozett (Eds.), *Dimensions of fatherhood* (pp. 115-140). Beverly Hills, CA: Sage.

Glaser, B. G., & Strauss, A. L. (1967). *The discovery of grounded theory.* Chicago: Aldine.

Goode, W. (1982). Why men resist. In B. Thorne & M. Yalom (Eds.), *Rethinking the family: Some feminist questions* (pp. 131-150). New York: Longman.

Goodnow, J., & Bowes, J. (1994). *Men, women and household work.* New York: Oxford University Press.

Haas, L. (1980). Role-sharing couples: A study of egalitarian marriages. *Family Relations, 29,* 289-296.

Haas, L. (1982). Determinants of role-sharing behavior: A study of egalitarian couples. *Sex Roles, 8,* 747-760.

Haas, L. (1988, November). *Understanding fathers' participation in childcare: A social constructionist perspective.* Paper presented at the National Council of Family Relations annual conference, Philadelphia.

Harkness, S., & Super, C. M. (1992). The cultural foundations of fathers' roles: Evidence from Kenya and the United States. In B. S. Hewlett (Ed.), *Father-child relations: Cultural and biosocial contexts* (pp. 191-211). New York: Aldine de Gruyter.

Hartman, H. I. (1984). The family as the locus of gender, class and political struggle: The example of housework. In A. M. Jaggar & P. S. Rothenberg (Eds.), *Feminist frameworks* (pp. 341-357). New York: McGraw-Hill.

Hawkins, A. J., & Belsky, J. (1989). The role of father involvement in personality change in men across the transition to parenthood. *Family Relations, 38,* 378-384.

Hawkins, A. J., Christiansen, S. L., Sargent, K. P., & Hill, J. E. (1993). Rethinking father's involvement in child care: A developmental perspective. *Journal of Family Issues, 14,* 531-549.

Hawkins, A. J., & Dollahite, D. C. (1994). Book reviews: Building a more complete model of men in families. *Journal of Marriage and the Family, 56,* 772-776.

Hawkins, A. J., & Dollahite, D. C. (1997a). Beyond the role-inadequacy perspective of fathering. In A. J. Hawkins & D. C. Dollahite (Eds.), *Generative fathering: Beyond deficit perspectives* (pp. 3-16). Thousand Oaks, CA: Sage.

Hawkins, A. J., & Dollahite, D. C. (1997b). *Generative fathering: Beyond deficit perspectives.* Thousand Oaks, CA: Sage.

Hawkins, A. J., & Roberts, T. (1992). Designing a primary intervention program to help dual career couples share housework and child-care. *Family Relations, 41,* 169-177.

Hertz, R. (1997). A typology of approaches to child care. *Journal of Family Issues, 18,* 355-385.

Hochschild, A. (1989). *The second shift: Working parents and the revolution at home.* New York: Viking Penguin.

Hock, E., McKenry, P. C., Hock, M. D., Triolo, S., & Stewart, L. (1980). Child's school entry: A stressful event in the lives of fathers. *Family Relations, 29,* 467-472.

Hood, J. C. (Ed.). (1993). *Men, work, and family.* Thousand Oaks, CA: Sage.

Ishii-Kuntz, M. (1993). Japanese fathers: Work demands and family roles. In J. C. Hood (Ed.), *Men, work, and family* (pp. 45-76). Thousand Oaks, CA: Sage.

Kraemer, S. (1991). The origins of fatherhood: An ancient family process. *Family Process, 30.* 377-392.

Krampe, E. M., & Fairweather, P. D. (1993). Father presence and family formation: A theoretical reformulation. *Journal of Family Issues, 14,* 53-593.

Kupers, T. A. (1993). *Revisioning men's lives: Gender, intimacy, and power.* New York: Guilford.

Kvale, S. (1992). Postmodern psychology: A contradiction in terms? In S. Kvale (Ed.), *Psychology and postmodernism* (pp. 31-57). Newbury Park, CA: Sage.

Lamb, M. E. (Ed.). (1981). *The role of the father in child development.* New York: John Wiley.

Lamb, M. E. (Ed.). (1987). *The father's role: Cross-cultural perspectives.* Hillsdale, NJ: Lawrence Erlbaum.

Lamb, M. E., Pleck, J. H., & Levine, J. A. (1986). Effects of increased paternal involvement on children in two-parent families. In R. A. Lewis & R. E. Salt (Eds.), *Men in families* (pp. 141-158). Beverly Hills, CA: Sage.

Lamb, M. E., Pleck, J. H., & Levine, J. A. (1987). Effects of increased paternal involvement on fathers and mothers. In C. Lewis & M. O'Brien (Eds.), *Reassessing fatherhood: New observations on fathers and the modern family* (pp. 107-125). Newbury Park, CA: Sage.

La Rossa, R. (1988). Fatherhood and social change. *Family Relations, 37,* 451-457.

La Rossa, R. (1997). *The modernization of fatherhood: A social and political history.* Chicago: University of Chicago Press.

La Rossa, R., Gordon, B. A., Wilson, R. J., Bairan, A., & Jaret, C. (1991). The fluctuating image of the 20th century American father. *Journal of Marriage and the Family, 53,* 987-997.

Leslie, L. A., Anderson, E. A., & Branson, M. P. (1991). Responsibility for children. *Journal of Family Issues, 12,* 197-210.

Levant, R. F., Slattery, S. C., & Loiselle, J. E. (1987). Fathers' involvement in housework and child care with school-aged children. *Family Relations, 36,* 152-175.

Levy-Shiff, R., & Israelashvilii, R. (1988). Antecedents of fathering: Some further exploration. *Developmental Psychology, 24,* 434-440.

Lewis, C. (1986). *Becoming a father.* Milton Keynes, UK: Open University Press.

Lewis, C., & O'Brien, M. (1987). *Reassessing fatherhood: New observations on fathers and the modern family* (pp. 1-19). Newbury Park, CA: Sage.

Lewis, M., Feiring, C., & Israelashvilii, R. (1981). The father as a member of the child's social network. In M. E. Lamb (Ed.), *The role of the father in child development* (pp. 259-294). New York: John Wiley.

Lincoln, Y. S., & Guba, E. G. (1985). *Naturalistic inquiry.* Beverly Hills, CA: Sage.

Lutwin, D. R., & Siperstein, G. N. (1985). House-husband fathers. In S. M. Hanson & F. W. Bozett (Eds.), *Dimensions of fatherhood* (pp. 269-287). Beverly Hills, CA: Sage.

Mandell, N., & Duffy, A. (1988). *Reconstructing the Canadian family: Feminist perspectives.* Toronto: Butterworth.

Marshall, C., & Rossman, G. B. (1989). *Designing qualitative research.* Newbury Park, CA: Sage.

Marsiglio, W. (1991). Parental engagement activities with minor children. *Journal of Marriage and the Family, 53,* 973-986.

Marsiglio, W. (1993). Contemporary scholarship on fatherhood: Culture, identity and conduct. *Journal of Family Issues, 14,* 484-509.

McBride, B. A. (1989). Stress and fathers' parental competence: Implications for family life and parent educators. *Family Relations, 38,* 385-389.

McCracken, G. (1988). *The long interview.* Newbury Park, CA: Sage.

Messner, M. (1987). Review essay: Men and families. *Social Science Journal, 24,* 337-340.

Miller, J. B. (1976). *Toward a new psychology of women.* Boston: Beacon.

Model, S. (1981). Housework by husbands. *Journal of Family Issues, 2*(2), 225-237.

Moustakas, C. (1990). *Heuristic research.* Newbury Park, CA: Sage.

Newman, P. R., & Newman, B. M. (1988). Parenthood and adult development. *Marriage and Family Review, 12*(3/4), 313-337.

Okun, L. (1986). *Woman abuse: Facts replacing myths.* Albany: State University of New York Press.

Osherson, S. (1986). *Finding our fathers: How a man's life is shaped by his relationship with his father.* New York: Fawcett Columbine.

Palkovitz, R. (1994, November). *Men's perceptions of the effects of fathering on their adult development and lifecourse.* Paper presented at the National Council of Family Relations, Minneapolis, MN.

Palkovitz, R. (1997). Reconstructing "involvement" : Expanding conceptualizations of men's caring in contemporary families. In A. J. Hawkins & D. C. Dollahite (Eds.), *Generative fathering: Beyond deficit perspectives* (pp. 200-216). Thousand Oaks, CA: Sage.

Palkovitz, R., & Copes, M. (1988). Changes in attitudes, beliefs, and expectations associated with the transition to parenthood. *Marriage and Family Review,* 183-199.

Parke, R. D. (1981). *Fathers.* Cambridge, MA: Harvard University Press.

Parke, R. D. (1988). Foreword. In P. Bronstein & C. P. Cowan (Eds.), *Fatherhood today* (pp. ix-xii). New York: John Wiley.

Parke, R. D. (1990). In search of fathers: A narrative of an empirical journey. In I. E. Sigel & G. H. Brody (Eds.), *Methods of family research: Biographies of research projects* (pp. 153-188). Hillsdale, NJ: Lawrence Erlbaum.

Parsons, T., & Bales, R. (1955). *Family socialization and interaction process.* New York: Free Press.

Patton, M. Q. (1990). *Qualitative evaluation and research methods.* Newbury Park, CA: Sage.

Pederson, F. A. (1981). Father influences viewed in a family context. In M. E. Lamb (Ed.), *The role of the father in child development* (pp. 295-317). New York: John Wiley & Sons.

Perry-Jenkins, M., & Crouter, A. (1990). Men's provider-role attitudes. *Journal of Family Issues, 11,* 136-156.

Pleck, J. H. (1982). *Husbands' and wives' paid work, family work, and adjustment.* Wellesley, MA: Wellesley College Center for Research on Women.

Pleck, J. H. (1984). *Working wives and family well-being.* New York: Garland.

Pleck, J. H. (1985). *Working wives/working husbands.* Beverly Hills, CA: Sage.

Pleck, J. H. (1986). Fatherhood and the work-place. In M. E. Lamb (Ed.), *The father's role: Applied perspectives* (pp. 385-412). New York: John Wiley.

Pleck, J. H. (1987). American fathering in historical perspective. In M. S. Kimmel (Ed.), *Changing men: New directions in research on men and masculinity* (pp. 83-97). Newbury Park, CA: Sage.

Pleck, J. H. (1993). Are "family supportive" employer policies relevant to men? In J. C. Hood (Ed.), *Work, family, and masculinities* (pp. 217-237). Thousand Oaks, CA: Sage.

Pruett, K. (1989). The nurturing male: A longitudinal study of primary nurturing fathers. In S. H. Cath, A. Gurwitt, & L. Gunsberg (Eds.), *Fathers and their families* (pp. 389-405). Hillsdale, NJ: Analytic.

Radin, N. (1988). Primary care-giving fathers of long duration. In P. Bronstein & C. P. Cowan (Eds.), *Fatherhood today* (pp. 127-143). New York: John Wiley.

Radin, N., & Russell, G. (1983). Increased father participation and child development outcomes. In M. E. Lamb & A. Sagi (Eds.), *Fatherhood and family policy* (pp. 139-165). Hillsdale, NJ: Lawrence Erlbaum.

Restrepo, D. R. (1995). *Gender entitlements in Colombian families.* Unpublished doctoral dissertation, University of Guelph, Ontario.

Riessman, C. (1993). *Narrative analysis.* Newbury Park, CA: Sage.

Russell, G. (1983). *The changing role of fathers.* St. Lucia, Australia: University of Queensland Press.

Russell, G. (1986). Primary caretaking and role sharing fathers. In M. E. Lamb (Ed.), *The father's role: Applied perspectives* (pp. 29-57). New York: John Wiley.

Russell, G. (1987). Fatherhood in Australia. In M. E. Lamb (Ed.), *The father's role: Cross-cultural perspectives* (pp. 333-358). Hillsdale, NJ: Lawrence Erlbaum.

Schwartz, P. (1994). *Peer marriage: How love between equals really works.* New York: Free Press.

Skinner, D. A. (1980). Dual-career family stress and coping: A literature review. *Family Relations, 29,* 473-480.

Smith, D. E. (1987). *The everyday world as problematic: A feminist sociology.* Toronto: University of Toronto Press.

Snarey, J. (1993). *How fathers care for the next generation: A four-decade study.* Cambridge, MA: Harvard University Press.

Starrels, M. E. (1994). Gender differences in parent-child relations. *Journal of Family Issues, 15,* 148-165.

Stier, H., & Tienda, M. (1993). Are men marginal to the family? Insights from Chicago's inner city. In J. C. Hood (Ed.), *Men, work, and family* (pp. 23-44). Thousand Oaks, CA: Sage.

Strauss, A. L. (1987). *Qualitative analysis for social scientists.* Cambridge, UK: Cambridge University Press.

Strauss, A. L., & Corbin, J. (1990). *Basics of qualitative research: Grounded theory procedures and techniques.* Newbury Park, CA: Sage.

Thompson, L., & Walker, A. (1989). Gender in families: Women and men in marriage, work and parenthood. *Journal of Marriage and the Family, 51,* 845-871.

Volling, B. L., & Belsky, J. (1991). Multiple determinants of father involvement during infancy in dual-earner and single-earner families. *Journal of Marriage and the Family, 53,* 461-474.

Webster's Ninth New Collegiate Dictionary. (1983). Springfield, MA: Merriam-Webster.

Weingarten, K. (1991). The discourses of intimacy: Adding a social constructionist and feminist view. *Family Process, 30,* 285-305.

Williams, M. G., Williams, R., & Radcliffe, M. (Producers), & Columbus, C. (Director). (1993). *Mrs. Doubtfire* (Video). (Available from Twentieth Century Fox Corp., Los Angeles)

Williams, N. (1993). Elderly Mexican-American men: Work and family patterns. In J. C. Hood (Ed.), *Men, work, and family* (pp. 68-85). Thousand Oaks, CA: Sage.

Yogev, S. (1981). Do professional women have egalitarian marital relationships. *Journal of Marriage and the Family, 43,* 865-872.

Zarestky, E. (1976). *Capitalism, the family and personal life.* New York: Harper Colophon.

Index

Cultural perspective, xi
  obstacles to co-parenting, 175
  popular culture and fatherhood, 13
  value of family, 194-196

Dance metaphor in parenting, 128-129
  readiness to dance, 129-131
  reshaping parenthood, 147-148,
    162-163, 178-179
  solo and partnered dancing, 131-135
  See also Reciprocal revisioning
Discourses, 10-11, 21
  comparative model, 185-186
  deficit model, 184-185
  dichotomous thinking, 196-199
  division of labor, 186-190
  dominant, of fatherhood, 11-15, 184
  expanding conceptualizations, 186,
    188-190
  family man, 192-194
  family, value of, 194-196
  father's involvement, quanity/quality,
    24-28
  individual/competitive and collective/
    relational, 190-192

Family life:
  cultural valuing of family, 194-196

dichotomous thinking, 196-199
family work, valuing, 181-182
father's involvement, 24-28, 175,
    193-194
philosophy of and shared parenting,
    169-170
structural-functional theory, 23-24
Fatherhood:
  acculturation holdovers, 143-146
  child care and family life, 24-28
  developing parenting skills, 141-142
  dichotomous assumptions about, 20
  dominant discourses, 11-15
  gender politics, 178-179
  historically, 21-22
  influence on child, 29-31
  men's transition to, 31-34
  popular culture perspective, 13
  reshaping, 147-148
  role inadequacy perspective (RIP),
    12-13, 20-21
  stay-at-home Dad, 44-45, 51-52,
    228-229
  types of, 7-8
  violence, intergenerational transfer
    of, 194
  See also Parenting; Reciprocal
    revisioning; Shared parenting
Fatherhood images, 4-6
  alternative view of, 9-11

language of, 6-8
Father involvement:
    deliberate choice, 193-194
    influence on children, 29-31
    men's experience of, 139-146
    personal resources, 197-199
    provider role, 197
    women's experience of, 136-139

Gender politics of co-parenting:
    balancing specialties/shared
        responsibilities, 179-180
    challenging accepted gender
        practices, 180-181
    equality in family work patterns,
        186-187
    reshaping motherhood/fatherhood,
        178-179
    valuing family work, 181-182
    voice and choice, 177-178

Labor, division of:
    gender equality in, 186-187
    specialization-based, 187-188

Meaning-making, 37, 38-39
Motherhood:
    acculturation holdover, 137-139
    displacement, feelings of, 137
    father involvement, 136
    gender politics, 178-179
    reshaping, 147-148
    stay-at-home Mom, 45-46, 52-53,
        229-232
    See also Reciprocal revisioning

Obstacles to co-parenting:
    cultural considerations, 175
    gender entitlements, 175-176
    institutional factors, 174-175

Parenting:
    co-constructive process, 65-73,
        127-128, 161

commitment to, 77-82
dance metaphor, 128-129
goodwill in, 96-98, 188
mother-father-child system, 30-31
multidirectional influences on child
    development, 199
parent-child attachment, 32-33
paths towards shared, 56-75
philosophy, 82-95, 169-170
play and fathers, 30
See also Fatherhood; Motherhood;
    Shared parenting; Tag-team
    parenting

Reciprocal revisioning, 149-150,
    162-163
    concordant steps, 157-161
    leading-following, patterns of,
        150-151
    matched steps, 154-156
    out of step, 151-154
Research methodology:
    convenience referrals, 208-209
    data analysis, 214-216
    data collection, 209-211
    grounded theory approach, 204-206
    interview process, 211-213
    legitimation practices, 216-219
    limitations of research design,
        219-221
    participant characteristics, 213-214,
        214 (table)
    participant selection, 206-208
    theoretical sampling, 206
    theoretical saturation, 209
Role inadequacy perspective (RIP), 12-13,
    20-21

Shared parenting:
    accounting equity pattern, 43-44,
        50-51, 226-228
    co-creating possibilities and
        arrangements, 65-73, 127-128,
        161
    decision-making process, factors in,
        73-75
    egalitarian ideology, 63-65

elements of successful, 169-173
family-of-origin precursors, 56-63
gender politics of, 176-182
interactive dynamics, 134-135
interchangeable partners, 41-42,
    48-49, 223-224
obstacles to, 173-176
research approach on, 15-18, 165-167
reserved specialties, 42-43, 49-50,
    224-226
stay-at-home Dad, 44-45, 51-52,
    228-229
stay-at-home Mom, 45-46, 52-53,
    229-232
stress and conflict in, 171-173
See also Reciprocal revisioning;
    Tag-team parenting
Social constructionist perspective, xi, xii,
    11, 21, 205
Social learning theory, 29
Structural-functional theory, 23-24

Tag-team parenting, 100-101, 125-126,
    170-171
agreements/arrangements, 116-118
deficit/comparative model discourses,
    184-186
matched team players, 102-106
negotiating agreements, 123-125
refusing a turn, 112-113, 115
specialization and interchangeability,
    118-123, 187-188
spelling each other, 106-109
stepping in/taking over, 114
turn taking, 110-112

Women:
child care responsibilities, 25-28
demanding change of men, 192-193
father involvement, experience of,
    136-139
personal resources and family life, 198
See also Motherhood

About the Author

Anna Dienhart received a PhD in Family Relations and Human Development from the University of Guelph, Ontario, Canada. She also holds master's degrees in Marriage and Family Therapy (University of Guelph) and Management Sciences (University of California at Los Angeles). Her research focuses on questions about gender relations in the family, especially exploring these issues from both cultural and individual perspectives. She has research interests in the clinical area, where she explores gender awareness and how it is applied in therapy with couples and families. Recent publications include articles on how family therapy practices may effectively engage men in family change, using narrative family therapy to engage fathers in responsible parenting of their children, a critique of cultural practices that may limit men's involvement in fathering their children, and collaborative parenting partnerships. She is an active couple and family therapist with clinical and approved clinical supervisor standing with the American Association for Marriage and Family Therapy. She came to this new profession after spending 15 years working as a consultant/advisor on international economic trends for multinational corporations.